BRUNO

BRUNO

CONVERSATIONS WITH A BRAZILIAN DRUG DEALER

Robert Gay

Duke University Press   Durham and London   2015

© 2015 Duke University Press
All rights reserved
Printed in the United States of America on acid-free paper ∞
Typeset in Quadraat by Graphic Composition, Inc.

Library of Congress Cataloging-in-Publication Data
Gay, Robert, 1958–
Bruno : conversations with a Brazilian drug dealer /
Robert Gay.
pages cm
Includes bibliographical references and index.
ISBN 978-0-8223-5841-1 (hardcover : alk. paper)
ISBN 978-0-8223-5849-7 (pbk. : alk. paper)
ISBN 978-0-8223-7577-7 (e-book)
1. Bruno, 1967– 2. Drug dealers—Brazil—Biography.
3. Comando Vermelho. 4. Organized crime—Brazil.
5. Drug traffic—Brazil. I. Title.
HV5840.B6G39 2015
363.45092—dc23
[B]
2014034851

Cover: The Corridor, photo by André Cypriano.

For Mum and Dad

CONTENTS

ACKNOWLEDGMENTS

I would like to thank Bruno, first and foremost, for making this book a possibility. I can honestly say I never saw it coming. I would also like to thank Lucia and her family for their friendship and generosity over the years. My only hope is that someday I can repay you.

Otherwise, my thanks go to Bill McNally and Neville Thorley for their enthusiastic reading of an early version of this manuscript; Raquel Heidorn for her invaluable help with transcription; my friends at the David Rockefeller Center for Latin American Studies for their support; Luis Eduardo Soares, Myrian Sepúlveda dos Santos, Javier Auyero, and Bryan McCann for their time and insights; and Gisela Fosado and Lorien Olive at Duke for just about everything else.

Finally, I'd like to thank my family, past, present, and future, for all their love, patience, and understanding.

In July 1999, I flew from New York City to Rio to begin the process of interviewing Lucia. I had known Lucia since the 1980s, when I first started doing research on Rio's shantytowns, or *favelas*. In the last few years, however, I'd hardly seen her. And that was because she'd become romantically involved with what turned out to be a series of drug dealers operating out of the western part of the state. But now she was back home, with her family, in Jakeira. And it was her experiences as a survivor of this cruel and largely undocumented world that I was there to investigate. Except that when I got there, to her house, there was a man, a man I'd never seen before.

His name was Bruno.[1] He was sitting on a white plastic chair on the veranda as I came in. Not knowing who he was, I nodded, extended my hand, and introduced myself as a friend of the family, before making my way through the living room into the kitchen. It was there that Lucia told me, while she was preparing food for everyone, that Bruno was her boyfriend, and that he had just been released, having spent the last eight years of his life in prison. But that's pretty much all I knew at the time, until a few days later, when Lucia told me to go talk to him about his experiences. And so I did.

Our conversation that day lasted around fifty minutes. During those fifty minutes, he told me how he'd become involved with dealing drugs as a corporal in the Brazilian navy while stationed at the

A view of Jakeira. Photograph by author, 2014.

border with Bolivia, and how years later he'd been arrested in Rio and sent to a prison where he joined the ranks of the Comando Vermelho (CV), the oldest and, until recently, most powerful of the region's criminal factions. Finally, he went on to describe how, over the course of the next few years, he rose through the ranks of the CV to become a prison leader. And I remember thinking to myself, "This is amazing. This is really incredible!" Because here was Lucia, on the one hand, telling me about drug gang life on the outside, and here was Bruno, on the other, telling me about the drug trade and the internal structure and dynamics of organized crime on the inside. I mean, how lucky could I be to be able to bring these separate but related worlds together? At the time, I was thinking that I'd get to interview him over and over, just as I planned to do, and eventually did, with Lucia. But I was wrong. Dead wrong. After that day he refused to talk to me about anything to do with his life, even though I tried. No, it was clear to me that that particular window had closed, and there was no way I was going to get it to open again.[2]

Until, that is, about seven years later, when Bruno literally turned to me one day and said, "I'm ready to tell my story." I remember thinking, "Why now, why after all this time?" Part of the answer, I believe, is that he'd seen what I'd done with my interviews with Lucia. He'd seen the final product and was impressed. The other part of the answer is that we had become close friends and, I guess, he felt that he could trust me. Between 1999 and 2006 I must have visited Rio a dozen times. Much of my time there was spent hanging out with Bruno, Lucia, and their family. Or, on occasion, I'd accompany Bruno downtown on an errand or to look for a job. Because while he was having a hard time finding work, because of his past, he never stopped trying to find ways to put food on the table. As he once said, "It's no use sitting around hoping something will fall from the sky. Because the only thing that falls from the sky, my friend, is rain!"

Once we decided to go ahead, I made it down to Rio as often as I could, six times in the next fourteen months, in fact. The deal was that when I got there, I'd call up and arrange a day and a time for Bruno to meet me at the entrance to the favela. Then we'd walk or take a motorcycle taxi to his home. At first things progressed pretty slowly, in no small part because in January and February his children were on almost permanent vacation. We'd try to persuade them to watch a movie or play a video game in their room. That never lasted long, however, and pretty soon they'd be out looking for us, sitting at the living room table or upstairs in the half-finished bathroom that Bruno was building for Lucia's daughter, Amanda. So then we'd stop, and we'd try to bribe them to give us a little more time. But that was okay, because by the time of my third visit, in June, they were back at school and we'd record two or three hours straight of interviews before they made it home again.

The other reason why, at first, things progressed pretty slowly was that we were both feeling each other out, as tends to happen on such occasions. I have to say, however, that Bruno was the perfect person to interview, for a couple of reasons. First, he was intensely aware of and interested in his surroundings, which meant that he was always trying to relate the things that he'd experienced to some broader context. Second, he was an outsider, in the sense that he found himself thrust into a world in which he didn't belong. He wasn't from Rio. He was from Recife, in the northeast. And he wasn't born or raised in a favela, in the midst of gun battles between drug gangs and the police. As a result, he had this incredible ability to see things clearly, and to communicate them in a detailed yet clear way to someone who had no idea what that world was about.

Finally, the other reason why Bruno was such a good person to interview was that he was so into it. And he was more into it the more we went along.

He made it very clear to me, from the beginning, that he was telling me things that he hadn't told anyone else, not even Lucia. And there were times when we'd stop, at the end of an interview, and he'd say, "I can't believe I just told you that!" At other times, especially toward the end, the conversation would become difficult for him. And I'd ask him if he'd like to stop, and he'd say, "No, no, we must go on, because I need to get this off my chest."

Now, obviously, since the controversy over *I, Rigoberta Menchú*, there have been many questions about the integrity and veracity of the testimonial tradition.[3] So what makes me think that Bruno's story is the truth, or close to the truth, or what he believes to be the truth? First of all, there was our initial conversation, all those years ago, which established the basic framework of the story, a framework that remained remarkably consistent over the years. Second, there was Lucia herself, who appears in Bruno's story toward the end, as his friend and lover, who was there to witness his time as a prison leader and the consequences of the near-fatal decisions he was forced to make, as a result of a split within the ranks of the cv.

Finally, there was the somewhat unnerving discovery, on my part, that some of what he was talking about was familiar. I'd known Bruno for seven years before we embarked on this project, and during that time, things had happened, and people had come and gone, that made little or no sense to me. But now they did. Like the time we were walking down the hill together, and this young man suddenly appeared from an alleyway and pulled Bruno aside. I knew that he was the leader of the favela, because Bruno told me afterward. What I couldn't work out, however, was why he wanted to talk to Bruno, of all people. Now, of course, I know. And I'm still not sure if I should be upset or relieved that I didn't know who my friend was for all those years.

Anyway, once the interviews were done I began the long process of transcribing, translating, and editing. Because in every interview there's a lot of redundancy, and a lot of repetition. And then, when you translate from Portuguese to English, you have to decide on a cadence and you have to try and stick to it. Then there are things that have to be taken out or moved around to ensure that the narrative is tight and consistent, and that it reads like a conversation, which is essentially what it is. And hopefully, that is how it comes across to you, the reader. And hopefully, it provides you with a window into a world that is largely hidden from view and, more importantly, that is misrepresented and little understood.

The book itself is divided into eight chapters, organized chronologically.

Chapter 1 begins with Bruno's decision to join the navy and ends with him making his first drug deals. Chapter 2 discusses, in detail, the nature of the drug trade and ends with Bruno's arrest in Rio. Chapter 3 focuses on his initial experiences, first in a navy jail, and then in a civilian prison, where he chooses to join the ranks of the CV. Chapter 4 deals with his transfer to a prison on the island of Ilha Grande, and chapter 5 his first attempt at escape. In chapter 6 Bruno is moved to a maximum-security facility on the mainland where he gets to know the Comando Vermelho's leaders and attempts to escape once again. In chapter 7 he finds himself in a prison that is in lockdown mode because of tensions generated by conflicts within the faction out on the street, a prison that he takes over with significant risk to himself. And finally, in chapter 8, he negotiates his exit from the CV, which paves the way for his eventual release. Interspersed with the sections of Bruno's narrative are short and, hopefully, informative discussions of issues raised by the text, including Brazil's border problem, the nature of and prohibitions against cocaine, Brazil's prison system in general and the Ilha Grande and Bangu prison complexes in particular, and the causes and consequences of rifts between Rio's various criminal factions.

My name is Luis Antônio Pereira da Silva, but my friends all call me Bruno. I was born April 16, 1967, in Recife. And when I was seventeen, I joined the navy.[1] Because I worked for this jeweler. I was his office boy, in charge of deliveries. And one day I went to this man's house. He was an officer in the navy, and he asked me if I'd ever thought of enlisting. And when I signed up I had one thing in mind, and that was to travel and make my own way in life. Because I grew up on a farm, miles from nowhere. So I imagined that joining the navy would be a great opportunity for me to see places like Rio and São Paulo.

Were there other opportunities to travel?

Not really, because although I was in school, the quality of the education was really poor. And as much as I tried to study, I could see that I wasn't going to achieve my objectives. So the navy was a big opportunity for me, for a poor boy like me.

But you weren't poor, right?

I wasn't poor poor, but I was poor, because my father had so many children, because he had three families.

How so?

Well, he had ten children with my mother. Then my mother died and he married this other woman, and had ten children with her.

And then there was this other woman who had four children of her own. So my father took care of three families, you see? So when I got the chance to enlist, it was a big deal for me. But I mean it wasn't easy, because I had to go to school at night. And from where I lived to my school was fifteen kilometers. And my last class ended at ten, so I only got home around midnight.

And you worked during the day, right?

That's right, because apart from all the chores I had to do on my father's farm, I worked at this jeweler's, in the city. And that's how I met this officer, this captain in the navy. And he told me all about the military, and what with my age, it all seemed to make sense. So I went to the recruitment center and I took the test.

So it was a way of escaping, then?

That's right, because the last thing I wanted was to stay there on that farm. Because I was already behind in my studies, because on a farm, no one thought that school was important. What I mean is, school was for rich kids, for other people's kids. Because kids who were raised on a farm were supposed to stay there and work, understand?

Doing what?

We raised cows and goats and pigs. My father had some land. I mean, it wasn't much land, but for growing corn and raising farm animals it was okay. And a lot of folks around there had never even been to the city. They only knew about it from TV. And we were the first family to own a TV, so people used to come over to our house all the time and watch. And we were the first family to own a refrigerator. And because I was always interested in making money, I used to make ice cream out of coconuts and sell it to friends and neighbors. Then, after I joined up, I spent a year in military school in Recife.

Did you like it?

I loved it, because I did really well. Then after a year of military school we were all transferred to Rio. And the day that we left was a great day for me, because here I was, a young man of eighteen, leaving Recife for the first time. And after three days of traveling, by bus, we finally arrived. We came down from the mountains and crossed the Rio-Níteroi Bridge to the base. And that's where we were split up, that's where we were divided. And the guys who were sent to the best places were the ones with connections.

What do you mean?

If you're a commander, and a friend's son arrives, you're going to make sure he's sent to work on a frigate, right? Or if someone knows someone who knows an admiral, he'll be sent to work in an office with air conditioning. And then there were recruits like me, who didn't know anyone, who were sent to work in what is called the first division. And the guys in the first division are the ones who scrub the decks, who do all the hard work to keep the boats clean. But you know what? It was fine by me, because I was happy to be out of Recife, that's all.

So where did they send you?

They sent me to work on a destroyer that they'd bought from the U.S. And I mean, the ship was a wreck, and it had these horrific-sounding cannons. Because I remember the first day of training—I remember thinking that my ears would explode! And when I first boarded that ship, there was this sergeant there who said, "You have two days to get to know the ship. There's port and there's starboard and there's forward and there's aft. Now get to it!" So then I went down below to put my things away. Then, after that, I went up on deck. And I was standing there, looking out at the Rio-Níteroi Bridge. And I'd never seen a bridge like that before. And I thought to myself, "You know what? This is something—this is really something!"

So you were a long way from home.

I was a long way from home! So then after a year, I was transferred to this base in Belém Novo, which is about fifty kilometers from Rio. And the time that I spent there was really useful, in terms of learning about ships. And from there I was transferred back to Rio to take a course to become a corporal of artillery. And I mean, that was all well and good. I mean, it was all very interesting. But even so, life in Rio wasn't easy.

What do you mean?

What I mean is, I was either at home or on board ship. And at first, we all slept at the base. But then a bunch of us rented an apartment, in Santa Teresa. Because it's no fun living in the city if you don't take advantage of it, right? So we got a place together. But I didn't stay there long, only about six months, because, like I said, I was transferred to Belém Novo. And by the time I was transferred back to Rio, I was no longer in Santa Teresa. I was living with other friends across the bay in Níteroi. I remember the officer saying to me, "Do you live somewhere here in Rio?" And I said, "No, I live in Níteroi." "Well, you know that you have to be here by five in the morning, right? Now is that something you can do? Because if you can't, you'll be punished." Because Níteroi was a long way away, which meant that I had to take the ferry. And by the time I got home at night, there were only a few hours left before I had to set out again. And this course I was on was really hard, because you had to learn about all kinds of weapons. You know, small arms, chemical weapons, mines. And you had to know how to fire a rifle, and you had to study the different parts of a submarine. And if you didn't pass, you went back to being a regular recruit. So I mean, there was a lot of studying, and a lot of tests. But I wanted it, I wanted it all. And I was going to do it all by the book, because I wanted to get on with my career.

Was it possible for a recruit like you to get ahead?

It was difficult because there's a lot of prejudice, a lot of discrimination in the navy.[2] To give you an idea, they only started letting in negros in 1983. I mean, there were already pardos by then, but no negros.[3]

When you say "negro," what do you mean?

Black, negro means black [laughter]. Black is black, white is white, and I'm pardo. Because there's this mixing of races in this country. And it's this mixing of races that causes all these problems. Because they say there isn't prejudice, but there is, if you know what I mean. And a poor guy's going to face a lot of difficulties, unless, of course, he has connections.

And negros don't have connections, right?

Have you ever seen a black admiral? [Laughter.][4]

What about pardos?

A pardo might become a lieutenant commander, or a captain of a frigate. But even then it's going to be difficult. So anyway, by the time I finished this course, I'd gotten to know this friend who grew up in this town on the frontier. His name was Valdoberto, and he was from Corumbá, in Mato Grosso do Sul. And if I thought I was a long way from home, my God! Because this country's enormous, I mean it's almost 9,000 kilometers square. And he was like me. You know, he wanted to experience new things. And this town where he grew up, the navy had a base there. And it was the navy's job to patrol the border with Bolivia. Because it's fresh water there, it's the Pantanal.[5] So I said to myself, "When I'm done with this course, I want to go to one of these places on the border."

Could you choose where you were sent?

You could ask, I mean you could petition. And the way I saw it, I had two options. And my first option was to go back home to Recife.

But I thought you wanted to get away.

I did! But the first thing that comes to mind, when you're in a strange place, is to go back home, because you feel homesick. Never mind all those dreams; never mind all those plans you made. But I think that's just a natural reaction, right? Because my second choice was to head for the frontier. I mean, if you can't go back home, you might as well go all the way, right? So when I completed the course, I packed my bags and I left.

Was it difficult for you to leave Rio?

Yes, yes it was. Because Rio's a big city, right? And there are lots of things to do. And I'd gotten to know the place. And now I was going to go somewhere new. So I was going to have to start all over again.

How long did it take you to get there?

It took twenty-eight hours, by bus. And when I got there, to Corumbá, I could see that the place was primitive, that there was almost nothing to do. And I mean, that was where I was going to be, that was where the real story was about to begin. Because I'd left home, right? And now where was I? In a small town in the middle of nowhere. So I was thinking to myself, "What was the point?"

You mean, it was like you were back on the farm?

That's right [*laughter*]. And I mean, I'd studied hard. And what did I have to show for it? So I was beginning to think that it was all bullshit. You know, the things that they tell you. And I realized that if I was going to make it, I was going to have to take matters into my own hands, understand? So then I started work.

When I first got to Corumbá, I was told that my job was to look after all the weapons on the base. And the guy that I was replacing had been there for five years already, and he was desperate to get out. He'd been given thirty days to teach me everything, but after a week he told the commander that

Brazil.

I was ready, that I knew everything I needed to know! So then he took off. And when he left there, I went through all the files, and I noticed that a lot of ammunition was missing. But you know what? I said to myself, "It's no big deal. I'm just going to go ahead and fill out all the forms." Because I was no longer that naive little farm boy [laughter]. I mean I knew right then that the situation on the border was a whole lot more complicated than it was in Rio. Because in Rio the navy just sits there, right? With nothing to do. But on the border it's different. Because there are things going on there. It's just that they didn't have the resources.

To do what?

To police the frontier. So then they sent me out to work on a patrol boat, that went out at night. And while I was on that boat I began to notice things [laughter]. I began to notice that some boats were treated differently than others, that some boats were allowed to go by, while others were stopped and searched. And you know what else I noticed? I noticed that some of my friends owned things that made no sense in terms of their salary. You know, cars, homes, businesses. And it was while I was out there, on the frontier, that I began to realize that being sent there

A Brazilian navy patrol on the River Paraguay. Photograph by Felipe Barra / Ministério da Defesa, 2012. Licensed under CC BY 2.0 BR: https://creativecommons.org/licenses/by/2.0/legalcode.

wasn't such a bad thing after all. Because there were guys there who made the same as me, who had all this stuff. And it wasn't like they were from wealthy families or anything. No, it was because they'd become involved in illicit activities.

What did you think, when you found out about this?

I thought, "Hey, I could do well for myself out here!" [*Laughter.*] I thought, "This could be my big opportunity!" I thought that if I could find someone who'd been there for a while, he could teach me.

Even though you might be risking your career? Did you ever think about that?

Not really. And perhaps it was because I was so desperate to have something of my own. You know, to leave that little life of mine behind. Because my career was moving along nicely, but I wasn't really getting anywhere. I mean, I never had money to send home or anything. Because I was earning more, but I was spending more as well. Because as a corporal, you're not going to live on the base, you're going to find a house, with air conditioning. And looking back, I think that it was also because of a lack of preparation on my part. Because if you're raised in a poor environment, right? And you find yourself in a position of responsibility, you have to be prepared. And I wasn't prepared, because my father was distant from us all. So no one ever said to me, "Look, be careful out there. Be careful who you choose as your friends, okay?" Because I think these things are important.

And it was a small city, right? I mean, there wasn't a lot to do.

There was nothing! I mean, there were nightclubs and everything, but they were all really expensive.

Nightclubs for whom?

For the coke dealers! Because at night, they owned the place [*laughter*]. And there I was, working really hard, while they all drove around in their imported cars. So I said to myself, "I've got to take advantage of this." And so then there was this party, at the base. And there were lots of people there. And a fight broke out, because sailors love to fight, right? And we wrecked the place, and the military police came in and arrested everyone. And we all spent the night in jail, so the commander could figure out who was responsible in the morning. And when I got there, there was this one guy alone in this cell. And I found out, from one of the guards, that he'd been arrested for drug trafficking. He was a corporal, like me, in the navy, and he'd been arrested at the airport. And I thought to myself, "Well, this is interesting!" Because there was this long corridor, with cells on either side. And there was this one big cell at the end, just for him. So I climbed up on my bed and I said to him, "Are you okay, sir?" And he said, "Yes, yes, I'm okay, and how about you?" "I was just posted here, from Rio. I've only been here a week, and I'm in trouble already! We had a few too many drinks at the bar, and there was a fight." So then he became interested in me, and he wanted to know more about me. And when I found out he'd been arrested for smuggling drugs, I figured he could be my contact. You know, he could be my guide.

So you sought him out?

In a way, yes, yes, I did. And then he asked me if I was going to be in jail for long, because he had this note that needed to be delivered to his wife. And I told him that I'd deliver it for him. So then he wrote the note and handed it over, and I hid it inside my underwear. Then the next day, after the commander let everyone out, I went to find his house. And it was a big house, a beautiful house!

Where was it?

It was about seven kilometers from the base. I took the bus to the town where he lived, and then I walked the rest of the way. And when I reached the front gate, I stood there and clapped my hands. And then his wife came out, and I gave her the note. And when I gave her the note I told her that I'd been with her husband, because there'd been a fight and I ended up in the cell next to him. And you know what? Because I delivered it, he felt like he owed me. So the next time his wife came to visit, he asked me if I could meet her outside. So when I came out, I saw her standing there. And she said to me, "Bruno, can I talk to you for a second? My husband asked me to thank you for delivering the note. And he was wondering if you needed anything, anything at all. I mean, like a place to live, because he has houses around town."

And what were you thinking?

I was thinking that I needed a place to live, so I could get away from the base. So she wrote down this address and said, "Come by the house and pick up the keys. Just keep the place clean, okay?" So then I said, "Well, can I at least pay you rent?" "No, no, there's no need. Oh, and Sunday's visiting day. Do you want to come with me?" "I'm going to be working Sunday, but I'll speak to the captain on duty. I'll have a word with him, okay?" And I didn't realize it at the time but, little by little, I was becoming involved.

You didn't realize it, really?

Well, on the one hand, I was being a little naive, right? But on the other, I wanted to find out more about his arrest, about his contacts. Because he'd spent a good deal of time in Rio, because that was where the package was going, when he was arrested. It was going to be shipped to Holland, or somewhere like that. And when he told me about it, I found it all really interesting. And he told me that I had a future. You know, in the business. It's just that I had to be careful not to make the same mistake that he had made.

And what mistake was that?

His mistake was that he was too involved. Because he was caught with the drugs, because he was being watched by the federal police. So then I asked him if he had any contacts in Rio. And he said yes, that he knew a lot of people in Rio, because Rio was an important point in the whole scheme. And he also said that if I needed anything I should tell him, because I could count on him. Then he said, "Do you know how to drive?" And I said, "Sure I know how to drive." "Then I have a car you can borrow. Because I can't drive it while I'm in prison." And you know what? At that stage in my life, I was desperate to be able to drive. So gradually, I became more and more involved. Because he had a lot of contacts, and a lot of deals that had come to a halt.

So you were going to do things for him, in his name.

That's right. So I made a point of talking to him whenever I could. Like when he was allowed out, to stretch his legs. You know, so I could ask him things. Because inside that base there were a lot of people like him. It's just that they hadn't been caught.

Part of my job at the base involved shipping munitions back to Rio. And I found out that the next batch was to be flown by the air force, and that someone from the navy had to go along. So when the commander asked me if I was willing to go, I jumped at the chance. Because I'd been in Corumbá for a month already, so I saw it as an opportunity to go back and see my friends. And so then I got in touch with my friend in jail. And he told me that a friend of his also had something that needed to be shipped to Rio. So then he made contact with his friend, and his friend asked if I would have dinner with him. You know, to listen to what he had to say.

Was he in the military?

No, no, he wasn't. But he had access to a lot of military personnel, and he was a big supplier of cocaine to the favelas in Rio. And me? I was a nobody. But I was about to take a big step. And I knew that I was taking a huge risk in agreeing to be responsible for that shipment. But you know what? I had no sense of what I was doing, of what I was getting myself into. So then they delivered the cocaine to me in a bag, the night before we left.

What kind of bag?

It was a big leather bag. And it was filled with ten packets of cocaine, each weighing a kilo. So then we flew to Campo Grande, where we stayed the night in a transit hotel. You know, for military personnel who were passing through. But I couldn't sleep, because my bag stayed on the plane, out on the runway. Because it was really really heavy, and we were only going to be there overnight. And besides, what was I going to do, walk around with it all the time? And Jesus Christ was I relieved when we took off again the next morning. And you know what? I didn't even notice when we touched down in Rio, because my part in the deal was through.

Did you hand it over to someone at the airport?

No, no, because the marines were there with their truck, to pick up the munitions. So I went to the base with them, and signed all the papers. And then I set out for this address that someone had given me.

Were you paid then, when you handed it over?

No, no, I was paid when I got back to base. And I made a thousand dollars a kilo. So I made ten thousand dollars, in cash, which is a lot. Because at the time, I was making six hundred reais (293 USD) per month as a corporal.[6] So ten thousand dollars was a lot.

Did you spend the money in dollars, or did you exchange it?

I exchanged it. There was this guy in downtown Corumbá who bought dollars. He didn't care where they came from, but he wouldn't change more than five hundred, or maybe a thousand at a time. So you had to change it in small amounts. Or you had to send someone else, or go different places. Because the federal authorities were always on the lookout. But there were lot of guys who bought dollars, especially at the frontier.

What did you do with all the money?

I bought a car. I bought a new car and a house. And I bought it all with cash. And I began eating out at restaurants, and going to clubs. You know, the ones I couldn't afford before. Because now I was someone, understand? I was part of a group of friends in town who were introduced to me, who were all involved. And that was important for me. Because before I felt excluded, and now I was a part of everything, understand? And I would say that 80 percent of the wealth in that town was made from drugs. Because it's like an exchange. I mean, it's as if drugs were listed on the stock market, as if they had a price, like coffee or oil or something. And because Brazil shares a border with countries like Bolivia, Colombia, and Peru, it's used as a route, both for drugs that are consumed locally and for drugs that are shipped out of the country. But the quantity of drugs that is consumed locally, that causes all of these problems, is nothing compared to the quantity that is shipped abroad. And when I got involved, I got involved with the idea of making contact with someone who could help me ship drugs abroad. But that was a long way off. I mean that was a long way in the future.

So you wanted to become a supplier?

That's right. Because when I made my first trip to Rio, I was a just courier, right? Who just handed over the drugs. So when I got back to the base, I put part of the money I made aside, because I wanted to get into the business of buying and selling. It's just that I didn't know who to sell it to, because I didn't have any contacts.

How much was a kilo of cocaine?

At the time, a kilo of cocaine was about two thousand dollars. And you could sell it for five in Rio.

So your friend bought ten kilos for twenty thousand dollars and sold it for fifty?

I don't know what he paid for it, but I know that he made good money. And so anyway, I went back home to Corumbá and those first few weeks were just party, party, party! What with me being twenty-one, and having no family, I was beginning to think that I was, you know, "the man."

What about your friend?

He was transferred to a civilian prison. He was held at the base until he was tried and then he was expelled from the navy. And visiting day at this civilian prison was Sunday. So I went there to visit him. And while I was there, I asked him if he had any contacts in Rio, so we didn't have to depend on these other guys. Because I wanted to sell the drugs directly, even though I knew that what I was doing was wrong. Because I was ambitious, understand?

So you never thought, "I've done it once, so now I'm going to stop?"

I thought about it. But then the money soon goes, because you spend it like water. And then it becomes a vicious cycle. Because you buy a car and you drive it around, and then you see one you like even more. So you think to yourself, "I'll deliver another load and then I'll be able to buy that other car." So you become addicted to buying things, because that's what capitalism's about, right? Especially in a country like this, where the gap between the rich and poor is so vast. I mean, it's the same thing in the favelas. I mean, a guy goes to the mall, and he sees a pair of sneakers for three hundred reais. Then he sees them on TV, and so he has to have them, right? So then he goes out and robs, and maybe he kills someone. And so the situation is really complicated.

Did you tell anyone about what you'd done?

No, no, no, I told no one. Because the house I bought was small. What I mean is, it was compatible with what I was earning as a salary. And I was also conscious of the fact that I couldn't just go out and buy everything, you know, all at once, because people would become suspicious. And you know what? I'd already convinced myself that I needed more. So I knew I had to get in contact with my friend again, because he was the one with all the contacts, even though he was in prison. Because even though he was in prison he was still able to manage his affairs. And when I told him that it would be better for us to deal with our own contacts in Rio, he said that it was a good idea, but that I should be careful, because it might be dangerous. Because he had heard rumors that there were drug gangs in Rio who killed their suppliers. You know, a supplier would show up with twenty, thirty kilos of cocaine, and he'd be given part of the money. Then, when he came back for the rest, they'd kill him. They'd cut him up into small pieces and burn him, and shit like that.

Was it true? I mean, surely, if a drug gang does that, no one's going to want to deal with them, right?

But they wouldn't say that they killed him to steal his drugs. They'd say that he messed up, that he stole from them or something. And that's when things get tricky. But I thought that if we knew someone we could trust, we could deal with the buyers directly. And this friend of mine, he had a contact in Rio. So he gave me his name, and I arranged a leave of absence from the base, and off I went.

My contact's name was Ademar. And he lived in the favela of Estrada do Paiol. And he was a dealer like me. You know, an intermediary. So he knew a lot of people we could sell to. And during the day he worked at an army barracks. But he wasn't a soldier, he was a civilian. So I went to the barracks to look for him and we set it all up for Sunday. And on Sunday, I went to his house and he introduced me to this guy, this leader of the favela. He said, "Let me introduce you to my friend. He's stationed at the frontier. He's in the military, and he's got a *carteira quente*, and so it's easy for him to get the merchandise here."

Carteira quente?

Carteira quente means that you have papers that can get you across the border, that can get you past the police. And this guy, this leader, seemed interested, because a direct contact with a supplier's a good thing, right? I mean, for them. So he asked me how much I wanted. And I told him five thousand dollars. And he said that five thousand dollars was a lot, because he wanted to buy fifty kilos. So I said, "Then it's four thousand." So then we closed the deal at four thousand dollars per kilo. Because if a guy buys ten kilos, it's five thousand dollars. But if he buys more, then there's a discount [*laughter*]. Because if you buy a lot at the border, there's a discount there as well. I mean, it's less than two thousand, because you're buying in bulk, understand? So then I returned from Rio and I went to see my friend in prison. And I told him that I'd spoken to Ademar, and that the whole thing was ready to go, and that all he had to do was contact his supplier.

Did you fill him in on all the details?

No, no, because it was my deal and I had my own way of doing things. Besides, I was going to get help from my friends [*laughter*]. Because there was this friend of mine, Valdoberto, who I knew from my time in Rio. And he was from Corumbá. And he was the one who told me that the military did well there, because of certain "opportunities." And when Valdoberto finished his training, he was posted to Corumbá, so we were there together. And by the time he arrived I'd been there almost a year. And he was surprised that I was already involved. So when Valdoberto got there, I confided in him. I mean, I told him everything.

What did he say?

He said that he wasn't going to let me go it alone [*laughter*]. So I told him that I was about to deliver a shipment of cocaine to Rio, to a favela. And he said that he'd go with me. So we bought a car and we made a *cafofo*. And a cafofo is a secret hiding place for drugs. You know, you take out the engine, and then you cut open a hole, and then you hide the drugs. Then you solder the car back together again, and you paint it, and off you go! You leave on a Friday night after work and then, by Monday, you're back at the base.

Where did you get the drugs?

There was this supplier I knew in Bolivia, through my friend in prison. I told him that I had this contact in Rio, and that this contact had other contacts, and that we could sell a lot of drugs together. And he said, "Okay." So I bought fourteen kilos. And it cost us sixteen hundred dollars per kilo. And the supplier told me that he'd bring in the drugs, that he'd deliver them to my house.

And where did you hide them, under the bed?

I put them in a bag and I drove them over to my friend Valdoberto's house. And when I got there I said, "Valdoberto, it's all here, in this bag!" And he said, "Are you crazy? My mom and dad are here. What am I going to do with it?" "I don't know, it's just that I couldn't leave it at my house, because the Bolivian was there, and the neighbors saw his license plate. So as soon as he got there I left." "Okay, okay, no problem. Let's do this: let's bury it in the backyard." Because his mom and dad were home watching TV. So we went around the back and we dug this big hole. Because he told his parents he was going to dig up a tree for me. "I'm going to dig up a sapling so he can plant it at his house, okay?" So then, after we were done, I went back to my house. But I couldn't sleep. Neither of us could sleep. Because I kept thinking, "What's going to happen next? What if his dad finds out?" Because I mean it was this big fucking hole. And we put leaves over it. You know, to cover it up. But still! And you know what? It even crossed my mind that Valdoberto might take off with it. Because I was the one who made the deal, right? I mean, I was the one who was responsible. Because I didn't have enough money to pay for it all. I only had enough to pay for six kilos. And the rest was on consignment. You know, credit.

So the supplier gave you the drugs without being paid up front?

That's right, because that's usually how it's done. You know, you pay the supplier what you can, and you leave your house or your car as security. Then you pay him when you get back. Or sometimes, if he's a good friend, he'll give you the drugs and tell you to pay him later. But he has to be a really good friend to do that. But in those days it was easy, because the suppliers had lots of drugs, and they were always looking for new ways to sell them.

And how long was it before you set off for Rio?

Three days. And everything has to be done in secret. I mean, you can't tell anyone where you're going or what you're doing.

And his parents?

You tell them that you're going around the corner. And that you'll be back real quick. And his parents always believed him anyway, because he was in the military. So he could pretty much do as he pleased—when in reality, we were dealing drugs. I mean, can you believe it? [*Laughter.*]

Were you nervous?

A little. But once we got going, once we crossed the border into São Paulo, I felt fine. Because there are so many cars on the road that you figure you'll never get caught, right? Because I mean all you have to do is to get there. I mean, it's that simple. Except that when we got there, to Rio, we parked the car in Santa Teresa, because my aunt lived there. Well, I called her my aunt, because when I lived in Santa Teresa she used to help me out. So when we got there, to her house, I shouted out, "Hey aunt, it's me!" And she said, "Hey Bruno, what a surprise! Are you here on vacation?" "I'm here to sort something out for the navy." "So you came by car then?" "Yeah, is it okay if the car stays here, while I run into town?" "Sure, of course, whatever you want." So then I left the car there and I took the bus to Ademar's place. And when I got there, I told him that I had the drugs with me. And he said, "But how? Did you bring them in by bus?" Because I didn't want to tell him about the car, right? Because I didn't know him that well, and the car was my security. So then he said, "Okay, let's go see the guy tonight." So then I went back to my aunt's house, and I sat there with Valdoberto waiting. And Valdoberto was scared. I mean, he was really nervous. And he said, "How well do you know this guy?" And I said, "It's not a problem. Everything's going to turn out fine, because he's a friend of a friend of mine." So then, at around ten o'clock at night, I said, "Come on, let's go!" And Valdoberto said, "You know what? You go, you go on your own. I'll stay here with the car." "Okay, you stay here then. And if anything happens you know where to find me." And so when I got to Ademar's house, he introduced me to his family. You know, to his wife and kids. And Ademar's story is really interesting, because both of his sons ended up dead. And one of them came to visit me in prison. And then they both became involved. You know, with dealing drugs. And Ademar ended up dead too. He died snorting cocaine in a hotel here in Rio. But he was the one who introduced me to the leader of the favela. Because the day I did the deal in Estrada do Paiol was my first. It was my first time, understand?

Where did they take you?

They took us to this *boca de fumo*.[7] They were all standing around with their automatic weapons and they took us to this place. And when we got there, the leader said, "Well, where's the merchandise?" And I said, "It's nearby, with a friend. It's just that I didn't know when you wanted to seal the deal." "Well, let's seal the deal! Now how much did you bring?" "Fourteen kilos." "Good, because the money's almost all here." And when he told me about the money, I began to feel relieved. Because without even seeing the drugs, he had already come up with almost all the money.

Where did he put it?

He put it in these shopping bags. You know, the brown ones, with paper handles. There were three of them, all filled with cash. And we took them from the boca de fumo to Ademar's house. And we were escorted there by two gang members carrying guns, like it was a bank delivery or something [laughter]. And then, when we got there, we began counting it. And pretty soon Ademar shouted out, "It's all here. The money's all here." So then I explained to him that the drugs were in a car, in Santa Teresa, because I felt that by then that I could trust him. So then he said, "Hey, this is great, man! I mean, we'll both get rich this way! Because I have contacts here in Rio, and you have contacts at the border." And so then I left the money with Ademar, and I went to find Valdoberto, at my aunt's place. And when I got there I said, "Everything's all set, so let's bring in the drugs." And Valdoberto said, "What, at this time of night?" "Look, there's no problem. Everything's cool, okay? So come on, let's go!" So then we drove to this garage. And then we opened up the cafofo and took out the drugs. And then we handed them over to the leader. And he checked to see that it was all there, and that was it!

That was it?

That was it. And this friend of mine, Ademar, who worked at the barracks, he had a lot of contacts in favelas that were controlled by the Comando Vermelho. In Estrada do Paiol, Linha Nova, Paraiso Boa, Vila Santana, Córrego do Curió, Formigueiro . . .

So you were well connected?

We were well connected and protected, because we got to know the leaders. We visited them in their homes, and we got to know their families. And because we were honest, and doing things up front, there was no way we could get into any trouble. I mean, there was no way we could get double-crossed.

What did you do with the money?

Well, there are two ways you can get the money home. You can bring it back in the same cafofo and exchange it at the border for dollars, which is what we did in this case. Or you can deposit it in a bank in Rio, in the current account of some business. Because the guys in the favelas don't deal in dollars, so you have to figure out the exchange rate. You know, someone will say, "How much is the dollar today?" Then you do the math and the gang's treasurer pays you the money, understand? It's like, "Hey, just tell me how much it is in reais, okay?" Because this whole business of the exchange rate is confusing for them. But in Bolivia everything's paid for in dollars, understand? I mean, they won't accept reais. So we were always at a bit of a disadvantage, because the dollar kept rising. You know, it kept increasing in value. So if you waited too long, you could lose money. So you had to exchange it fast. And where I was stationed, at the border, it was never a problem.

So you went back to Corumbá . . .

With the car and the money, and then I contacted my friend in prison. And he said, "Let's exchange it with this friend of mine." Because dollars are sold every day at midday, after they are brought up from São Paulo. And then me and my friend Valdoberto, we threw this enormous party with some of the money that we'd made.

How much did you make?

We made a lot. Because we bought fourteen kilos for sixteen hundred dollars per kilo, right? And we sold it in Rio for four. So we made 2,400 dollars per kilo.

Which is a lot.

Yeah, it's a lot.

THE BORDER

For much of Brazil's history, borders have meant little in terms of regulating or stemming the flow of people or commodities. One reason for this, clearly, is the enormity of the border itself. Brazil rubs shoulders with every country in South America except Chile and Ecuador along a 16,885-kilometer line

A bridge between Brazil and Bolivia across the River Abunã. Photograph by Ariel Mariano Silber, 2013. Used by permission.

that traverses vast expanses of tropical rain forest and equally vast stretches of freshwater. By way of contrast, the U.S-Mexico border runs a mere 3,169 kilometers across relatively open and easy to monitor land.

The second reason why borders have meant little is that they have rarely been in dispute. The last war of any consequence between Brazil and its neighbors ended in 1870, meaning that the country's attentions have been focused, firmly, on its relationships with trading partners in Europe, the United States and, more recently, China.[8] The situation began to change in the mid-1990s, however, as fiscal reforms brought inflation under control and the economy began to burgeon. Suddenly, Brazil found itself outperforming its neighbors, who flooded the country with illegal immigrants and illicit goods.

There are an estimated 600,000 illegal immigrants in Brazil, mostly from Paraguay, Bolivia, Peru, Colombia, Chile, and Argentina.[9] Attracted by the prospect of better jobs and opportunities in life in general, they have crossed the border at various points, often with the assistance of professional traffickers, or coyotes, who are paid thousands of reais to bring their clients in. In fact, with access to countries of the developed world becoming

Downtown Ciudad del Este. Photograph by Ekem, 2007. Licensed under CC BY: http://creativecommons.org/licenses/by-sa/3.0/legalcode.

more and more restricted, Brazil has become a destination for immigrants from as far away as Senegal, Nigeria, Bangladesh, China, and Haiti.[10]

For illicit goods, the primary point of origin is Ciudad del Este, a city of a quarter of a million people on the Paraguayan side of the Bridge of Friendship. It is estimated that the illicit smuggling of DVDs, toys, cigarettes, textiles, guns, stolen cars, computers, and electronics from this region alone generates revenues of sixteen billion reais per year, and employs an army of twenty thousand women and men. The problem is that the ever-increasing volume of activity, fueled in part by Brazil's economic growth, and in part by widely disparate import tax regimes, makes border control extremely difficult.[11] By way of example, between thirty and forty thousand people and twenty thousand vehicles cross the Bridge of Friendship each day, with only limited and, ultimately, ineffectual monitoring by an understaffed federal police, to say nothing of the myriad other routes and ways that traffickers employ to get their goods across.[12]

Of course, the most significant illicit activity, for our purposes, is the cross-border trafficking of drugs. Brazil has never been a major producer of illicit drugs, although marijuana is grown fairly extensively in the northeast and the country is an important source of precursor chemicals for illicit drug manufacture. Since the mid-1970s, however, Brazil has become an important transshipment point for cocaine as the global increase in trade and the U.S.-led war on drugs have prompted producers in Colombia, Bolivia, and Peru to seek out alternative routes and markets in western Europe and Africa.[13] Not surprisingly, the emergence of Brazil as a transshipment point has led to a significant increase in local use, such that the country is now the largest consumer of cocaine—and its derivative, crack—in the world.

It is estimated that ninety tons of high-quality, pure cocaine enter Brazil each year, half of it from Bolivia and an additional 40 percent from Peru. This wasn't always the case, however. Initially, most of the cocaine that found its way to Brazil was flown in by small plane from Colombia. Then, in the early 1990s, under significant pressure from the United States, both Colombia and Peru increased their ability to monitor and control their airspace, pushing drug-trafficking operations toward their borders with Brazil.[14] And it was the subsequent invasion of Brazilian airspace by unauthorized, drug-related traffic that prompted the federal government to introduce its own version of the shoot-down law, or Lei do Abate.[15]

The Lei do Abate was first approved by the Brazilian congress in March 1998. It was not signed into law, however, until six years later, in October 2004. The law in essence grants the Brazilian air force authority to shoot down planes that are suspected of carrying drugs, but only after a wide range of precautionary measures are taken. These include attempts to establish visual or radio contact, attempts to change the plane's course, and, finally, the firing of warning shots. In addition, the Lei do Abate stipulates that the entire process has to be videotaped and that planes cannot be brought down over densely populated areas or if the pilot attempts to land.

The authorities claim that the law had an immediate impact, reducing the number of unauthorized flights from Colombia, Bolivia, and Peru by as much as 60 percent. Others argue, however, that the law is basically unenforceable, given that SIVAM, the Amazon surveillance system, is inadequate to the task and that, if anything, it has forced traffickers to adopt new methods, such as transporting drugs by plane to the border, from where they are brought in by land or by boat.[16] Alternatively, pilots have been known to fly for twenty minutes into Brazilian airspace, drop their load at a GPS-specified location, and then return, with the knowledge that they have time to cross the border before being intercepted.[17]

Either way, the attempt to restrict the trafficking of drugs by air has done little to stem the flow of drugs into the country. Fueled by increasing domestic prosperity and new opportunities in markets abroad, drug trafficking, drug use, and drug addiction have all been on the rise. Perhaps the most visible and disturbing manifestation of this increase is the crack epidemic that is ravaging Brazil's cities.[18] In São Paulo, for example, police seizures of crack cocaine increased from 595 kilos in 2006 to 1,636 kilos in 2009. And in Rio, crack-related arrests increased from 546 in 2009 to 2,597 in 2010.[19]

Taken together, the ease with which illegal immigrants, illicit goods, and drugs, in particular, make their way into the country has prompted the federal government to unveil an ambitious program to build a ten-thousand-mile "virtual fence."[20] The system, known as SISFRON, will use a combination of satellite technology, electromagnetic signaling, tactical communications, unmanned drones, ground vehicles, and river and naval craft to monitor border areas.[21] The plan is projected to cost somewhere in the region of fourteen billion dollars and will be completed in stages over the course of a decade, the first stage targeting, for obvious reasons, the border between Brazil and Bolivia, and Brazil and Paraguay.

In the meantime, the Brazilian military has launched a series of operations in the border region, including forays into neighboring countries to destroy illicit crops. As Brazil flexes its muscles, it has been compared, at times, with its neighbor to the north. Pedro Taques, a senator from Mato Grosso, said, "It pains me to say it, but I've heard people say we're the new gringos. Controlling the border is a problem that Brazil never thought it would have to face . . . and it's forcing us to do some uncomfortable things."[22]

Part of the profit that I made from my trip to Rio, I invested in a hotel. Because there was this guy, selling this hotel, in downtown Corumbá. And he was selling this hotel because he was in debt. And he was in debt because we were out on patrol one night and we stopped his boat. Because he was a drug trafficker, and now he owed his suppliers money, so he had to sell his hotel.

Were people bringing in drugs all the time?

All the time. And when they came across the Pantanal, from Bolivia, they'd bring in five, ten kilos at a time. And sometimes we'd catch them. And whoever was in charge that night would say, "No one saw anything, right?" And we'd say, "Right!" And so we'd catch them, and we'd keep the drugs.

And the people you caught?

We'd let them go, so they wouldn't say anything. Because it was a game, understand?

And this happened often?

It happened all the time. So I had to be careful, because I went to Bolivia a lot on business, because I had a lot of contacts there. So I had to be careful not to be seen in a bad light. Because most of the time we knew when boats were coming across, because it wasn't by accident, you know?

You mean someone would tell you that a boat was coming across?
That's right.

But why would someone do that?
To settle a score, to put someone out of business. And the federal police were totally unprepared for all these boats, because they just didn't have the men.[1] And so it was the navy's responsibility to police the frontier, except that a lot of people in the navy were involved, so no one was ever caught, understand? And this friend of mine, this friend of mine Valdoberto, who made this trip with me to Rio, he had this incredible knack for recruiting people. I mean, we'd go out one night, and by morning, we'd have two or three others tagging along.

People you could trust?
Absolutely. But then the navy sent two agents from CENIMAR to investigate.[2] Because we were having too much fun. Because we were hanging out at nightclubs, and driving around in imported cars, and shit like that.

So they suspected something?
That's right. And you know what? We managed to turn one of them. We managed to persuade him to come over to our side [*laughter*]. Because we all went out one night, because a friend in the department of communications had warned us. He said, "Watch out for the two guys that have just arrived, because there's something suspicious about them." So we already knew who they were, and what they were up to. So one night, when we were out, one of them was there dancing and having a good time. And we sat down together and had a few whiskeys. And I told him that I knew all about him. And so then he confessed. So I said, "How can we get around this?" And he said that he'd write up a report. So I told him that it should say that my father owned a business, and that he was always sending me money. You know, to calm things down.

And did it?
For a while it did. Except that do you know what happened? My friend Valdoberto, he became addicted, to cocaine. He began throwing these huge parties. And he'd do stupid things like stand on a table and set fire to a hundred-dollar note. And I tried to tell him. I tried to tell him that

he was going about it the wrong way. Then, on one of our trips, we were arrested.

By whom?

By the police, in São Paulo. Someone must have told them. Someone must have said there were drugs in the car. Because they stopped us as we were crossing the border from Mato Grosso do Sul. But then a few days later, we were released, because they didn't have enough evidence. Because we told the judge that we were delivering the car to someone in Rio, and that we didn't know anything about the drugs. And he believed us—the judge believed us.

And the drugs?

The police kept the drugs. They only reported a small amount, because I read about it in the newspaper. Because it's a double game. Because they get to arrest someone, and they get to keep the drugs, understand? And so after this, after being arrested, I stopped traveling with the stuff, because it was too much of a risk. Because there are people who make money this way, you know, who drive the drugs one way and then bring back the money. I mean, there's no shortage of people willing to do this, because that's how they make their living.

And where were you headed when you were arrested?

We were headed to Santos. And from there the drugs were going to be shipped to Germany. So it was a step in the right direction. I mean for me. It's just that we didn't have our own contacts.

How much were you selling it for?

We were selling it for six thousand dollars per kilo. And I knew the deal was doomed from the start, because there were way too many phone calls. Because the more phone calls you make, the more vulnerable the deal becomes. Because the ship was ready to leave. And it was my job to get them the drugs. And it was my haste to get them the drugs that was our undoing. And so then I said to Valdoberto, "Let's split the loss between us." And do you know what he said? He said, "You mean let's split *your* loss! Okay, let's split *your* loss, but from now on you take care of your business and I'll take care of mine, okay? Because I told you not to bring them the drugs, because, I mean, we already had their money." Because the guys in Santos sent us the money, so we could buy the drugs. They sent these two guys in a car with the money hidden inside a cafofo.

Was that usual?

No, no, it wasn't. And so all we had to do was to tell our suppliers that we needed so many kilos. Because the guys in Santos had heard that I was reliable, that I could be trusted. And that's when Valdoberto said that we should sell the drugs to someone else. He said, "What are they going to do, come after us, two guys in the military?" But I didn't agree. Because I thought that we had to be honest, because I've always been honest, understand? And you know what? I had serious misgivings about traveling that day. But on the other hand, I'd given them my word. And the guy who usually delivered the drugs for me was off somewhere else. And the guys from Santos kept calling, calling, and calling, because they wanted to leave. But the business of transporting drugs is complicated. I mean, you can't just make a deal and take off, understand? You have to follow the rules. And if you are so interested in the money that you don't follow the rules, that's when you get into trouble. So these guys kept calling me and saying, "Where the fuck's our drugs?" And there's me saying, "Don't worry, they'll be there." And then, when we reached the border with São Paulo, we were arrested. And so now I had to go to Santos to explain myself. And the situation was complicated because they didn't believe me, because only two kilos were reported in the press. So they thought we'd kept the rest. So I had to go there and explain to them that their drugs had been in the car. So you see how complicated it is? Because you buy and you sell, and sometimes you win and sometimes you lose, understand? And if you're not careful, if you're not up front about all this, you'll end up dead. And so now I had to pay off my debt, because when someone takes a loss like this, they have to be paid, no matter what it takes, understand? And so when I went back to Corumbá, the first thing I thought about was selling my hotel. Because that's how I started out, right? By telling you about the hotel. Because I bought the hotel and I used it to put up the Bolivians who brought over the drugs, even though it was across from the police station! [Laughter.]

And in all these years of drug trafficking, had you acquired much property, much money?

No, no, because the money soon goes. I mean, you live a good life, right? But you never own anything, because nothing's ever in your name, understand? I mean, it's almost as if you don't exist. And so I reached a point where I wanted to quit, because the whole business was beginning to irritate me. But then again I didn't, because I liked certain things, like the respect you were given. Because people looked to me, you know, to help them out. Like my aunt who lived here in Rio. Because her husband needed a taxi, so I bought him one. So you see, I was involved in a lot of good things. I mean, it wasn't all bad, right? And it was because of this attitude that when we got back to Corumbá, I said to Valdoberto, "Okay, Valdoberto, now we have to pay our debt." And he said, "Fuck that!" "Come on, Valdoberto, let's split what we owe between us. I mean, we were in this together, right?" "No, no, we weren't. Because I told you not to do business with those guys. Because they appeared out of nowhere, and we knew nothing about them, and then look what happened!" "Look, I'm going to pay up, even if you don't. I mean, I'll sell whatever it takes."

How much was the debt?

Sixty thousand dollars. Because that's what they sent us. And they were shipping the cocaine to Germany, where they'd sell it for five times that amount. Because they had this opportunity, and then, just like that, it was gone. Because the business is like that. I mean, you can have everything at your fingertips one day, and then, the next day, it's gone. And so after we were arrested in São Paulo, I got rid of Valdoberto as my partner. We split because he wanted to go it alone. And that's often what happens in this world. You start out as partners, you know, as friends, and then, after a while, you become rivals.

And did Valdoberto continue to do drugs?

Yes, yes, he did. He became more and more addicted and he turned into one of those, you know, crazy guys. And he ended up being killed here in Rio. He was killed in Linha Nova because he made a deal and took off with the money. And we were great friends in those days, because we went into the business together. And I went through what I went through. And because I had a sense for the business, I was able to get out alive. But him, no, he ended up dead. Because I warned him that this business was dangerous, ever since I left him there that one time with my aunt. I told him that to deal with these guys from the favelas, you had to know how to talk to them. And when we drove into town to deliver the drugs, do you know what he said? He said, "Bruno, they've already given you the money? Let's split, and sell the drugs to someone else!" And I told him that no, that's not the way to do business, that you have to be honest. And I believe that it is because I have always been honest, that I am still alive today. I mean, it's a reputation that I have to this day.

You mean inside of crime?

That's right. And you know what? There was even talk that it was Valdoberto who told the police. You know, when we were arrested on the way to Santos. But I didn't take it seriously. I mean, it just wasn't possible, was it? I mean, I guess anything's possible in this world.

So like I said, when I finally got back to Corumbá, my first instinct was to pay off my debt by selling the hotel. But the hotel wasn't in my name, it was in the name of this lawyer guy from Rio. And do you know what he did? He sold the hotel and took off [*laughter*]. Because a lot of our stuff was in his name, so he could move it around. But he took off for Boston and we never heard from him again. And some of my friends wanted to go after his family, you know, to punish him. But I disagreed. I wouldn't let them.

Is this type of punishment common?

It's extremely common, but it depends on who's involved. Because I've never been one for violence. Because the way I figure, you either win or lose in this game, so why make things more complicated? Of course, not everyone thinks like this. And the guy should have known that the moment he messed with someone's money, his life and the lives of his family were in danger. And anyway, by then I was working with a different guy. I mean, I was with a different partner.

What was his name?

His name was Wagner, and I met him at a party. And it turned out that he was this big bank robber from São Paulo.

How did you know?

I asked around. Because inside the world of crime there's this vast network of information. So it's no use robbing someone and trying to hide, unless you go far away.

Like Boston?

Like Boston, exactly. But if you stay here in Brazil, they'll find you. I mean, it might take them a year or two, but they'll find you. And so this Wagner guy was in Corumbá because he was owed money. And we got to know each other, because he stayed at my hotel. And one day, he turned to me and said, "How can you afford to own a hotel, if you're a corporal in the navy?" And so then we decided to go into business together, because he also had contacts in Rio. But before I could do this, before I could go in a different direction, I had to clear it with friends. Because it's never a problem doing business with someone. But you have to be careful, understand? You have to be careful that no one thinks you're moving in on their territory. Because if they do, you can end up losing everything, understand? And then you're going to have to start all over again, so you can make money and pay off your debts. Because there's always someone willing to give you credit, especially if you have a reputation for being honest, like me. I mean, I'd sell anything to pay off my debts. I'd sell cars, jewelry, anything. Because then I'd be given more credit, understand? I mean, I guess I could have just quit. But then I would have lost everything. You know, the nightlife, the money, the prestige, everything. And I didn't want that. Because I was always after more, you see.

So when you say credit, you mean the ability to get drugs without paying for them?

That's right. Because the deal was you'd pay your supplier later, because you had a line of credit. I mean, it's like any business. And my line of credit was pretty much open. It had to be, because I had a lot of debts. I mean, a few of my friends had money. You know, stashed away. But I'd stopped doing business with them. Like my friend Valdoberto. Because Valdoberto was a great guy, but he had the wrong attitude when it came to the business of crime.

What do you mean?

He'd lie. He'd say that he brought twenty kilos with him to Rio, and that the police had taken it all away. You know, shit like that. And since he never paid his debts, he was always asking for more credit. And I didn't think that was right, and that sooner or later someone would find out. And you know what? He didn't last long in this business. He didn't last long once he went out on his own.

But you always tried to pay your debts, right?

Always. But then something would happen to leave me with more, understand? I mean, it was like a vicious cycle. I mean, I'd supply this one favela, right? And it would be invaded by the police, and the police would take everything. And just like I had credit with my suppliers, I'd give credit to the guys I supplied in Rio. And that often made things more difficult for me, because as a dealer I had less credit to give than my suppliers, understand?

Could you give me an example?

Let's say, for example, that I supply this one favela with thirty kilos of cocaine. And they pay me for fifteen, which means they owe me for another fifteen, which they say they'll pay later. And then the police come in and take everything, which means they don't have the money to pay me, which means they're going to have to go out and rob. Or, alternatively, I can give them more credit, so they can pay me from what they make. Because if I'm going to continue selling to them, I'm going to have to give them more credit, understand? Because if I don't, I'll be seen as a guy who's a friend when things are good, but who doesn't want to know when things are bad. Because then you'll lose that contact, and then maybe something will happen to you in another favela. Because word will get around that you're not to be trusted, and that it's okay to steal your stuff. And I didn't want that kind of reputation. I mean, I did everything I could to keep everyone happy. Except that I wouldn't give them as much as I did before, because of my credit situation in Bolivia. Because I didn't tell my suppliers about my losses, because it would affect my credit. And I mean, I had stuff taken from me all the time.

So your suppliers didn't know about your end of the business?

No, and they didn't want to know. And then there were some who did away with intermediaries altogether and made contact with their buyers directly. And nowadays, a lot of them ship coca base and distill it right here in the city, in a laboratory. Because it's much easier to get a hold of the liquids. You know, the ether, the acetone, and the hydrochloric acid.

Where do they distill it?

Out of town, in the countryside. It's something that's been going on for a decade or so. And I was looking to expand my business, because I wanted to make one more deal and get out. So I came to the conclusion that I needed someone to help me ship the drugs out of the country, because it was a lot more profitable and a lot safer, because you didn't have to deal with the favelas. And this new friend of mine, Wagner, he knew a journalist who lived in Rio who had a contact in Italy. And there were these ships that belonged to this company that were stranded in all these ports abroad, because the company was going under. And there were all these

A typical setup in a *boca de fumo* in a Rio favela. Photograph by AP / Felipe Dana, 2012. Used by permission.

sailors who were getting rides home to see their families, because they'd been away for so long. And we knew one of them, who lived here in Rio, and he was about to head back to his ship. So we figured he could be our courier.

What sort of quantity were you thinking of?

Ten kilos, because that was the most he could carry in his bag. But I mean, that was more than enough, because we could sell it in Italy for twenty thousand dollars a kilo. So ten kilos meant 200,000 dollars, which was four times our usual profit. And so we made contact with this guy, with this sailor, so he could deliver the drugs to another contact we had made in Italy. And the money from the deal was going to be transferred back to Brazil via an import-export business. Except that when the cocaine base arrived, it turned out to be no good. Because we weren't buying cocaine this time, we were buying cocaine base, because we were going to distill it ourselves. But hey, it was no big deal. It just meant that we had to send for more, that's all.

What about the stuff you bought that was no good?

We sold it here in Rio, in the favelas. Because you can sell anything here in Rio, because the guys who live in the favelas, they'll stick anything up their noses. And when the leader of a favela buys a kilo of cocaine, he mixes it with all kinds of shit. I mean, it's incredible.

So you mean when someone in a favela buys cocaine, it's 50 percent?

Less, much less, 25 percent maybe. Because the guys who live in a favela don't have any money, understand? Because the market's not in the favelas. So there are all these different products of different quality and price. And when there's a *baile funk* they sell a lot of cocaine for five, ten reais.[3] But it's not good quality, understand? Because the good stuff's sold to the people who live outside of the favela. You know, who have money. But anyway, getting back to the story, it was in the process of distilling this cocaine base that everything fell apart. It was in this house in Rio where we'd set up this laboratory that everything came to an end.

There were six of us, including Wagner who, after he got to know me, told me he wanted in. Except that he was unsure about the whole drug trafficking thing, because he thought that robbing banks was safer [*laughter*]. So anyway, it took a week or so before the new batch of cocaine base arrived. And when it arrived, I made arrangements to have it shipped to Rio, so we could distill it.

Had you ever distilled cocaine before?

Once or twice, because buying cocaine base and chemicals was cheaper. And I was always looking for ways to make more money. So yeah, I had a basic idea of what I was doing. So then, when the cocaine base finally arrived, I called my friend in Rio and said, "Get the place ready, because it's on its way."

Who bought the liquids?

A friend of mine, who had a contact in a pharmacy. Because you can't just walk into a pharmacy and buy the stuff, because it's restricted.[4] So this friend of mine, he bought us the liquids. And then he said, "All we need now is a place." And our first thought was to find somewhere out of town. You know, in the country. But there again, we had so little time that we ended up doing it right here in Rio, in a house in Barra. This friend of mine got us this house, down toward Recreio, a small house in a neighborhood. And so we stored all the liquids there and we waited for the cocaine base to arrive.

A cocaine brick is prepared for cutting in a Rio favela. Photograph by Loretta van der Horst, journalist and filmmaker, 2013. Used by permission.

And no one in the neighborhood was suspicious?

No, because we brought everything over at night. And there really wasn't that much stuff. And we were all really anxious to get on with it. Because we'd found a house, right? And we'd bought all the liquids, and all the other materials. So now all we needed was the base. Because a courier was bringing it in. Because after what had happened to me on the way to Santos, I didn't do that kind of thing anymore. So I paid someone I could trust, because you can't give it to just anyone you know.

How did you get there, to Rio?

I flew. And then I waited. And the key to the whole deal was keeping it a secret. Because it was our chance of getting out of the business. So when the cocaine base finally arrived, we were all set to go. And I mean, it's not a difficult process. You just have to know what you're doing, and the place has to be right. I mean, under no circumstances can you light a match, or a cigarette, or anything.

Because otherwise?

Because otherwise, boom! [*Laughter.*] But basically, what you do is, you take the cocaine base and you soak it in ether. Then you strain it through a sheet. You know, some sort of fabric, to filter out the impurities. Then, when you're done with that, you pour in the acetone and so many milliliters of hydrochloric acid. Then you let it sit for an hour. And we figured that it was best to do two kilos at a time. And since we had to process ten kilos, it was going to take us five, six hours.

So one hour for each two kilos of base.

That's right. And we decided to do it at night, because that's when all of us were available. And we were running a huge risk in doing it in that house, because of the smell of the materials. But I mean, we had no choice, because it was the only place that we could get. And because we were going to distill it in one night, everything had to be carefully planned and coordinated. And I had the feeling that night that something was wrong. And something kept telling me to get the hell out of there. But then again, I kept thinking about the money. I mean, a whole bunch of different things went through my head. And then there were these two other guys there, who I didn't know. And I didn't like it, because I knew nothing about them. And another thing—I didn't know the layout of the house. You know, where the bathroom was, and where the hallways led, in the event that we needed to escape.

So you felt vulnerable?

I felt extremely vulnerable. And like I said, I had a feeling that night that something was about to go wrong. And then of course it did. Because they broke in. And then it was, "Hands on your heads, everyone!" You know, like they'd set a trap.

Who were they?

The police, the civil police.[5] They were looking for a safe house, where kidnappers hid their victims. And they came across us instead. At least I don't think we were who they were looking for.

So no one told on you?

No, no, no, I don't think so, because we were all so careful with everything.

And was everyone still inside the house?

No, because most of the guys had already left, because they didn't need to be there. The only ones who were still there were me and this other guy who was responsible for delivering the cocaine to the sailor who was going to take it to Italy. And I asked this other guy if he had a gun. And he said that he didn't. So I said, "What the fuck do you mean, you don't have a gun?" "Hey, you're the one who should have a fucking gun!" Then someone shouted, "Open the door! It's the police!" Because the smell of the materials was unbelievable. So then I said to this other guy, "Is there any way out of here?" And he said, "No, no, there isn't." "Then for fuck's sake hide!" "Hide, hide, but where?"

Where were the drugs at this point?

The drugs were in the front room on a table next to a weighing machine, and two microwaves that we used for drying. I mean, we'd turned the fucking house into a laboratory. And then more police arrived, and they broke down the door. And then they started firing shots into the air, and then it was, "Nobody move!" Because the police have this whole way of breaking into houses.

And how did you respond?

"We give up. We give up." You know, so they wouldn't shoot us. Then one of them said, "Where are all the others?" And I said, "There aren't any others." "Of course there are, you motherfuckers! And you're going to tell us where they are! And what's this? Are you motherfuckers distilling cocaine?" "No, no one's distilling cocaine." "So what's this, then, popcorn? Shut your mouth, you son of a bitch." And then one of them kicked me in the stomach. And then he said, "Lie down, you asshole, lie down on the floor. Now where's the rest of the stuff?" Because they wanted more. They wanted money too, but there wasn't any.

And what were you thinking?

I was thinking, "Holy shit, it's over before it's begun." That's what I was thinking. Because my folks in Recife, they didn't know what I was up to. I mean, occasionally I'd write them a letter or something. But I wasn't going to involve my family in any of this, no way. And all my stuff was back at the frontier. And here I was in Rio, on my own, with no one to help.

And did the police take away the cocaine?

Of course! There were ten kilos there ready, and they only reported four. And they made up this whole story about how they knew we were there. You know, nothing about the fact that they broke in without a warrant, or anything like that. I mean, I guess they just got lucky. Because we were almost done. I mean everything was almost ready. And the last two kilos were drying in the microwaves when they came in.

And that was the beginning of your journey, right? Your journey to prison and your involvement with the CV?

I already knew the guys from the CV. And they said to me, "Hey, if anything ever happens to you, make sure you come over to our side, okay? Because we're family."

So you weren't scared, then?

On the contrary. I knew I was going to be treated well, because of my reputation. I mean, it helped me survive. Because I knew I'd be safe in there. You know, I'd be able to sleep at night, and I wouldn't have to buy a knife or anything. Because before it wasn't like that. But with the Comando Vermelho, you could show up with nothing. I mean, you could leave your money on the floor and no one would touch it. Because the Comando Vermelho's a family. And I noticed this right away, as soon as I got to prison, that there was this brotherhood. And I also noticed that they were organizing, and that they were making contact with other leaders in other places. And these alliances that you hear about these days, between the CV and PCC, they go way back.[6] I mean, when I got to prison, they were already being made.

COCAINE

Cocaine (benzoylmethylecgonine) is a crystalline tropane alkaloid that is derived from the leaves of the coca plant, which indigenous peoples of South America have been harvesting and chewing for centuries.[7] There are two species and four varieties of the plant, which resembles a blackthorn bush and grows to a height of seven to ten feet. Once harvested, coca leaves are made into coca base. First, the leaves are placed in an aboveground container, or in a plastic-lined pit, together with an alkaline material such as sodium carbonate. Then, a water-immiscible solvent, such as kerosene, is added and the mixture is stirred. This initiates a process whereby the solvent extracts water-insoluble cocaine alkaloids from the alkaline solution.

Once the cocaine alkaloids and kerosene separate, the water and leaves are drained off. Then the cocaine alkaloids are extracted from the kerosene by adding diluted hydrochloric or sulfuric acid. The mixture is then filtered and potassium permanganate added. After standing for four to six hours, the mixture is then filtered again and ammonia added. This forms an off-white, dough-like precipitate, which is cocaine base. Cocaine base is made into cocaine by dissolving the base in acetone and then filtering it to remove impurities. Hydrochloric acid diluted in acetone or ether is then added to the solution. The addition of the hydrochloric acid causes the cocaine to precipitate out of the solution as cocaine hydrochloride. The cocaine hydrochloride is then filtered out for drying under heat lamps, in microwaves, or with the aid of fans.[8]

The stimulant and hunger-suppressing qualities of coca have been known for centuries. The Spanish used coca to increase the endurance and productivity of their slaves, especially in the mines, recognizing early on that it allowed them to go without eating meat for days and instilled in them a sense of "force and courage."[9] It was not until the mid-nineteenth century, however, that the isolation of the cocaine alkaloid was achieved. In 1855, a German chemist, Friedrich Gaedcke, published a treatise on an extract of the coca leaf he called erythroxylinal, though little progress was made in isolating its active ingredients. Then, a year later, another German chemist, Friedrich Wöhler, obtained a large quantity of coca leaves from an Austrian frigate that had circumnavigated the globe. Wöhler gave the leaves to Albert Niemann, a PhD student at the University of Göttingen, who isolated the primary alkaloid, which he named cocaine. The first synthesis and elucidation of the structure of the cocaine molecule was subsequently achieved by Richard Willstätter in 1898.

With the discovery of this new alkaloid, attempts were made to explore and exploit its potential commercial use. In Europe and the United States, it was marketed as a stimulant; an anesthetic; an additive to cigarettes, wine, and soft drinks, most notably Coca-Cola; and a treatment for morphine addiction, sinus infection, and hay fever. As cocaine use gradually increased, however, and its addictive qualities and links to antisocial behavior became better known, steps were taken to restrict its distribution and sale.[10]

In the United States, Georgia was the first state to ban the sale of cocaine in 1902. A more common approach, however, was to restrict who could sell it and whom it could be sold to. A 1907 California law, for example, limited the sale of cocaine to those with a physician's prescription. And in 1913, a New York State law limited pharmacists' supplies to five ounces.[11] The federal government's first intervention was in 1906, when it instituted a national labeling requirement for cocaine and cocaine-based products through the Food and Drug Act. This was followed, in 1914, by the Harrison Narcotics Tax Act, which established a regulatory and licensing regime. The Harrison Act did not affect cocaine producers, however, who were left

Drugs captured during a police raid in a Rio favela. Photograph by Marcello Casal Jr. / ABr, 2010. Licensed under CC BY 3.0 BR: http://creativecommons.org/licenses/by /3.0/br/legalcode.

alone as long as they conformed to federally mandated purity and labeling standards. In fact, restrictions on cocaine manufacture were not imposed until the Jones-Miller Act of 1922.[12]

With the imposition of federal restrictions, cocaine use in the United States fell sharply until the 1970s, when cultural attitudes toward drug use began to change. In 1962, there were fewer than a million users of cocaine in the United States. By 1985, however, there were an estimated twelve million.[13] The rise in cocaine use, and in drug use in general, was the impetus behind the declaration of the now four-decade-old war on drugs, which has cost taxpayers more than a trillion dollars and filled our prisons with low-level, mainly nonviolent offenders.[14] Not surprisingly, a principal target of the war on drugs has been cocaine producers and traffickers in South America.

The current U.S. strategy began in Colombia in 2000, with an eight-year, seven-billion-dollar campaign to stop the flow of cocaine to the United States. During Plan Colombia, thousands of square kilometers of coca plants were sprayed from the air and destroyed, and heavy investments were made in training and equipping Colombian army counternarcotics battalions. The effect of Plan Colombia has been to decrease the country's share of global coca production from 74 percent in 2000 to 42 percent in 2011.[15] The other effect has been to increase coca production in the neighboring countries of Bolivia and Peru and to reorient supply routes from the Caribbean toward Central America and, more significantly, Mexico.

In 1990, just over half the cocaine imported into the United States came through Mexico. By 2007, that had risen to more than 90 percent. In response, the U.S. government entered into an agreement with the governments of Mexico and the countries of Central America. The Mérida Initiative, or Plan Mexico as it is sometimes known, budgeted 1.6 billion dollars to be spent on equipment, such as transport helicopters and surveillance aircraft, but also on judicial reform, institution building, and rule-of-law issues, in recognition of the fact that one of the biggest enemies in the war on drugs is corruption. The effect of the Mérida Initiative has been to force traffickers to adapt, once again, by shifting their focus to the countries to Mexico's immediate south.

This brings us, finally, to the latest iteration of U.S. policy toward the region, which is the 165-million-dollar Central America Regional Security Initiative. The operation is focused on Central America's shipping lanes and coastline, the route of choice for 90 percent of the estimated 850 metric tons of cocaine per year that is headed for the United States.[16] The goal is to make it so difficult and dangerous for traffickers to move drugs north that they will eventually quit the U.S. market, where cocaine use is falling, and look for easier routes to expanding markets in the countries of western Europe and Africa. One of the most important routes for this trade is to the south and east through Brazil.

When the police found out I was in the military, they took me to a precinct and opened an investigation. And I told them that I wasn't going to talk to anyone without a lawyer, because that was my right. And so they kept me there all night until the navy came and took me away. And when I got to the navy jail I was interrogated, because the navy wanted to know who else was involved. But my friends at the frontier had nothing to do with my arrest. And I wasn't about to give them any names, because that's not the way I operated. So then they started the trial process. And within thirty days they'd handed me over to the civilian authorities. And as far as I was concerned, the sooner the better.

How come?

Because I wasn't sure how long I could take it. Because they'd blindfold me, and put me in the back of a car, and drive me around. And then they'd take me to a building and put me in a room. And they'd tell me that the other guys who were involved were in the next room, and that they were talking. And the whole time I kept telling myself that they were bluffing, as much for my own survival as anything else. Because once you become involved, the situation becomes a lot more complicated, even if you're a nobody, like me. And so anyway, I told them that I'd done everything myself, so they wouldn't investigate any further. Because all they were interested in was getting rid of me, you know, in turning me over to the civilian authorities.

You mean to make the whole thing go away?

That's right. And that was fine by me because I could breathe freely again, because I wouldn't have to give them any names.

So what was navy jail like?

There was almost no one else there. And I had my own cell, and there was a snooker table and a TV. And I thought that all the prisons would be alike. You know, that I'd serve a little time and then get out. I mean, when I think about it, I was completely deluded.

Did anyone come to visit you, while you were there?

No, no, no, because no one wants to expose themselves in that way. And because the guys who say they're your friends, they're your friends when things are going good. But when things are going bad they don't want to know. It's like, "Who? Who's been arrested? No, no, I don't know him." And you know what? You can't really expect much from friends. Family, maybe. And my family was all in Recife. But when I was arrested, I decided not to tell any of them. So I sort of disappeared.

And no one suspected, I mean, no one came to look for you?

Eventually they did. I mean, eventually they found out what had happened. But at the time, I didn't want them there. I said, "Look, if you really want to help me, then get on with your lives, okay?" Because I knew that it would be really painful when they saw me in prison, when they saw the situation I was in. And so then I started to think about things. And I realized that back then, I had no idea what I was getting myself into. Because I imagined it was one thing, right? And it turned out to be another. And I remember thinking to myself, "But why are drugs illegal? I mean, I just don't get it."

Did you do drugs?

No. I mean, I tried them, but I never liked them, because I could see that they were no good. But you know what? In those days it wasn't such a big deal. I mean, guys would be arrested and then before you knew it, they'd be back out on the street. Because that was the way it was at the frontier. I mean, it was pretty much out in the open. And the level of corruption there was incredible. So I said to myself, "Am I going to get rich in this place or what?" Except that if it's one thing at the frontier, it's another thing everyplace else. I mean it's one thing when you're transporting the drugs, and it's another when you're dealing with the favelas. And then it's another thing when you are in prison. Because each situation has its own logic, each situation has its own dynamic, understand? And as a consequence, there are guys who never leave the frontier. I mean, there might be millions to be made elsewhere, and yet they still don't leave. But not me! Because I wanted everything, I wanted it all. So no, I didn't tell my family. I took time to reflect, to think things through instead. But it was my arrival at a civilian prison that scared me. It was that that scared me the most.

On the day that I was transferred, I was taken to a police precinct in Novo Horizonte. And there was this policeman there who was beating everyone as they came in. He told all the prisoners to strip naked and then he beat them with a shovel. And when I arrived, he took a look at my papers and moved me to one side. Then he started beating the guy next to me. And I mean he was beating him hard! And yet he didn't lay a finger on me, because I was in the military. He said, "Hey, you were in the navy, right?" Then he told me that that's how he dealt with scum, with *vagabundos*.[1] And that if I wanted to get out of there, I'd have to give him money. Because only prisoners with money could be transferred.

Transferred where?

To Aranha Filho, which is this prison in Rio Claro where they held prisoners until they were sent to where they'd serve out their sentence. So then they sent me to this cell where there were just these two other guys. And all the other cells were full. I mean, they were overcrowded, with everyone huddled together. Because in Brazil, if you've been to school or you have a job with the government, they'll put you in a different cell, in a much nicer cell. So then I said to myself, "You know what? I'm no different from all these other guys." So when the guard went to put me in with the two prisoners, I said, "No, put me in that cell over there, with all those other guys." And the guard said, "Are you sure?" And I said, "Yes, I'm sure. Put me in with all those other guys." Because I didn't want to be in that other cell. Because the cells were the same size, right? But in one of them there were just these two prisoners, and in the other, there were thirty or forty guys. And some of them were standing up, and some of them were lying down, you know, trying to get some sleep.

Was there a bathroom?

No bathroom, just a hole in the floor in the corner. And at night the hole had to be cleaned and covered up, so someone could sleep there [*laughter*]. I mean, the place was filthy. I mean, it was disgusting. So then I sat there listening to everyone talk about how they'd been arrested, and where they were from. And I didn't want anyone to know I was in the navy, so I kept that to myself.

So people asked each other, "Hey, where are you from?"

That's right. And you know what? Everyone in that cell was Comando Vermelho. Because the guard said to me, he said, "Are you sure you want to go in there? Because everyone there is Comando Vermelho." And I said, "That's fine. That's where I want to be."

Were there other options?

There were cells for those who were Terceiro Comando.[2] And there were cells for those who were neutral, who weren't part of a faction. But then you were on your own. You know, you had no one to support you, and no way of being transferred. Whereas I could be transferred to any prison that was controlled by the cv, understand? And when all the prisoners in that cell started talking, it turned out that some of them were from favelas that I had supplied. And so there were guys there who knew the guys who bought drugs from me.

You mean they came up to you and said, "Hey, don't I know you?"

Not exactly, but then one thing leads to another, right? Because when anyone new came in, they'd write their name, their nickname, and where they were from on a piece of paper. And so I told them that my name was Luis, that my nickname was Bruno, and that I was from Estrada do Paiol, which is where I did most of my business. Because that's where most people knew me.

And that was it? That meant you were in?

It was like night and day. It was like, "Hey Bruno, come over here, brother. Look, I've brought you some coffee!" I mean, it was like all of a sudden I was a celebrity [*laughter*]. And most of the guys in that cell were from the favelas. And they had no sense of their rights, and of how they were being abused. And a lot of them couldn't read or write. And you know what? I was already thinking of ways I could help them, of things that I could do. So when Ademar's son came to visit me the next day, I said to him, "Jesus Christ, there are guys in here who have served out their sentence already. I bet it wouldn't take much to get them out." And he said, "Look, Bruno, take care of yourself first, okay? Forget about these others." But still, there was something really wrong with the situation. I mean, the way that everyone was beaten when they came in. It just wasn't right. But you know what? He didn't last long. I mean, it wasn't long before that guard was taken out.

You mean he was killed?

That's right, because someone sent a message, you know, to the outside, to have him killed. Because that's the way it had to be, understand? Because they had to start organizing. Because how can you call yourself an organization, if you're suffering that kind of abuse inside of prison? But this process of organizing took a long time. Because they were always fighting among themselves, because they didn't know any better.

How long did you spend there, in that precinct?

Fifteen days. And then I was transferred to Aranha Filho.

And you'd already been sentenced, right?

That's right. I'd been tried and sentenced and expelled from the navy.

And the other prisoners who were there?

Some of them had been sentenced. But there were others there who were awaiting trial. I mean, it was a real mixture. And so I said to Ademar's son, "Hurry up and get me those three hundred reais." Because that's what it cost to be transferred. "Hurry up and get me those three hundred reais, because I can't stand it here any longer. And you see that guard over there? Give the money to him, so by next week I'll be gone."

Where did these three hundred reais come from?

From the cv, from Estrada do Paiol. And you know what? I'd convinced myself that Aranha Filho was going to be a better place, that there'd at least be enough space to lie down. But when I got there, I realized that I was wrong, because the situation was a whole lot worse. Because there were these two guards there with clubs. And they beat the prisoners as they got out of the back of the truck. And when I got there, when I saw what was going on, I said to myself, "Holy shit!" Because it was obvious that no one had any rights in that place.

Were you beaten?

No, no, I wasn't. Because I arrived with these three other guys, from the same precinct. And these other guys were leaders, you know, of favelas. And when we arrived, one of them recognized one of the guards, because they were from the same neighborhood. And this guard took us all aside. And I found out later that he'd been paid a thousand reais not to beat us. So then we were taken to the *cela de espera*, which is a cell where they send new prisoners so the guard shifts can check them out.[3] And then, after two weeks in there, we were taken to Cell Block 2. Because Aranha Filho consists of four cell blocks. There's Cell Block 1, which is underground. And then there's Cell Blocks 2, 3, and 4, one on top of another. And Cell Block 4 was for prisoners who were educated, or who worked for the government. And I could have gone there if I wanted to, except that I didn't. Because I was already involved, right? And so now I was going to run away and hide? "No way," I said to myself. "There has to be something in this for me. There just has to be."

What do you mean?

I was thinking that I had to take advantage of the situation, because I had eight years in front of me, right? And who knows? Maybe I'd be in there even longer. Because what if I got into a fight, what if I killed someone? But you know what? I noticed that these guys were a family, that they shared things, and that they called me "brother."

So you felt protected?

That's right. And there were guys there who had money, who helped the other prisoners out. Because they'd pay to smuggle things in. I mean, really stupid things like pizza, or a TV. Because TVs weren't allowed back then, and so they'd pay a guard to put one in front of the cell. And if you didn't have money, you couldn't afford to be transferred, which meant you had to stay there and sleep on the freezing cold floor, which meant you'd get sick. And so you had to try to find a way out of there. And how were you going to do that? By bribing someone, by giving a guard some money. And I mean, a lot of people died in that place, a lot of people who didn't have family, who didn't have anyone to support them. And like I said, after two weeks I was sent to Cell Block 2, which was this enormous hall with five different wings. And each wing consisted of four cells facing each other. And each wing was closed off by these huge metal gates. And these gates would be opened during the day and locked again at night. And everyone in that cell block was CV, everyone.

How many prisoners were in each cell?

There were sixty, seventy men. And each cell was about eight meters square, and everyone slept on the floor. And there was this tiny space in the corner to go to the bathroom, and to take a shower. Because there was this pipe sticking out of the wall—except that there was never any water. So when there was water, everyone took turns. And the toilet, the toilet was a hole in the ground. So you had to make do with a towel. You know, you wrapped the towel around you, so no one could see.

So there was no privacy?

No privacy, none at all. And then in the morning, they'd bring you coffee. And the coffee was awful. I mean, it was more like sludge. And sometimes there was bread, and sometimes there wasn't. You know, a small piece of stale bread. And then you had to wait until lunchtime. And they claimed that they spent more than a thousand reais per month to feed each prisoner. But it was a lie, it was a huge fucking lie. And I mean, what were you going to do, complain? And then there was this canteen there that sold things for breakfast, but only to those who had money. But then what? You're going to sit there and eat while everyone is watching you? I don't think so. So the prisoners who had money bought things, and they shared them with the others. And that's how the guys who were Comando Vermelho gained the other prisoners' support. Because a lot of prisoners who didn't have money came over to their side, understand? Because the guys in the Comando Vermelho were beginning to organize, and they were arranging for all these things to be brought in. I mean, cases and cases of things like toothpaste, soap, and toilet paper would show up, all of them sent by communities on the outside. And the director of the prison would accept them. I mean, he'd let them in. Because the authorities weren't giving the prisoners anything. And when I saw what was going on, I said to myself, "Holy shit, look at this!"

So in a way, the director of the prison was helping the CV to organize?

In a sense, yes, he was. I mean it all started when they divided the prisons by faction, when they decided that certain prisons were only for the CV. But you're right, by letting all of these things in, they were helping them to organize. Because the guys who were running the prison would say, "Ah, but this way everyone's happy. This way there are no revolts." But at the same time the CV was growing, and it was getting stronger and stronger. And it got to the point where prisoners began escaping from the roof. Because they'd pay the military police. Because the inside of the prison is guarded by the Department of Corrections. But the roof and the perimeter are guarded by the police. And the prisoners paid them to let them escape. And I mean, a lot of prisoners escaped that way. And at the time, it cost around thirty thousand reais to escape from Aranha Filho. I mean, all you needed was the money and the next day you'd be back home in your community. So when I found out about this, I said, "Well, this is interesting!" Because I also wanted to escape. And so they asked me, they said, "Do you have any money?" And I said, "No, but I'm going to get in contact with friends, on the outside."

You mean Ademar?

That's right. Because he found out what had happened after I was arrested, because he wasn't in on that deal. Because I wanted to be done with dealing with Ademar and the favelas, because I wanted to make more money, understand? And you know what? I would have helped him out, if things hadn't come undone. Because he wasn't making much money either. Because unless you sell a lot, you don't make a lot. And so he sent his son to get a pass, so he could visit me in prison.

Did you ask him for money, so you could escape?

Of course! And in Aranha Filho there was also this business of writing down your name, your nickname, and where you were from. And it was organized by the president of the Comando Vermelho in that prison. And he had his group of men. And if someone had to be killed, the president had to give his permission. And I found all this extremely interesting.

The same deal as in a favela then?

That's right. Because this way of organizing developed first inside of prison, and then it spread to the favelas, understand? So when I told them my name, everybody started clapping. And I thought to myself, "Hey, this is okay! This is a good thing." Right? And you know what? I could put my things down on the floor of that cell without worrying. And I could go to sleep without worrying. I mean, I didn't have to worry that someone would rob me or mess with my stuff.

But surely, there must have been fights.

It was forbidden. And if you did fight you'd be punished. And that was a good thing, right? Except you know what? There were a lot of drugs in that prison. There was a lot of marijuana and a lot of cocaine. And when families came to visit, they'd give the prisoners money, and that's how they'd spend it.

Did the guards know that the prisoners were selling drugs?

The guards were the ones who brought the drugs in! And then they'd sell them to the prisoners, who'd sell them to the other prisoners. But drugs didn't interest me, because all I was interested in was escaping. Because I didn't think I was going to be able to take it. I mean, can you imagine, eight years? So if there was a way to get out of there, I was going to take it. It didn't matter that I was welcome in that place. It didn't matter that everyone clapped their hands when I came in. Because there's nothing like freedom, understand? But then again, I noticed that there were leaders in there who liked it, who'd gotten used to the place.

Why?

Because in prison they were protected. Because they were the ones who gave the orders, right? They were the ones who decided what went on in their communities on the outside. But I mean, they weren't involved in shootouts with the police. They weren't the ones who were putting their lives on the line. And they had their drugs, and their money, and their weekly visits.

Weekly visits by whom?

By their women. Because women were allowed in every Thursday. And there was this place there called the *ratão*. And it was this tiny place, this tiny bathroom that was about two meters square, where you could fuck a woman standing up. And the guards used to charge you money. Because no one can go without sex, right? [*Laughter.*]

How much did it cost?

Back then it cost around twenty, thirty reais. I mean, the guards would exploit the prisoners every which way they could. Except that you had to know who was in charge that day. Because there were some guards that weren't interested, that couldn't be bothered. And then again, we must be careful not to generalize. Because during the whole time that I spent in prison, I came across some wonderful people, who helped me a lot in terms of opportunities. So we must be careful not to generalize, okay?

In my cell in Aranha Filho, there was this old guy, who'd escaped and been recaptured a number of times. And he started to tell me about his life, about how he'd been in and out of prison since the age of eighteen. And initially he was in for assault. And then for drugs, and then for drugs again. And he explained to me that one of the best prisons he'd been to was Ilha Grande, and that now he was going back there again—and that if you knew someone with a boat, it was easy to escape from there. And I thought to myself, "I know someone with a boat!" And another thing—if I escaped from Ilha Grande, I'd be able to go it alone. I mean, I wouldn't have to hang out with the guys from the favelas, because, I mean, this was their life.

You mean, favela, prison, favela, prison . . .

That's right. And by this time I'd managed to figure out that anytime anyone new came in, it was a chance for the leaders to find out what was going on in their communities. Because the guys on the outside took their orders from the leaders in prison. Because a leader in prison was someone to be feared. Because if a guy fucks up on the outside, he can be punished or killed. But if he's good, he'll be treated well if he ends up in prison. And so the guys on the outside did everything they could to support their leaders in prison.

Like how?

They'd send them money, money that they made from drugs. And they'd send them supplies that they'd distribute to the other prisoners. Because every prison that's controlled by the cv has a leader. And then there are some leaders that are more important than others, because there's a hierarchy. And it's the leaders of the faction that determine everything that goes on, and who is to be the leader in all the other prisons. And Ilha Grande used to be the most important prison, because that's where the faction was founded, and that's where all the important leaders were held until they were transferred, in 1988. And this old guy, this prisoner I'd gotten to know, he asked me if I'd like to go with him, to Ilha Grande. And I said yes. I said yes and I put my name on the list of prisoners to be transferred. Because every Thursday morning this prisoner would come by with a notebook. And he'd ask who wanted to go to Ilha Grande, because there was room for more prisoners there.

How long had you been in Aranha Filho?

By then, almost four months. And because Ilha Grande was going to be closed down, they only sent prisoners there who had less than ten years to serve. Because they were building new prisons in Rio, maximum security prisons. And because I had less than eight years to serve, I put my name down on the list.

Did you have to pay to be transferred?

You did if you wanted to be transferred right away. But then again, you could always pay later. And so the old guy said to me, he said, "Hey, you're going to have to give that guard some money." So I said, "How much?" "Three hundred reais." And so I paid him. I told Ademar's son to get it for me, because I was going to Ilha Grande. And I told him that I needed his father to go to the frontier, because I had a friend there who had a boat— and not to forget to visit me, because I was depending on him. I said, "For Christ's sake, make sure nothing happens to you, okay? Because I'm going to need you." So then he said, "But Ilha Grande? Ilha Grande's so far away!" "But I need you. I mean, this is a big opportunity for me."

You mean to escape?

And to get to know the place. Because Ilha Grande's historic, because that's where the Comando Vermelho started. And also to get out of Aranha Filho, because Aranha Filho was a hellhole. Because there, you were either standing up or lying down, trying to sleep with everyone on the floor. And when they did let you out, it was only for a half an hour. And the old guy told me that Ilha Grande was an open prison, and that there was a soccer pitch and room to run around. And at the time, it was everything that I wanted. So when the guy came by, he said to me, "Your name's on the list. You're leaving Friday." And the day that I left, the old guy left with me too.

And that was a good thing, right?

It was a really good thing. Because he'd spent more than ten years on Ilha Grande. And now I was going there with him, and he was going to look out for me. And he wasn't a bad guy. I mean, he was a good guy. And because he'd escaped from Ilha Grande, everyone treated him with respect. And because he was with me, everyone looked at me a little bit differently—you know, as someone who was smart, as someone who also needed to be respected, understand?

PRISONS

In November 2012, the federal minister of justice, José Eduardo Cardozo, told a group of São Paulo businessmen that he would "rather die" than spend time in a Brazilian prison, describing conditions in such places as "medieval."[4] Few would disagree with him. In fact, the Brazilian government has regularly and routinely been taken to task by the UN, Amnesty International, and Human Rights Watch, among others, for failing to prevent what are described as gross and systematic violations of prisoners' rights.[5]

On the face of it, the formal protections provided by Brazilian law are considerable. Brazil was one of the first countries to introduce a national plan for human rights in 1994, following recommendations made by the UN World Conference on Human Rights the previous year. And Brazil's prison rules, which were also adopted in 1994, are based on the UN Standard Minimum Rules, which are widely considered to reflect international best practices.[6] The problem is that the existence of formal legal protections has little to do with actual conditions on the ground, where prisoners are forced to endure poor sanitation, inadequate medical and legal care, torture and physical abuse, a lack of personal security in general, and severe overcrowding.

In 1992, the year that Bruno was transferred to Ilha Grande, there were 114,377 inmates in Brazil. Twenty years later, in 2012, there were 548,003 in a system that was built to accommodate a little more than half that number.[7] A major factor contributing to overcrowding is the steady increase in the incarceration rate. In 1992, there were seventy-four prisoners for every 100,000 people. In 2012, there were 274, an increase of more than 365 percent.[8] As in the United States, the increase in the incarceration rate has a lot to do with drugs.[9] Brazil, like the United States, has committed to fighting the war on drugs by any means available, including arresting and locking up as many of those suspected of being involved as possible. The result is that in 2013, one in four inmates in Brazil was in prison because of involvement with drugs, the highest percentage since this statistic was first published in 2005.[10]

Ironically, the recent increase in the prison population involved with drugs is the product of legislation that was designed to achieve the opposite. For much of Brazil's history, a distinction was made between drug

Overcrowded conditions in Rio's Polinter Prison. Ninety-eight prisoners are kept in a twenty-five-square-meter (eighty-two-square-feet) cell where temperatures in the summer reach 50 degrees Celsius (122 degrees Fahrenheit). *Cell Block, Rio*, photograph by Gary Knight / VII, 2005. Used by permission.

users, who were seen as dependents, and drug traffickers, who were seen as criminals. Beginning in the 1960s, however, this distinction was set aside as Brazil signed on to a series of UN-sponsored conventions whose focus was on prohibition and repression.[11] The ultimate expression of this approach was the Lei de Crimes Hediondos, passed by the Brazilian congress in July 1990, which eliminated the possibility of bail, provisional release, pardon, amnesty, progression, or commutation of sentence for the aforementioned "heinous crimes," including drug trafficking, broadly defined.[12]

In August 2006, however, a new law was passed whose goal was to decriminalize drug possession for personal use.[13] The idea was to distinguish users, and those who engaged in small-scale trafficking to pay for their habit, from traffickers who engaged in it for profit, and to deal with them accordingly. The law stated that users should not face jail time but should be required, instead, to be educated about the potential harm caused by drugs and to perform community service. Since the law failed to specify in any detail, however, the distinction between one form of activity and another, the decision to charge an individual with drug use or drug trafficking was left to judges and the police, who took it upon themselves to fill Brazil's prisons with low-level and mostly nonviolent offenders.[14]

This brings me to a second factor contributing to overcrowding, which is the chronic inefficiency and fundamental unfairness of the criminal justice system. According to the 1988 Constitution, the Brazilian judiciary is duty-bound to assume that pretrial prisoners are innocent, and that unless they are charged with a so-called heinous crime, they should be detained only as a last resort. Yet 38 percent of the more than half a million prisoners in Brazil are currently awaiting trial, a wait that, in some cases, lasts longer than the eventual sentence. Part of the problem has to do with the fact that 80 percent of prisoners in Brazil cannot afford a lawyer. This means that they are dependent on the services of underresourced public defenders, which means that they have virtually no chance of being granted bail.[15] The other problem is that lower-court judges in Brazil face such a huge backlog of cases, and the judicial system is so slow, that they end up giving in to public pressure to detain suspected criminal elements—and not just those charged with trafficking drugs—before they have the chance to be tried or sentenced.[16]

In most cases, pretrial detainees are warehoused in places that are designed to be temporary holding cells, such as jails inside police precincts. According to Brazilian law, criminal suspects, upon arrest, are to be held for only a few days before being charged or released. A suspect who is not released is supposed to be transferred to a jail or house of detention to await trial and sentencing. Then, if convicted, the prisoner is transferred to a separate facility, the type of which is determined by the nature of the crime and the circumstances of the accused.[17]

The government in Rio has taken significant steps since the late 1990s to build enough houses of detention to allow them to empty the police precincts, where some of the worst abuses take place.[18] However, the prison system in Rio is still a long way from resolving the issue of overcrowding. According to the secretary of prison administration, as of December 2012, there were 24,215 spaces, in fifty-two separate establishments, for 33,826 inmates. And the situation is only going to get worse as more and more people are arrested and enter the system.[19] And then, finally, there is the issue of criminal factions.

As Bruno's testimony makes clear, Rio's prisons have been under the control of factions for a long time. According to one study, eleven prisons in Rio are currently dominated by the Comando Vermelho, four by the Terceiro Comando, and three by the Amigos dos Amigos.[20] This means that only those who identify with those factions are sent there, a situation that the authorities openly acknowledge. And then there are other prisons where members of the various factions are confined to different wings or cell blocks.[21] What this means, in terms of overcrowding, is that there are often spaces within the system, but only for certain types of prisoner. It also means that some prisons and cell blocks within prisons are overcrowded while others are not.[22]

The government has made various attempts to deal with the situation, even going as far as to argue that most prisoners would prefer to be housed in prisons that are neutral.[23] Be that as it may, whenever prisoners from different factions get together, the outcome is always a disaster. The most infamous of these events took place in the Benfica house of detention in May 2004. The house of detention had been open for only a month and housed 600 members of the Comando Vermelho, 150 of the Terceiro Comando, and 110 of the Amigos dos Amigos. On the morning of May 29, fourteen inmates escaped when a group of armed men attacked the prison from the outside, blasting a hole in the main gate. This escape attempt subsequently sparked a rebellion that lasted for sixty-two hours until a local priest could intervene and negotiate a peace. When all was said and done, one guard and thirty inmates lay dead, many of them mutilated and charred beyond recognition. By all accounts, the Comando Vermelho had taken advantage of the confusion caused by the situation to settle accounts.

Events such as the Benfica massacre have the perverse effect of encouraging the watching public to call for even harsher treatment of prisoners who, in their eyes, are barbaric and beyond redemption. The reality of the situation, however, is that the cruel and inhuman treatment of prisoners serves to consolidate and reinforce the power of criminal factions and plays directly into their hands.

That Friday afternoon, the guard called for all the prisoners who were being transferred to Ilha Grande. There were eighteen of us. And we were all handcuffed together in the hold of this boat. And when the boat docked, we were loaded onto a truck that drove us seven kilometers to Vila de Dois Rios. And Vila de Dois Rios was this spectacular place on the other side of the island. And when we got there, when we were coming down from the mountain, we saw the prison below us. And the prison was called the Devil's Cauldron, because a lot of bad things happened there. And I remember thinking to myself, "So this is where I'm going to be. This is where I am going to spend the next few years of my life!" And the prison itself was enormous, because there were five hundred prisoners in that place. And they were housed in three cell blocks. Cell Block 1 on the ground floor, and Cell Blocks 2 and 3 above it.

How many prisoners were in each cell?

There were two, in cells of about three meters square. Because there were two beds in each cell, one on top of another. And there was a chest of drawers to put your clothes in. And if you had a television, you had a television. And if you had a stove, you had a stove. So you could even make your own meals. And then there was a bathroom for the two of you. But when I got there, the prison was completely quiet. And the old guy who came with me, he told me that when the prison was completely quiet, something was going on. Because he was my eyes and ears in that place [laughter]. And because it was such a big prison, my fear was that he'd be sent to one end, and I'd be sent to the other. Because I was a nobody, understand? But you know what? As soon as we got there, he said, "I'm going to introduce you to the leader, I'm going to introduce you to the president." And the president's name was Zezinho. And he was this tall thin guy, with eyes like a cat. And he walked around all day in this coat, even if it was a hundred degrees outside. And inside this coat he had these two enormous knives. And his bodyguards were always with him. You know, five or six of his men. And the prison, I mean, Jesus Christ, it was like the Comando Vermelho owned the place. Because they controlled everything, and I mean everything.

Where did they put you, when you first got there?

They put us in the cela de espera, like they always do, in Cell Block 1. And on the first night I was there, they killed this guy Marcão.

Why?

They claimed that he was a snitch, that he was giving information to the authorities. Because his sister came to visit. And on the ride over, she heard one of the guards say that some of the leaders were going to be transferred. So she told her brother. And her brother told the president. Except that when the leaders were transferred, a few days later, the president figured that Marcão must have given the authorities some names. Because the authorities were always trying to figure out who was in charge of the prison so they could be transferred. Because in 1988 there was this massacre. And that was when the prison was divided, you know, between the Comando Vermelho and the Terceiro Comando. And the authorities wanted to find out who was responsible, except that they didn't know who was responsible, which meant they had to try and find out from the prisoners. Because the group that carried out the massacre was beginning to organize and to represent a threat. So they had to get their hands on the leaders, understand?

But I still don't understand what this guy Marcão did wrong.

He did nothing wrong. It's just that the leaders didn't like him, because they didn't trust him, because he was one of the prisoners who worked on the outside. He worked on the outside of the prison chopping wood. So they thought that perhaps he'd given the authorities some names. But you know what? Marcão was this simple guy. He was big and dumb, that's all. And he would never do anything to hurt the CV. But I only found out about this later, after he'd been killed. And I thought to myself, "Holy shit, I'd better be careful. I'd better figure out how this place operates. Because if they killed this guy Marcão, and he was innocent!"

How did he die?

These three guys showed up at the entrance to his cell block. And they called out his name. Because Marcão went inside his cell at six o'clock every evening, and he never came out. So they called him, and they told him that they had food for him, that was sent by the president. So then he came out. And when he came out, one of them went and hid inside his cell. And when he went back inside his cell, the guy who was hiding there stabbed him. So Marcão came running out of his cell with this knife sticking in his back, between his shoulder blades. And that's when the other guys jumped him. And one of them stabbed him in the stomach, and another one went at him with an axe. And they chopped him into pieces. Because this guy Marcão had an axe that he used for chopping wood. Except that he kept his axe in his cell. And so they went inside and asked his cellmate where it was. And it was under his bed. So they used it to kill him.

Right there in front of you?

Right there in front of my eyes. So then one of the guys shouted out, "You see this guy here? This motherfucker? He's a traitor! And this is what we do to traitors. Because no one fucks with the CV, understand?" So then some people came and took the body away, I mean all the pieces. And then they washed away all of the blood. And the rest of the day the prison was locked down. And the two that killed him went and assumed responsibility.

What do you mean?

They told the guards that they were the ones who killed him. So then they had to serve more time, understand? And so then they sent me to Cell Block 2, because the old guy spoke to the leader, and Cell Block 2 was where he was. Except that they put me in this cell with this really strange guy. And on the third day we got into a fight, because he was so difficult to live with. Because at ten o'clock at night he refused to turn off the light. And he chain-smoked, and he dropped all his ashes on the floor. And he made a mess of the bathroom. You know, he left his clothes all over the place. So I said to him, I said, "You know what? You're a pig." And he said, "You know what? You're neurotic." And then he jumped off his bed and came at me with a knife. So then I hit him, because I was ready for him, and I made him drop his knife. And then I said, "What's fucking wrong with you?" But you know what? You're not allowed to fight. No one's allowed to fight. And so the next day, I was told that I had to go and meet the president. Because these guys showed up and they said, "You two, tomorrow morning at ten, upstairs!" Because the president lived on the third floor. And so the next morning, the old guy came by and said, "Bruno, what the hell happened to you?" And I said, "I got into a fight. So what's going to happen to me now?" "You're going to have to meet with the leader. Now I'll speak to him, okay, but there's really not a lot that I can do." "Hey, I don't need anyone to defend me, okay? Don't worry, I can handle it." And so when I went up to meet the president, the next day, I explained myself. I explained how I liked a clean cell, and how I was just trying to defend myself. And you know what? The whole time this guy Zezinho just sat there looking at me. And he said, "Hey kid, where are you from?" And I said, "I'm from the frontier. Because I was in the navy, and I used to supply drugs to your friends in Estrada do Paiol." "So who do you know inside this prison?" "I don't know anyone really, just the old guy I came here with. But I don't want him involved, okay?" And he said, "Okay, okay, but this can't happen again, understand? Now I want everybody out." So then everyone left except for me. And I stayed there talking to him, and he became my friend.

Just like that?

Just like that. Because he found me interesting. Because I wasn't from a favela, you know, like the guy I got into a fight with. Because that guy was scum. Because he'd been in prison so long, he'd gotten used to it. But you know what? There was no way I was going to get used to it. Not that mess in my cell, not the way they killed that guy the first night. Because it's one thing to read about it in the newspapers, or to see it on TV. But to have it happen right in front of you? I mean, Jesus Christ, I couldn't sleep that night. Because I kept thinking that it could happen to me! And so when everyone else left, this guy Zezinho, this president of the prison, explained to me that I'd be moving to a different cell. Because it was clear that me and this other guy couldn't get along. And so then the leader said that one of these days we should hang out together. Because Ilha Grande was this enormous prison. And there was lots of space to move around. And every morning at six o'clock, they'd open up the cell blocks.

And the cells?

The cells were never locked, but the cell blocks were locked from six o'clock at night until six o'clock in the morning. And at around six thirty, breakfast was served in the kitchen, in Cell Block 1. Except that some prisoners didn't go to breakfast, because they had breakfast in their cells. And like I said, some of the prisoners had their own stoves. And they had pots and pans and food and everything, so they didn't need anything from the kitchen. And then there was this deal whereby the leaders would get the best food. You know, their food would be better than everyone else's.

Who made the food?

The prisoners. Because like I said, the prison was run by the prisoners. I mean, it was considered a maximum-security prison, but only because it was so far away. Because everyone knew that it was a joke, because the prisoners controlled everything. To give you an example, when Escadinha, who was one of the founders of the CV, escaped from Ilha Grande by helicopter, no one said anything about the fact that he was living on the outside. Because in those days, some of the prisoners were allowed to build their own houses, outside the prison, and have their families come live with them. So they lived outside the prison in a favela that was built for the CV.

And the authorities let them do this?

They let some of them. You know, the prisoners who were in good standing. And then there were these big parties that went on for three days. And there were families there, and children. I mean, it was as if the prison was transformed into a giant amusement park [laughter]. Except that while these parties were going on, no one was allowed to escape.

What do you mean?

There was an agreement between the president and the authorities. Because the authorities would say, "If you want to enjoy this privilege, don't abuse it, okay?" And before these parties started, twenty or thirty prisoners would be allowed out to collect things to decorate the place. I mean, it was incredible the amount of freedom the prisoners enjoyed there. And so the day-to-day life of the prison wasn't that bad. What I mean is, it wasn't that stressful, except that everything had to be done a certain way. You know, you had to play by the rules, because the CV controlled everything.

Was this a privilege the CV had won, that they had managed to achieve?

Yes, but to achieve it, there had to be this massacre. Because before the CV took over, the prisoners fought among themselves. I mean, young guys would be raped, and prisoners would have their things stolen. And there were all these gangs. I mean, I was even told of cases, a long, long time ago, where a prisoner would kill himself rather than be sent there. And that was why it was called the Devil's Cauldron. I mean, can you believe it?[1]

When did the situation begin to change?

It changed when the military sent political prisoners there in the late 1960s and early 1970s. Because they were the ones who told the prisoners to stop fighting among themselves. They were the ones who told them to take their fight to the authorities instead. It was like, "Look, you guys, you need to unite, because this whole deal of killing each other, it can wait until you're on the outside, okay?" And there was this one group of prisoners there who accepted these ideas, who saw this as the way to go. And then there was another group there who didn't, who wanted nothing to do with it. And so there was this fight, this massacre. Except that some of the guys who were killed didn't deserve to be, because they'd done nothing wrong. It's just that they had enemies, and so their names were placed on the list. And so when the killings started, they barricaded themselves in on the third floor. And that's when the prison was divided.

You mean between the Comando Vermelho and the Terceiro Comando?

That's right. And the Terceiro Comando got its name because the guys who were being targeted took refuge on the third floor. Except that there was this domino effect. You know, once it happened on Ilha Grande it started happening in all the other prisons as well. And I only found out about this because I asked around. Because I asked guys who'd been there a long time. And a lot of guys wanted to get to know me because of my past. It was like, "Hey, you see that guy over there, he was in the navy!" So then they'd ask me to have dinner with them, in their cells.

So you were somewhat of a novelty?

That's right, because they'd never had someone like me there before, at least not with a history like mine. And then they'd see me speaking with the leader. So they knew I must be someone who's smart, who's intelligent, right? And I mean, I was going to need all of my intelligence to survive in that place. Because my only contact was Ademar's son, who visited me in Aranha Filho. And so when I got to Ilha Grande, I had to make friends. And they had to be good friends, right? I mean, if I was going to survive. And from then on they told me that I didn't have to eat with all the other prisoners, because there would be better food for me. And I thought to myself, "Hey, not bad, Bruno, not bad at all!"

In other words, they accepted you. The leaders, I mean.
That's right, they accepted me, and they protected me. Except that I had to figure out exactly what that protection meant. Because after a while, I realized that there was a Right and a Left in that prison, that there was a politics of crime.

What do you mean?
Because the president of Ilha Grande is treated with the greatest respect, right? Because Ilha Grande's famous, because that's where the faction got its start. So whatever the president needs, he gets. You know, in terms of money, or drugs. Or say, if someone needs to escape. Because if someone needs to escape, all of the favelas on the outside will help finance it, with the understanding that it's someone who's needed. You know, someone who's useful to the organization.

So not everyone could escape?
That's right. Only prisoners who robbed banks, or who were involved in things like kidnapping. You know, prisoners who could fill the organization's coffers. And so the president of the prison has control of everything. I mean, all the money in the prison passes through his hands. And he's the one who decides who's going to live and who's going to die, because he's the leader. Except that when I first met him, I could see that he wasn't that smart, that he wasn't the revolutionary I had imagined. And then I began to wonder about his group, about his men and their attitude toward the authorities. Because I'd been told that the leaders who'd been transferred were good at protecting everyone. But that was clearly no longer the case. Because by the time I got there, it was a different era. It was a whole different situation.

What do you mean?
Well, to give you an idea, it was the government's responsibility to send food to Ilha Grande, to feed the prisoners. Except that by the time the

food arrived, a lot of it had been stolen. But no one said anything, no one said a word.

But why?

Because the prisoners were in charge of the prison. And so if the prisoners said it was okay, it was okay, understand? Because there was supposed to be meat on Monday, chicken on Sunday, and so on and so on. But there wasn't. And so someone was taking advantage of the situation. I mean, it just wasn't possible that the government was spending a thousand reais per month to feed each prisoner, if the food never reached his plate, right?

So who took it?

Someone in the administration. But as far as the president was concerned, everything was okay, because whatever food was left was given to him, to do as he pleased. Because like I said, the authorities turned the prison over to the president and his group. And so it was up to the president what he did with the kitchen, what he did with the food. Except that there was never enough. And whenever it was close to one of those parties I was telling you about, they'd start cutting back. They'd start saving food for the barbecue. So there'd be three months to go before a party, and there'd be no meat. And then there was this canteen inside the prison. And it was run by the president and his group. And it sold everything—you know, rice, beans, tomatoes, pasta, you name it. I mean, can you believe it?

So the president participated in the scheme of stealing food.

That's right. And because of this he made a lot of enemies, on the left, understand? And even though I knew what was going on, there was no way I could say anything. But I could see what was going to happen, because they were causing people to suffer. You know, the prisoners who were weak, who didn't have anything. And so the prison was becoming divided. And I spoke to the guys on the left who were beginning to organize. And I realized that at any moment there could be a revolt, because they were upset with the president. And so I thought to myself, "I've got to find a way out of here. I've got to find a way of escaping." Because I had no idea what was going to happen. And I mean, I may have been a nobody when I came in, but, like it or not, I was now one of them, because I was spending a lot of time with the leaders. But I made sure to talk to the guys on the left as well. Because I didn't want to be identified just with one side and not the other, understand?

My escape from Ilha Grande began one day when I was talking to my friend, the old guy. Because at six thirty one night, this tall guy came by, carrying a bucket of fish. And I said to my friend, "Who's that?" And he told me that he was one of the prisoners who were allowed out to fish. And I said, "Jesus Christ, you have to introduce me to him then!" And he said, "No problem, because I watch the news every night in his cell." And so that night my friend said, "Come on, let's go watch the news." And so when we got there, we knocked on the door and we went in.

How long was he in for?

Thirty years. And I made friends with him because I wanted to escape. And he became my best friend there in that prison. But you know what? He ended up trusting me too much. And it was only on the day of the escape that I told him, that I said, "Let's escape. Now!"

Why didn't you tell him before?

Because I didn't trust him. And I mean, he did everything for me. Because he's the one who got me out. He's the one who got me work on the outside, because he gave my name to the authorities. But I just didn't trust him, because he was really timid. And in prison, it's the ones who are really timid that are the most dangerous. Because they're scared. And because they're scared, they're the ones who are likely to talk. And so anyway, this friend of mine, this old guy, he took me to this other guy's cell and introduced me. And when he introduced me, the guy who went out to fish just stood there like a statue. And then he said, "Hi, how's it going?" And I said, "Is the news going to be on?" And he said, "Sure, but how about some coffee?" And so then he got up and turned on his stove. And then he carefully measured out how much coffee and water we would need, because he was extremely meticulous. And so after he'd made the coffee, I said to him, "It's a long time since I've seen the news, because I don't have a TV. And if I'm going to watch TV with someone, it's got to be someone special, someone I trust. And my friend here says you're someone I can trust. So that's why I'm here." Because I was trying to make him feel good, to gain his confidence. Because, I mean, he left the prison first thing in the morning and he only came back at night. So he was someone I had to get to know, right?

Was it just him who left the prison each day?

There was him and three others. So I said to him, "Tomorrow I'll be back, okay?" And he said, "Okay." And so the next night I went back there. And because he was late getting there, I talked to his cellmate. I said to him, "How long have you been living with this guy?" And he said, "Here, in this cell? Six years already." "And how long has he been going out to fish?" "Oh, a long time, because he's the leader of the group." "So do you think I'll be able to persuade him, you know, to get me out to fish?" "Yes, yes, of course. All you have to do is talk about fish. Talk to him about fishing, because that's what he likes."

And did you fish?

Me? Never. I mean, I knew there were fish in the sea, but I'd never fished! [*Laughter.*] And this part of the story's really interesting, because as soon as he got back, I said to him, "Barbicha," because he had this big bushy beard and that's what everyone called him, "Barbicha, is everything okay?" "Yep, everything's okay. I'm going to make us some coffee. Now, do you want some fish? Because I brought you some fish." And I noticed right away how comfortable he was. And I said, "What type of fish do you have there?" "Well, I have a *xererete*, because they're the best." And then he showed me the fish and I said to him, "In Mato Grosso do Sul, we have *pacu, pintado, dourado* . . ." "You mean you know how to fish?" "Yes!" "With a net?" "Yes!" "Well, I can't promise anything, but I'll have a word with Seu Albinate, okay?"[2]

All this after just two days?

After just two days. Because I was interested in finding work. It's just that I didn't want to work in the kitchen. I wanted to work on the outside.

Because you were also thinking of escaping, right?

I went to Ilha Grande with the idea of escaping. So of course that was part of it. And I was thinking that if I was out there fishing, someone could come by and get me. So then we stayed there a while talking. And the next day he was allowed out and I stayed behind in prison. And when he came back, he said to me, "I didn't speak to Seu Albinate today because the season's ending, and we're putting all the fishing equipment away." Because I'd arrived in July, when it was winter, when there weren't any fish. And then he said to me, "Do you know how to do anything else? Because in Vila do Abraão," which was where the boats came in, "there's this house that belongs to a military policeman. And the roof's rotten, and they want us to replace it. So I was thinking that if you knew how to do that sort of thing, I could put in a good word for you. Because there are guys in prison who are carpenters, it's just that the authorities won't let them out." Because after the massacre I told you about, a lot of the prisoners were under suspicion. In fact, I was the only prisoner, in the final years of the prison, to be allowed out.

Because you weren't part of this past?

And because I was in the military, which was a positive thing for me. And so anyway, at around eight o'clock in the morning, the next day, they called my number. Because when you arrived in that prison you ceased to exist as a name. And they called you by your number until the day you left that place.

What about the prisoners? Did they call each other by their number?

Oh no, never, not even as a joke, because you could be punished. You could be sent upstairs to see the leader. And I had to learn all of these rules. And to come in not knowing anything was really hard. And so when the director called for me, I went to see the leader first. And I said to him, "The director's calling for me. And it might be about a job. Now is that okay with you?" Because I hadn't been there long, right? And now I was off to see the director? And so when I reached the director's office, he already had my file open on his desk. And he looked at me and he said, "But you're so young! And you were in the military. What happened to you?" And I said, "You know what, sir? I've already been sentenced for what I did." Because I didn't want to go into any details. "And these are all things I'm trying to forget, sir, if you don't mind. What I'm looking for is work, something for me to do." So then he asked me, "Do you know anything about carpentry?" And I said, "Yes, yes, I do."

And did you?

No, of course not! [*Laughter.*] I knew nothing. All I knew about was guns and ammunition. So then he said, "Well, there are these houses that need to be repaired. And I'm trying to find something for the guys who go out fishing to do. And so we want to send them to Vila do Abraão to take a look at these houses. So listen up, okay? Tomorrow morning you'll be leaving early, around six o'clock. Make sure that you are ready." So then he signed for my release and sent the papers over to the guardhouse. And that night, I couldn't sleep. I just lay there with my eyes open. Because I'd been there for four months already. And a lot of shit had happened since then. And now I was going to be allowed out! But what was worrying me was all the things I said I could do that I couldn't. I mean, how the hell was I going to get around that? But that's okay, I thought, because I'll just stay close to Barbicha, because he knows how to do everything. Because he was a bright light in my universe. He was my hope! And like I said, I lay there the whole night with my eyes open, thinking about the next day.

But you weren't thinking of escaping—or were you?

No, not that day. I just wanted to get out of there. In fact, it was more than a year until I escaped. Because I mean, I would have been a fool to try and escape right away. And so when we left the prison the next morning, we all went out through the front gates. And there was this military police jeep there waiting. And so we all got in and off we went. And the others, they were all used to being on the outside. And so they knew where to go. They knew all the different trails. Because Ilha Grande is this enormous island with over a hundred different beaches. And there I was, riding along in this jeep, thinking about all the things that had happened in my life. I mean, it was really incredible! So then, when we got there, to this house, we climbed up on the roof. And I could see that the job was going to be difficult. But then luckily, as we were taking off the shingles, all these termites came running out. And so we called the military policeman who was guarding us, and Barbicha said to him, "Look, the place is infested with termites, so we can't fix it, okay?" And the policeman said, "Okay then, let's go back and talk to Seu Albinate." Because Seu Albinate was in charge of us. He was the one who got us out each day, and we were his responsibility. So we had to go back and tell him about the house.

And what were you thinking?

I was thinking, "What am I going to tell them now, that I used to work as a fumigator?" [*Laughter*.] But then, when we got back to the prison, Seu Albinate remembered that there were things to do in the shed where they stored all the equipment. You know, for fishing. And he said that since we were out already, we might as well spend the day working there. And when we got there, there were these huge canoes, and all these nets. And

Seu Albinate said, "There are no fish right now, but by August the water will be warm again, and we'll be able to get back out there. Now, do you know how to sew? Because these nets are in bad shape. And if we repair them now, we won't have to repair them later, okay?" And I said, "Yes, yes, I know how to sew." So then Barbicha came over and stood beside me. And he said, "Look, it's like this. Put this through there, and then bring it over, understand?" Because repairing a net isn't easy. And at first I was getting everything wrong, I mean, I was getting everything tangled. But then, after watching Barbicha and the others for a while, I began to get the hang of it. And then, when we were finished, Seu Albinate said, "Okay, let's put everything away." And then he turned to me and said, "Now listen, there's no work for you tomorrow, understand? Because you were allowed out just to work on the house. And since we're not going to be doing that anymore . . ." So then I said, "But Seu Albinate, I'll do anything. I'll paint the shed, I'll repair the nets, I'll do anything!" I mean, the only thing I didn't do was get down on my hands and knees and beg [laughter]. So then he said, "Okay, okay, I'll see what I can do, because it's really hard to get prisoners out these days."

Because of the massacre.

Precisely. Because there were a lot of families living in that town, and they were afraid of the prisoners, like they were diseased or something. And Seu Albinate tried to explain all this to me. And I said to him, "Seu Albinate, I know what it's like to be a prisoner, I really do. I just want you to know that you can trust me, okay?" And then he said to me, "So you're not going to try and escape?"

He said that?

Yes, he said, "So you're not going to try and escape?" And I said, "Look, if I told you I didn't want to escape, I'd be lying. Because every prisoner wants to escape, right? But on the other hand, if I told you I was going to escape, I'd also be lying. I mean, they'd both be lies, understand?"

Because you were thinking of escaping, but not right then?

Exactly. But I wasn't going to tell him that, right? "Hey, I'm going to escape, but not right now" [laughter]. And so the next day Barbicha left the prison and I didn't. And after a few days I thought to myself, "It must have been something I said." And so I knew I had to speak to Seu Albinate again somehow. And so when all the prisoners were allowed out of their

View of the grounds of the Vila de Dois Rios prison during the last few months of its operation. *Garbage Dump*, photograph by André Cypriano, 1993. Used by permission.

cell blocks in the morning, I went and stood at the front gates, because I didn't want to spend any more time in that prison.

So on Ilha Grande, the prisoners were allowed out, inside the prison?

That's right, because the prison was open for the entire day. I mean, you could wash your clothes, you could run around, and you could play soccer. Because they had teams there. And the favelas sent uniforms. And we had referees and everything. And when there was a tournament, the prisoners and the staff would come out and watch. I mean, it was incredible how well it was organized.

Was there gambling there?

There was *jogo de bicho*.[3] And there was gambling on horses, and soccer. All done via the radio. And the gambling was controlled by the president, because the president controlled everything. So anyway, after a few days of me standing there, I caught sight of Seu Albinate. And I called to him, I said, "Seu Albinate, I'm still waiting for that opportunity." And he said, "What opportunity?" "It's me, Bruno, remember?" "Ah yes, I remember. I'll talk to Barbicha, so you can be allowed out tomorrow." And so the next day I left the prison after breakfast, in the morning.

To do what?

To go back to where they stored the fishing equipment. And I worked there every day until we were ready to go out and fish. And that's how I got to know Seu Jeferson. Because Seu Jeferson was in charge of the group that went out to fish. And when he first met me, he said, "From now on I'm going to call you Naval." Because Seu Jeferson called everyone by their names, I mean, by their nicknames. And they were a great bunch of guys to work with—so much so that, when it came time to escape, I didn't escape while I was working with them, because I didn't want to cause them any trouble. So anyway, on the first day we went out, Seu Jeferson said, "Naval, since you were in the navy, why don't you man the rudder?" And I said, "Okay." But you know what? I had no idea what I was doing. And so when we pushed off that morning, the first wave hit us, and then the second, and then Barbicha shouted out, "On the third wave, row!" And so then I said, "Seu Jeferson, are you sure you don't want to steer? Why don't you let me go up front?" And so then I went up front with Barbicha. And I started to paddle. And my paddle got caught with Barbicha's and almost fell out of my hands. And so then I started paddling again. And when we finally got to where we were going, Barbicha said, "Okay, let's stop here." And then we started feeding out the rope that was attached to the top of the net. And then we attached the rope to the buoys until we made a circle. And then the fish swam in, and they stayed there swimming around and around. Then, when we went back in the afternoon, we lifted up the net and grabbed hold of the fish. And it was when we were grabbing hold of the fish that Seu Jeferson turned to me and said, "Naval, you don't know anything about fishing, now, do you!" [*Laughter.*] And I said, "But Seu Jeferson, I'm used to fresh water. And the fish here are a lot smarter!" And so then he laughed and he said, "Look, Naval, I can tell you know nothing about fishing. But that's okay, because everyone here likes you, and I can see that you're eager to learn. And you know what? We'll make you into a fisherman!"

And so then I stayed. And it was a lot of hard work, because the fish were really heavy. And then you had to fill up these huge containers with ice and churn it all around. And by the end of the day you were exhausted, and then you had to get up at four the next morning and start all over again.

How many fish did you catch in one day?

It depended. Because we used to check the nets once in the morning and once again in the afternoon. And I remember one day we ended up with two tons of fish, because we managed to catch a shoal. And it also depended on the type of fish. And I stayed there working for more than a year, for almost two years, because I couldn't figure any other way of escaping. Because it was a long time before my friend Ademar's son came to visit. So it was a long time before I received any news. And when he finally got there, I was already working on the outside. Because I remember him saying, "You've got a job already?"

Did they pay you?

Yes, minimum salary. Prison wages, at the end of each month. And during the fishing season, they gave us a few kilos of fish to take back to the prison. And Barbicha would sell most of his and give one or two to the president, to keep on his good side. But I took all of mine back to give to friends. You know, the ones who didn't have anything. The guys on the left. Because I figured that sooner or later they would try and take over. And so I knew I had to be friends with them, and with the group in power. Because while you are in prison you always have to be thinking about life on the outside. Because if you don't, you're screwed. And so I always kept an eye on what was going on, on the outside. And I made sure that I made friends with everyone, with guys on the left and guys on the right. But at the same time, I was looking for ways to get out of there. You know, to escape.

So the trick was to escape without enemies?

That's right. You had to leave there with a clean slate. And so anyway, getting back to the story, each of the prisoners who were allowed out was given five kilos of fish. So when I came back to the prison at night I'd give them to someone. You know, someone whose family was visiting, because they'd be there for three days.

Three days?

If you wanted, your family could stay with you for three days. Or your girlfriend, because a section of the prison was set aside. But very few people came to visit, because it was so far away. And since no one in my family came, I depended on Ademar's son. And so I sent him a letter, from Ilha Grande. Because a friend of mine there was from Estrada do Paiol. And his family came to visit, and so I gave them this letter and I said to them, "Go find this guy for me, okay? And give him this letter." And the letter said, "Look, I need you here." Because now that I was working on the outside, I thought that if he visited me, he could tell me if he knew someone with a boat. Or he could go to Corumbá, because I knew someone there who had a boat. You know, a motorboat.

But wasn't that a bit far?

But he could have put it on top of a car, or on a trailer or something. Because that's what I was thinking. Because when you're in prison, when you're deprived of your freedom, you exist in this fantasy world. Because even though it was really hard to get to that prison, on visiting day, you'd say to yourself, "So how come no one's come to visit?" And the families that did come to visit were almost always the families of the president's group, because they were the ones who were able to support them, the ones who could give them food. Because the money that was being sent by the favelas was being spent by the president and by the guys in his group. And when there were these parties, these three-day parties I was telling you about, it was the leaders who celebrated—you know, who drank and ate well. Not the others, not at all.

So did everyone else feel left out?

It depended. It depended on the individual. Because there were a lot of prisoners there who felt abandoned, who had given up hope. And a lot of them couldn't read or write. And a lot of them had served their time already, but they were still there because they didn't know how to get in touch with a lawyer. And a lot of the prisoners had rotten teeth, and they were in a lot of pain, because there was no dentist there. And I tried to tell the president to write a letter to the director, to demand that he send for a dentist. But I had to be careful. I had to be careful so no one would say, "Who the fuck does he think he is, a leader?" Because you had to know how to talk to these guys. And like I said, I made sure that I was friends with everyone, so I talked with everyone. And so anyway, I sent Ademar's son this letter. And a few weeks later I received a reply that he'd be there, the next month. And when he got there, I said to him, "So how are things?" And he said, "Not good. Because my brother's now involved, and he killed these two guys. And my father's into drugs." And you know what? He was thinking about becoming involved too. Because he'd been looking for a job, but he couldn't find one. And so now he was thinking of taking over this boca de fumo, in this favela. And I tried to get him to calm down. I tried to talk him out of it. And I told him that when I got out, we could work together. But he told me he couldn't wait that long. And there I was, hoping that he'd find someone with a boat, and there he was, thinking about taking over a favela. Because I already had a map of the island. And I'd already picked out a spot where a boat could come by and get me. And so then he said, "Okay, okay, I'll see if I can find someone." But you know what? I never saw him again. Because he died, because he did exactly what I told him not to. And when I found out he'd died, I said to myself, "Holy shit, now I'm really screwed!" Because he was my only contact. But then, after a while, I made contact with another friend of mine. And this guy's name was Ronilton. Because whenever I went to Rio on business, we'd hang out together. And so I told him, because I stayed at his house one night.

Told him what?

That I was a drug trafficker. He worked at a bank in the city, and so I told him, I said, "All the money that I make from now on I'm going to give to you, okay?" And so he began to take care of my money. You know, he took it to an exchange house and converted it into dollars. And so he became involved as well. But you know what? He was really into it. Because he only dealt with the money. I mean, it was not like he was dealing with drugs. And so after Ademar's son died, I sent Ronilton a letter. Because this woman who lived near him came to visit her son. And after talking to her for a while, I realized that she knew him. And so I sent him a letter. And he didn't come and visit me. But do you know who did? His mother. And I thought to myself, "Well, this is interesting!"

Did you know her?

Of course, because whenever I came to Rio, I'd often sleep at his house. And whenever they needed something, like milk or a loaf of bread, I'd go out and get it. I mean, I was the perfect houseguest! And she got a hold of the letter. Because I sent the letter to him, but she was the one who opened it, understand?

Did he give it to her?

No, she kept it to herself. And then she came to visit. Because I saw my name on the list of prisoners who had a visitor.[4] But the thing was, I didn't know it was her. Because I sent the letter to Ronilton, so of course I imag-

ined it was him, right? And because I imagined it was him, I didn't prepare anything. Because a guy's only going to stay one night, right? And
so I went down to Cell Block 1, which was where visitors stayed, with just
a mattress. I mean, I didn't take any food or anything. And then when I
saw her, with these bags full of groceries and winter clothing, I thought
to myself, "Holy shit!" Because I was doing okay. What I mean is, I was
surviving. And the money I was making from fishing was helping too.
But it was difficult to buy things there. I mean, what was I supposed to
do? Send someone to buy me something, and then wait for a month? And
so she was my salvation. And when I saw her, I said to her, "Hey, how's it
going?" And she said, "Bruno, what happened to you?" And I said, "Look,
this is the situation I'm in. This is what happened to me." And she said,
"But how come you never said anything?" And I said, "But how, how
could I have told you?"

THE VILA DE DOIS RIOS PRISON

The island of Ilha Grande is located one hundred kilometers to the south-
west of the city of Rio de Janeiro. It is reachable by ferry from the towns of
Mangaratiba and Angra dos Reis on the mainland. The island itself covers
an area of 193 square kilometers and its highest point is the Pico da Pedra
D'Água, at 1,031 meters. When it was first discovered by the Portuguese, in
1502, it was inhabited by Tamoios Indians, whose territory extended from
Cabo Frio to the east of Rio to Ubatuba on the northern coast of the state
of São Paulo. The Tamoios named the island Ipaum Guaçu, which literally
means Big Island.

In the eighteenth and nineteenth centuries, coffee and sugarcane were
produced by slave labor on the island. With the decline and eventual aboli-
tion of slavery, however, the island's economy went into a decline.[5] Then,
in 1884, the federal government purchased two large *fazendas*, or farms.
The Fazenda do Holandês, located in the port town of Vila do Abraão, was
purchased for the purpose of building a quarantine facility for immigrants
arriving by boat. The facility, which at the time was considered state of the
art, opened its doors in 1886 and could accommodate up to fifteen hundred passengers who were segregated according to the class of their berth
on board ship. Between 1886 and 1913, the Lazerota da Ilha Grande, as it
was called, received visits from 4,232 ships, 3,367 of which had to be disin-
fected.[6] Then, for the next few decades, it was used occasionally as a place

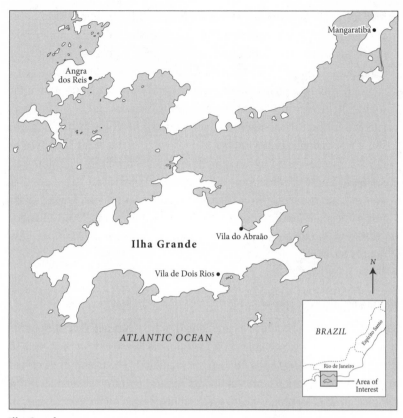

Ilha Grande.

to detain political prisoners until it was officially transformed into a prison under the name of the Colônia Penal Cândido Mendes in 1942.[7]

The other property purchased by the federal government was the Fazenda de Dois Rios, located on the other side of the island. Initially, the Fazenda de Dois Rios was used to produce supplies for the quarantine facility in Vila do Abraão, until in 1894 it was transformed into the Colônia Correcional de Dois Rios. During the first two years of its existence, the colônia accommodated very few prisoners, which led, ultimately, to it being closed down in 1896. In 1903, however, it was reopened and used, increasingly, to relieve overcrowded conditions in the prisons on the mainland.[8]

This second incarnation of the Colônia Correcional de Dois Rios was supposed to be more structured and organized than the first and to provide inmates with medical care, education, and opportunities for work. In reality, however, the distance between what was prescribed by law and what existed

Archival photo of the Vila de Dois Rios prison in 1943. Photograph by Cyro Manhães, 1943. Used by permission of Edison das Neves Manhães. Courtesy of the Arquivo Nacional do Brasil. Fundo / Coleção: Série Justiça-Administração-IJ2 (AF)—Notação: IJ2 1287.

on the ground was vast, resulting in repeated calls for the prison to be discontinued. Far from being an instrument for the rehabilitation of prisoners, as envisioned by the penal code, it was a place where inmates were isolated, abandoned, and subjected to extremely harsh treatment and conditions.[9]

As was the case with the Lazerota da Ilha Grande, the Colônia Correcional de Dois Rios was also used, on occasion, to imprison dissidents. These included sailors involved with the Revolta da Chibata in 1910, and members of the Brazilian Communist Party who were violently suppressed by the Vargas regime of the 1930s.[10] The most famous of these political prisoners was Graciliano Ramos, a nationally known author from the northern state of Alagoas, who wrote of his experiences in his *Memórias do cárcere*, published posthumously in 1953. Ramos described, in detail, the lack of adequate bedding, the inedible food, the appalling sanitary conditions, and the brutality of many of the guards.[11]

Then, in 1938, plans were made to build a new prison in Vila de Dois Rios. Part of a national program of prison building and reform, the facility was designed to allow prisoners on good behavior to serve out the last part of their sentence in relative freedom. Soon after the prison was completed, however, its name and function were changed from the Colônia Penal Cândido Mendes, which was moved to the site of the Lazerota da Ilha Grande in Vila do Abraão, to the Colônia Agrícola do Distrito Federal.[12] The reason for this change was the deactivation of the prison on the island of Fernando de Noronha, off the northeastern coast of Brazil, which, historically, had been where the more dangerous of the so-called enemies of the state had been held.[13]

Once again, it was these political prisoners, who were transferred en masse to the Vila de Dois Rios prison, who brought to light the horrendous conditions suffered by inmates, even though they themselves were afforded special privileges, and their stay on the island was not that long.[14] With World War II coming to an end, and Brazil entering a democratic phase, a general amnesty for political prisoners was declared on April 18, 1945. Following their departure, the Colônia Agrícola do Distrito Federal reverted back to what it was before, a repository for poor, dark-skinned, uneducated, and defenseless men. And that's the way it stayed until the next wave of political prisoners arrived in the 1960s, except that this time the consequences were very different.

On September 29, 1969, a severely weakened congress passed Law Decree No. 898, otherwise known as the National Security Law.[15] Article 27 of the law stipulated that any attempt to rob a bank would be punishable by ten to twenty-four years in prison, or more if the act resulted in a civilian death. The law was introduced by the military as a means to incarcerate, for as long as possible, members of so-called revolutionary groups that were targeting financial institutions as a means to fund resistance to the regime. The outcome of Article 27 was to bring together these aforementioned revolutionaries and common criminals in Cell Block B of the Vila de Dois Rios prison.[16]

Whether by direct influence or through demonstration, the common criminals in Cell Block B learned from their highly politicized colleagues the advantages of organization, loyalty, and discipline, both as a means of survival and, more significantly, as a means of mounting a challenge to gangs that, up until that point, had dominated and terrorized the lives of the inmates of that prison.[17] The situation finally came to a head, after the political prisoners had gone, in September 1979, when, following a provocation, the prisoners in Cell Block B confronted and took out their rivals.[18] From that point on, the Vila de Dois Rios prison was firmly under the control of what would eventually become known as the Comando Vermelho.[19]

Her name was Jandira, and as soon as she arrived she started organizing things. "Why don't we prepare some food, okay? Here, I've brought you a towel and some toothpaste. Now how about your family, how are they?" "Uh, I don't really want my family to know, because I'll be out of here soon, because I wasn't sentenced for very long."

But that wasn't true, right?

No, I was lying, because I was anxious to escape, and go back home to Recife. It's just that there was this problem of me escaping and causing trouble for Seu Albinate and Seu Jeferson. And so the whole thing was becoming more and more complicated. And then Jandira said, "Look, don't try and escape, okay? Because I'm here to help you."

Did she know Ronilton was involved?

Well, there was this one time when I left some money with him, in a shoebox underneath his bed. And she found it while she was cleaning. It was about forty thousand reais, which was way too much money for him, in terms of his position at the bank. And so I told her that we lent people money, and made money from the interest. Because it wasn't drugs that she found, it was only money. And so when she came to visit, she told me that ever since that day, she figured that I was up to something. Because I was always flying in from Mato Grosso do Sul, and she wasn't stupid, right? And that was why she came to visit me first, before telling her son, because she wanted to know if he was involved. And I told her that I'd never involve her son in any of this, and she believed me, and she told me that she appreciated my honesty. And then she said, "Look, how about next month I bring Ronilton, okay?" And that meant that it was going to be even more difficult for me to escape, because there were days when I spent the whole time on my own. I mean, all I had to do was take off. But the question was how, because from the prison to Vila do Abraão was seven kilometers, right? And from there to the mainland was another eleven. So I mean, it was way too far to swim. And so every morning that I was allowed out I'd visit a different beach. Or I'd go by Seu Jeferson's house, or visit the sisters. Because there were these sisters in town, from the Order of São Francisco, who looked after the prisoners when they got sick. And they'd try to get them to a doctor on the mainland, because there were no medical facilities there. And a lot of prisoners died trying to make that trip.

Was there a problem there with AIDS?

There was a huge problem with AIDS. I mean, a lot of prisoners died of AIDS. Because they had these big parties, right? And they didn't take precautions. And I mean, how are you going to tell a guy that he can't have sex? Or that he has to use a condom?

Sex with whom?

With the woman he hooks up with, with a young girl from the favelas. Because there were always orgies at these parties, because a lot of women, a lot of prostitutes would come. Because the leaders of the favelas would pay them to go there. And they'd stay there for all three days. And if you were lucky, the president would let you have one of them. I mean, can you imagine?

For three days?

No, no, in three days a woman would have sex with thirty different guys. Because that's why she's there, understand? And then someone would say, "Hey, Bruno, do you want some?" And, I mean, it's not easy, because you know you want to fuck her. So now you're going to tell everyone that you're afraid? But I mean, I already knew about AIDS. I knew that you had to be smart, that you had to try to figure out things about a woman's life, to see if she used drugs, or if she had a lot of partners. Because when I first met Lucia, we talked a lot before there was anything between us. I mean, I could see that she was smart and everything. But we talked a lot before we were, you know, intimate.

And what about Jandira? Did she go back there again?

She went back there many times. And the second time she brought Ronilton, and we hung out together. And then she said, "Ronilton can't come next month, because of work. But I'll come, okay?" And I noticed then that she was really keen to visit me. And I mean, I didn't mind. It was just that I didn't want to cause her all that trouble. But she insisted, because she was falling for me! [*Laughter.*]

Was she married?

No, her husband had died in an accident.

How old was she?

She was forty, and she was way too needy. And by her third visit, we were, well, you know. Because I was needy too. And I said to myself, "Is this the way it's going to be?" And it was interesting because after we'd been together she held on to me even tighter. And she told me that she'd be there till the end, even though her children were against it. "But Ma, three days there! Who knows what could happen to you!" But it was no use, because no one could dissuade her. Except me, that is. Because I sent her a letter, telling her not to visit me anymore, because I had a new girlfriend. Because it was the only thing I could think of, even though she was helping me so much. Because there was this one time when she arrived in the middle of a storm. And they were told, when they reached Vila do Abraão, that there was no truck to take them to the prison, but that if anyone wanted to, they could walk. And do you know what time they got there, to the prison? One thirty in the morning!

Boy, she must have really liked you!

Too much, she liked me too much! And you know what? During that first year she visited me almost every month. And it was in December, right before the Christmas party, that I decided to end it. Because I told her that my new girlfriend was coming to the party, and that I was in love with someone else.

But that wasn't true, right?

No, no, no, it wasn't, but it was the only way to tell her, so she wouldn't suffer. And I mean, it was a difficult letter for me to write, because she had supported me so much. And she gave me a certain amount of prestige, because I had someone to visit me, and that's always a good thing in prison.

Even though she was older?

It wasn't a problem, because I told everyone she was my aunt. So no one knew. And older women like younger men. You know, even if they are in prison. And so that was the situation I was in.

But what about your privacy?

We had privacy. Because we were in a room, with a door you could lock, and a shower with hot water. I mean, it was a whole different situation. And as I told you, because I thought Ronilton was coming the first time, I didn't do anything to get the room ready. But the next time I made an effort—I made up the room and brought down sheets for the bed. Because I mean, Jesus Christ, it was only every thirty days. And it was my only contact with the outside.[1] And she'd do my nails, and we'd talk, and she'd make us food. And so I sent her this letter, because I said to myself, "I can't let her visit me anymore." Because she'd fallen in love! And so I sent her this letter, and the letter said, "My dearest Jandira, I am very grateful for all that you've done but please don't come here anymore because there's this other woman . . ." And I know it was hard for her to take. And after that, she didn't visit me again.

You mean she gave up?

That's right. And then, after I'd dealt with that situation, I asked around to see if anyone was interested in an escape. Because there's always someone interested in an escape, because that's what prisoners do, right? And that's when I got to know José Carlos, Carlinho, and Espanõl, because they were the guys in charge of the plumbing.

What do you mean?

They were the prisoners who were in charge of the plumbing. You know, on the inside. And José Carlos's wife had an uncle who was a fisherman, who owned a boat. And so I said to him, "Jesus Christ, you have the keys to the fucking kingdom right there in your hand!" And he said to me, "Yeah, but I'm not the one who's allowed out!" "Well, what if I can get you out? Listen, we'll wait for the month of June, okay? Because I'll be outside working on the houses by then, so I'll have more time and freedom." "Okay, you figure out a way of getting us out, because I can get us a boat." Because his wife's uncle could come over from the mainland. But the question was, how was I going to get them out?

Then came the winter that we'd all been waiting for. And I was already thinking about how I was going to keep my promise, because that's what it was, a promise.

How many guys were you thinking about?

Well, there was me, José Carlos, Carlinho, Espanõl, and one other guy— and that other guy was Barbicha. Because I wasn't leaving without him.

Did he want to escape?

No, but I told him that if the opportunity arose, he had to go, because he had been there for twelve years already, and he had another eighteen to go. But like I said, I was afraid to tell him in case he told someone else. So I was only going to tell him when the time came, because he'd been there for such a long time that he'd gotten used to it. And it really would have upset him if he knew I was planning an escape. So anyway, then winter arrived, and the days got colder, and all the fishing equipment was put away, and no one was allowed out. And if you were used to being allowed out, it made things worse. So I hung out all day at the entrance to the prison. And when this guy Seu Jonas came by, I shouted out to him, I said, "Seu Jonas, any chance you can find me a job now that the fishing season is over?" Because Seu Jonas was a guard who fished with us. And he liked me, because he knew I was a hard worker. And he said to me, "Well, there's always my house, because the veranda needs painting." And I said, "I know how to paint. I'm good at that!"

And were you, or were you lying again?

I was kind of telling the truth, because you don't have to be a genius to know how to paint, right? So then he said, "Let me talk to Barbicha." Because they trusted Barbicha. And in the winter, he was the only one who was allowed out, because he knew how to do everything. And that's what I wanted to be, someone who knew how to do everything, because I couldn't stand being inside that prison all day. And so Barbicha told Seu

Jonas that it would be okay to let me out. And so the next day I went with Seu Jonas to his house. And there were these two cans of paint there, and some brushes. And he said, "You can have lunch here and stay the whole day." And then he went back to work at the prison.

So he left you alone at his house?

That's right, but he told his wife to keep an eye on me. And so then we got talking. And she asked me if I had a long time left to serve. And I said that I didn't, you know, to reassure her. And then she said, "Okay, make yourself at home. And if you need anything, let me know."

Did you know her?

I knew her a little. Because whenever we came back from fishing, I'd drop one or two off at her house. Because she loved fish but she hated cleaning them. So I cleaned them for her. And it was important for me to get to know her, so she would trust me, and find more work for me to do. Because I had to get out of that place. Because like I said, I didn't feel safe. And you know what? Looking back, maybe my mistake was that I got too involved too soon. I got involved too deeply. Because there was no need to. I mean I could have just served my time and been granted a conditional release.[2] But that's not what I did, right? Because from the moment I arrived, I got involved. Because ever since I was a child, I thought to myself, "How is it, that in a country like this, there is so much misery?" I mean, something must be wrong, right? So I said to myself, "There must be some group somewhere that sees things the way I do."

And you thought the Comando Vermelho might be this group?

That's right. Except that when I arrived on Ilha Grande, I quickly became disillusioned, because they were criminals, that's all. I mean, occasionally they'd do something for someone in their community, but otherwise, it was all about crime. And at first, things were pretty good, right? Because the president told me he liked me, and that he liked my ideas. But after a while, I figured I had nothing to learn from him, because he was a killer. I mean he had already killed nine or ten guys.

Did he do it himself, or did he get others to do it for him?

Sometimes he did it himself, so prisoners would fear him. And believe me, they feared him, because he was willing to use force. But at the same time he was exploiting the prisoners, together with the authorities, because it was like an agreement. You know, "I'll let you do what you want if you don't complain about anything, okay?" And I could see what was going on, but I couldn't say anything. Because that's the way the president chose to run the prison. And then he'd turn to us and say, "Aren't you the lucky ones! Because you get to throw three parties this year!" You know, as if he was doing us a huge favor. And right before these parties he'd start rationing our food, so there'd be almost nothing to eat for lunch or dinner. And in the meantime, he operated a canteen that sold food to the prisoners. I mean, it was like a king exploiting his own subjects!

Even though most of the prisoners were CV?

They were all CV, and there was nothing you could do or say. Because if you said anything negative about the CV, you could be punished. But like I said, there was this other group that was organizing. And my fear was that the prison was about to go up in smoke. Because if a prisoner is oppressed by the system, it's one thing. But if he's oppressed by the system within the system that's run by the prisoners, it's another, right? And so my only hope was to escape with these three other guys, because they had the means. But I mean you had to be smart about it, because if you tried to escape and failed, it looked like you were going against the president's wishes, which meant we couldn't talk about it, because the leadership couldn't be trusted. And so, like I said, if you tried to escape you had to be smart about it. Even if it meant betraying someone. You know, someone's confidence.

Like Seu Jonas, for example?

Like Seu Jonas, exactly. Because even though I liked him, I had to take advantage of his friendship. Because there was just no other way. And so I figured that there had to be a problem with the drains. You know, to get José Carlos and the others out of the prison. But my biggest fear was that there wasn't enough work at the house. But then, at around four o'clock in the afternoon, Seu Jonas arrived. And he said, "So, Bruno, how's the painting going?" And I said, "Well, it's going well. And by the way, did you know that there's some wood here that needs scraping?" "Okay, I'll get Barbicha to come out and work with you in the morning." And that was a good thing, right? Because it meant that I was going to be there for another day. Except that now that Barbicha was going to be there, it was going to complicate things. Because I knew that if there was a problem with the drains, Barbicha would try and resolve it himself. And so that evening, I asked José Carlos what I should do. And he told me to stuff some clothing down the toilet, so the water would back up into Seu Jonas's house, but to make sure that I filled it with dirty water first, so it looked like the problem was with the drains. So, the next day, I filled up this container with water from a sewage ditch that ran by the house. And I rolled up this shirt that I found in the laundry basket, and I stuffed it down the bowl. And then, when I flushed the toilet, it overflowed. And so then I called Barbicha. And Barbicha called Seu Jonas's wife, who called Seu Jonas at the prison. And when Seu Jonas arrived, he and Barbicha tried to figure things out—except that they couldn't, because they didn't know where the problem was. And I kept telling Barbicha that the guys inside the prison could fix it really easily. So then he finally said, "Seu Jonas, why don't we get José Carlos and the other guys out from the prison tomorrow?" And Seu Jonas said, "Well, it might be a problem. But maybe we can get them in and out really quickly."

Because prisoners weren't allowed out?

That's right. And so when I went back to the prison that night, I told José Carlos to tell his wife that her uncle should come by tomorrow.

Was she there already?

She was there visiting. Because José Carlos was a drug dealer. And she brought him his drugs. And he always made sure to give some to the leaders, so his wife could stay as long as she wanted, because she was a good person to have around. And so anyway, José Carlos said, "It's tomorrow? Are you sure?" And I said, "Absolutely." And that night I couldn't sleep. None of us could sleep. And then the next day, Seu Jonas had trouble getting the other guys out. And so at around eleven o'clock, I said to Barbicha, "I'm going over to the boat shed, okay?" And he said, "Okay." And when I got there, I saw the boat. And so I took off my shirt and I waved it in the air. But because it was winter, and the sea was so rough, the boat couldn't come in close to shore. And so the driver of the boat shouted out, "Well come on then, let's go! Because I can't stay here any longer, because it's a restricted area." And so I said, "But what about the others?" "Why don't you come now, on your own, and I'll explain it to José Carlos later. Come on, let's go!"

So he was basically saying he couldn't come back later.

That's right, and that I should go. And believe me, I thought about it, because I was desperate to get out of there. But then again, I knew that

I'd be seen as a traitor, and that the other guys wouldn't understand. And all the time he kept shouting, "Don't worry about it. I'll explain it to José Carlos later." But explain it how? When he came to visit? And so I had to think fast, because the situation was extremely complicated. And so then I said to him, "No, no, I'm not going. Just promise me you'll come back, in an hour, okay?"

And what did he say?

He said that he would try. And I said, "Okay, okay, that's good enough." And so then I went back into town. And on the way back, I ran into Seu Jonas and the others. And Seu Jonas said, "Well?" And I said, "I was on my way to Seu Jeferson's house, to see if he had anything we could use. But since you guys are already here, I'll just come back with you." And he said, "Okay." Because Seu Jonas was a good guy, he was a really good guy and he had no idea what we were up to. And so then we opened up the drain. And I said to José Carlos under my breath, "I've seen the boat. Your uncle says he's coming back at noon."

And what time was it?

It was around eleven thirty. And so then Seu Jonas went back to work at the prison. And I said to José Carlos, "It's got to be now. Go tell Barbicha." And Barbicha said, "Tell me what?" And I said, "Barbicha, there's a boat. And we're escaping. Now are you in?"

And what did he say?

He said, "I'm in. Let's go, because I know a shortcut."

Did you think he'd say no?

I wasn't sure, because he was so attached to his things, to his life in that prison that he surprised me. Because he had to make a decision. And he said to me, "Are you serious? There's a boat?" Because he thought we were joking. And then he said, "Okay, let's go!" And so then we took off. But because it was so cold, everyone was hanging out at the store in the main square, drinking wine, including Seu Albinate. And when he saw us he said, "Barbicha, Naval, are you guys working on the outside today?" And I said, "Yeah, there's a problem with the drains. So we're working on it, with these other guys." "Okay then, I won't keep you." And so then we left. And we climbed up this hill and went down the other side—except that when we got there, there was no boat. It wasn't there! Because the sea was too rough. I mean, there was no way he could've gotten close to shore. There was just no way.

So then I said to the others, "They must already know we've escaped. We've been out here so long, they must be wondering where we've gone." Because Seu Albinate saw us when we passed by the store. And by now, Seu Jonas would be coming back home for lunch. And so I knew there was no way we could go back. No, we were on the run.

What about Barbicha?

Barbicha was upset. He was really anxious. And he said, "I know a way that will lead us to the sea, on the other side of the island." And I said, "Barbicha. Barbicha, why don't you go back? Go back and leave us all here." "Are you sure?" "Sure I'm sure. Because although they must know we've escaped, you can run back there and tell them that you were looking for us." "Really? That would be great!" Because I realized that, although he'd agreed to come with us, I had to get him out. I mean, I couldn't take him with us. And there was time, there was still time. And so he went back.

And said what, that he wasn't part of the escape?

When he went back, he ran into the police, who asked him where we'd gone. And when he said he didn't know, they didn't believe him. And so they beat him, and put him in handcuffs, and he spent fifteen days in solitary. And it was only after we testified, after it was all over, that things began to improve for him. But he was punished, and he lost all of his privileges. And so anyway, Barbicha went back, and the rest of us headed into the forest. And I said to Espanõl, I said, "Hey, Espanõl, follow me. Because I know there's a town on the other side of the island. And maybe when we get there, we can get ourselves a boat." Because we were about an hour ahead of the guys they sent to find us, and so it made sense to push on into the forest. But you know what? That night was terrible. Because we'd left prison with nothing, because we thought we were going to escape by boat. And so all I had was what I was wearing. You know, shorts, T-shirt, and sneakers.

And you had to cross the island, right?

That's right. And my plan was to go from village to village until I reached the place where I was told there was this Christian community. And I thought, who knows? Maybe they might help us. Except that the other three were completely useless, because they kept getting caught in the undergrowth. And I thought to myself, "If I stick with them, I'm going to get caught." And so I said, "Hey, guys, you know what? I'm going to head off on my own, okay?" And they said, "No, no, let's go back the way we came, and take a different road." Because they wanted to take the main road, the road to Vila do Abraão. And I told them, I said, "But guys, if they've already sounded the alarm, that's the place they're going to go first!" But it was no use, because the other guys were basically lazy. I mean, it was almost as if they'd given up already.

So you left them there?

I left them there and I took off. And by then it was getting late, and I was really tired. And I knew that they were coming for us, that they'd put together a team to hunt us down.

Who was on the team?

Seu Jonas and some other guys who knew the forest well. And then there was this one guy who was a killer. Because he wasn't sent to bring us back, understand? He was sent to kill us. Because to be brought back alive, you had to be caught near a town where there were witnesses. Because otherwise, you'd end up dead, in the middle of nowhere, and nobody would know about it. And so I said to myself, "I'm going to have to stop somewhere and spend the night. Because there's no use wandering around in the dark." And so I picked out a spot in the forest and started trampling things down. And when I lay down, I said to myself, "I won't sleep, I'll just take a nap." And it was freezing that night, and pretty soon it started to rain.

Were you afraid?

I was more anxious than afraid, because I wasn't prepared for what had happened. I mean, I wasn't prepared for things to go wrong. And when the guy in the boat said he'd come back, in my heart of hearts, I knew that he wouldn't. And then I went and involved someone who was innocent, who I said nothing to beforehand. And believe me, he would have been happy to escape with me. But on the other hand, he would have been mad if we had failed. But you know what? At least I kept my promise. And perhaps if we had escaped, I wouldn't be sitting here now, telling you this story. Because we had very little time. And the police told us afterward that they would have sent a helicopter, and that we would have been killed on the open sea. And then, like I said, no one would ever have known. Because they liked to make out that the prisoners on Ilha Grande were evil, that they were really dangerous. But it just wasn't true. Because most of them were crooks. You know, petty thieves. But in any case, when the next day came, I took off again. And then, after walking for a few hours, I came across this beach. And at the end of this beach I could see these three guys, and it was José Carlos, Carlinho, and Espanõl. And when they caught up with me, I said, "Where the fuck have you guys been?" And they said, "We got lost!" And by then José Carlos could hardly walk, and neither could Carlinho. And then Espanõl said, "Let's rest here for a while." And I said, "But we can't, because they're right behind us! Come on, guys, we've got to keep moving. We've got to put some distance between us!" And so the four of us walked along the beach for an hour or so, until we heard someone shout, "Stop! Right there!" And then there were shots. And when they started shooting at us, I ran into the water. And then they shouted again, "Stop, stop, stop!"

How many were there?

There were six of them. And they all had guns and knives. And then José Carlos surprised me, because he started crying and begging for his life. And you know what? They were all afraid, all three of them. And so then one of the guards kicked me and forced me to lie down. And then another one smashed José Carlos over the head with the butt of his rifle. And then two of them started punching and kicking Carlinho and Espanõl. And so I said, "For the love of God, Seu Jonas, get everyone to calm down! We give up, okay?" And Seu Jonas said, "Jesus Christ, Naval, I really trusted you." "And I trusted you, Seu Jonas. So we both trusted each other, okay? And, I mean, thank God you were sent on this detail, because I know you won't let them kill us. I just know you won't." But then one of the guards said, "Let's finish them off. Come on, give me the shovel." Because the ones who were tired, the ones who had had enough, wanted to kill us and bury us right there in the sand. And so I said, "Seu Jonas, you're a smart guy. So you know it's to your advantage to take us back, right? Because then they'll think more highly of you, right?" And all I was trying to do was to get him to think. You know, to think twice about the situation. Because it was one thing to beat us. But, I mean, I didn't want to lose my life. Not there, not like that. And so Seu Jonas looked at me and he said, "No, Naval, I'm not going to let them kill you."

It was lucky that you knew him, then!

It was really lucky. And so then he said, "Okay, let's make our way back. Tie them all together." And so then we walked through the night, because they had lanterns and flashlights. And by midmorning, the next day, we were back at the prison.

When we got back to the prison we were all put in solitary confinement. And since Barbicha was already there, I was dying to know what he had told them. Because after being in solitary, there would be a hearing, where we'd all get to have our say. But first we had to serve our thirty days, which could be extended to sixty if necessary.

Where?

Jesus Christ, in this awful place. Because they put us all in this dungeon, in this underground cell, with no light, no bed, no mattress, no anything. And only one meal a day. And it was August, which is a month that is really cold. And so when you got out of there, you swore you'd never try and escape again! [*Laughter.*] And when we were all in there, I said to Barbicha, "So, are you mad at us?"

You were all in the same cell?

That's right. And there wasn't enough room for us all to lie down. So I spent most of my time exercising. You know, trying to stay warm. And I tried to get everyone else to do the same. And we were all in there together, except that Barbicha was only there for fifteen days. And when they held this hearing, I told them that if anyone was innocent, it was him.

And that was the truth, right? Because he only tried to escape at the last minute.

But we didn't even say he tried to escape. We said that he came after us, to find us. And I said as much to the director. And then the director said that when I got out of solitary, I wasn't going to be allowed out, for anything, because he now knew who I really was. And I tried to explain to him that it was something I decided to do on the spur of the moment. And he said, "So what about the boat?" And he wanted to know whose boat it was, so the police could go after him. And I mean, if they had put us in different cells, it might have been easier for them to find out what had happened. But they didn't. And so we were already up one to zero, right? [*Laughter.*] And so I told everyone not to worry. And after that, I never went fishing, obviously. And I never was allowed out. I just stayed there, passing the time. And the interesting thing was that I didn't say anything to Jandira, I mean about the escape. All I told her was that one day I might be able to surprise her. Except that I didn't, right?

So you continued to write to her, even though you told her not to visit?

Because she continued to write to me. And so I wrote her, so that she wouldn't come and visit. I mean, especially now that I'd lost everything, because I didn't know how she'd react. "Jesus Christ, I did everything for him, and then he doesn't trust me? He tries to escape and he doesn't tell me anything?" Because I told everyone to keep it a secret, and that the only person who could know was José Carlos's wife. And so I wrote Jandira a letter saying, "Wait until this place is closed down. Because then I'm going to be transferred to Rio. And I can explain everything to you then." And you know what? When she found out what had happened, she wrote me another letter saying, "I heard you tried to escape. So that's why you didn't want me to visit!" So there I was, trying not to make her suffer, and there she was thinking that I'd made up the story about a new girlfriend because I was trying to escape. Because she was in love with me, and she wanted to see me again.

Even if it was only for a few days a month.

It didn't matter. And I really didn't mean to hurt her. It's just that I needed someone, that's all. And now she was saying that she wanted to help me all over again. But I didn't let her. I wanted her to wait. And who knows if, down the road, in another prison or something, I mean, who knows?

And she did come to see you, right? After you were transferred?

That's right. And by that time I was with Lucia. And that's what they told her, at the prison. They told her that I was with another woman. So she turned around and left. And you know what? I never got to tell her. I never got to explain the situation to her face, because by the time I was released she was already dead.

How did she die?

Ronilton wrote me a letter, telling me that she got sick and died. Because he didn't know, you know, about us. I mean, he suspected, right? But she never told him. And so I told him, because he was my friend, because I was the one who involved him in all of this. And then I went and involved his mother, because she read the letter I sent him, remember? And then she started visiting me. And I didn't do anything to stop her. Because at that time I needed to be with someone.

And when they told her that you were with another woman, did she believe them?
No, no, she didn't. And it was better that way. I mean for her.

And so then the prison started to be emptied out. And what they'd do is, they'd call fifty, sixty prisoners at a time. You know, on a Sunday, when the guards did their rounds. They'd say, "You, you, and you, get your things together, because tomorrow you're being transferred." And then the prisoner would go to sleep knowing that the next day he'd be gone. And my group was the last to go. And in the end, there were only fifty of us left. And the day that I was transferred was a horrible day, because there were these policemen there who kept intimidating us, who kept threatening to beat us.

Why?
Because we were CV. They kept telling us that the Comando Vermelho was finished, because they thought that the CV was strong in that prison. But in reality, it wasn't. But you know what? The faction was about to reorganize, and I was a part of that process.

So if the Comando Vermelho wasn't strong there, why was Ilha Grande shut down?
Because the press found out about what was going on there. You know, about how much the government was spending, and about how it was the prisoners who were running the place, and about how the leaders had all these special privileges. I mean, all of that came out in the press. And all the prisoners could talk about was being transferred. And many of them were scared, because they knew that they were going to a prison where they'd have far less freedom. Because Afonso Costa was a maximum-security prison. And for the first few months, that's exactly what it was. What I mean is, it took a while before the CV turned it into the headquarters of their operations. Because in terms of physical structure, it was a prison just like in the U.S. But the problem was, they didn't have the men, they didn't have the personnel to keep it that way. And if the authorities thought they were weakening the CV by isolating its leaders, they were wrong. Because by isolating them, they made the CV even stronger.

And when Ilha Grande was shut down, was everyone transferred to Afonso Costa?

No, because Afonso Costa still wasn't built. And so the prisoners were sent to other prisons. And like I said, I was one of the last fifty prisoners to leave that place, along with the leaders and all the other prisoners who tried to escape. But you know what? Nothing ever happened to us. Because we were afraid we might be punished—you know, by the president. But we weren't. And in the end, everything turned out okay. And a few days after our escape there was a party, for Father's Day. I mean, in reality, the only ones who showed up were mothers. Because every prisoner has a mother, right? But a father? Very few fathers visit their sons in prison.

Was Father's Day the last party to be held there?

No, the last party was for New Year, a couple of months before the prison was shut down. And man, was it a party. I mean, it was incredible. Because everybody knew that it was coming to an end, and that soon, there'd be no more prisoners left on that island.

And what about the leaders? They were going to lose power, right?

That's right. Because when they made it to these other prisons, who knew what would happen to them? And because of this, they were afraid. And so it had to be a party to end all parties. Because they had to make out that they were the good guys, that they treated the other prisoners well. And in the last few days before the party, more than a hundred prisoners were allowed out to collect things, and to swim in the sea. But not us, because we were closely guarded. You know, "Uh uh, not these guys." And so then, on the day of the party, at around five o'clock in the afternoon, all these people showed up. And there was beer, and there was cachaça.[3] Because they brewed cachaça right there in the prison, in these huge metal containers. They made it out of sweet potatoes, manioc, and rice. And on the day of the party they'd set up stalls and they'd sell the cachaça to the visitors. And the interesting thing was that the prisoners dressed up as if it was a real party. You know, on the outside. And then they'd wait for their families to arrive. But it was really difficult for families to get there, because it was hard to get to the island. And then there was the truck ride, and the road was always in terrible shape. And so a lot of families were afraid, and so they walked to the prison instead. And then there was the whole business of the search, even on days when there was a party, because the military police would search everyone when they got to Vila do Abraão.

A serious search?

It can't have been that serious, because a lot of drugs found their way in. A lot of marijuana and a lot of cocaine. And then at around seven o'clock, all these prostitutes showed up. And when they got there, they were traded like goods. And the cells were all left open, and there were all these children wandering around. And there was music too. You know, funk, *samba, pagode*. I mean, it was a miniature version of hell, with all these little devils running around [*laughter*]. And even though there weren't a lot of prisoners left, it was a great party. And it went on until early the next morning. And when it was over, I looked around, and I said to myself, "Jesus Christ, it doesn't take much to make these prisoners happy!" But the reality of the situation was that it was over, and that the prison was about to be shut down. And a lot of them were sad because they knew their lives were about to change.

It must have been especially sad for prisoners with long sentences, right?

Yes, because they had a lot more to lose, because life for everyone in prison was changing. And the night before I left, I started wandering around, knowing that the next day I'd be transferred. And I thought to myself, "Now what? What's going to happen to me next?" And I knew that I was going to be transferred to a maximum-security prison. And I knew that I wouldn't have the freedom to run around. And everyone was saying that when the leaders from Ilha Grande got to these other prisons, there would be trouble, because of all the things they'd done. Because a lot of innocent people died on that island. And when the leaders took over, they didn't run the place the way they should. Because it was the authorities who established the rules, and the leaders just followed along. And in return, they were given control of the prison. But that wasn't true of the leaders who were there before, who had already been transferred. Because they stood up to the authorities, and they were the ones who established the rules. And in those days, all of the other prisons would do as they were told, because the leaders on Ilha Grande were respected, because they were strong. But not anymore, because they were being manipulated by the authorities.

But you got along with them, right?

I got along with them, but I didn't agree with their politics, because a lot of prisoners who tried to escape, or did something to annoy them, were punished. And a lot of prisoners were killed too.

You mean like Marcão?

That's right. Except that one of the prisoners they killed was a friend of one of the leaders in Bangu. And it caused a lot of problems.

So why did they kill him?

He worked in the kitchen, and these knives disappeared. Well, they didn't disappear, they were hidden, by the guys in Zezinho's group, so they could kill him. Because they told the leader that the guys in the kitchen were looking to take over. So he said, "Go ahead and kill them, after they come back from the kitchen at night." Because by the time they'd washed the dishes, and put away all the things, they were the last ones to go to bed. And that's when they killed them.

But isn't it dangerous to kill someone who has powerful friends?

It's really dangerous. So then they sent a letter to Bangu. But by the time they received a reply, telling them to remove the guys from the kitchen but under no circumstances to kill them, it was too late. Because Ilha Grande is a long way away. And it took time for the message to get there. So then guess what happened? What happened was that the knives reappeared. So the leader in Bangu knew that the guys in the kitchen had been killed for no reason. And he was so mad that he put someone else in charge.

You mean he removed the president?

That's right. But it wasn't long before the new president and his group were transferred to another prison. So the leader in Bangu had to reinstate the former president, until the prison was shut down, because he was the one with the most experience. And when he reinstated him, he ordered him to kill everyone who was involved with the killing of the guys in the kitchen, which he then did! I mean, the guy was Machiavellian, I mean he was pure evil! And not only that, he also took advantage of the situation to kill a bunch of other guys. Guys he didn't like, just for the hell of it. I mean, can you believe it?

And you couldn't say anything, obviously.

That's right. Even if the person who was to be killed was my friend. So I had to find another way to make him understand. And sometimes I could, and sometimes I couldn't. Like this one time, before the prison was shut down, I heard the president say, "Before we all leave, we're going to kill this guy, this guy, and this guy, okay?" And one of the guys he was talking about was my friend.

A prisoner stirs a cauldron in the kitchen of the Vila de Dois Rios prison. *Kitchen's Cauldron*, photograph by André Cypriano, 1993. Used by permission.

So what did you do?

I tried to make him understand, I mean, I had to. Because I knew what they were going to do to him. They were going to take him out and break every bone in his body. So I told him to tell the authorities that he had to leave with the next group. And he said to me, "But why are you telling me this? Do you know something I don't?" And I said, "No, no, I don't. I just want you to do this for me, for our friendship, okay?" "But how the hell am I going to speak to the authorities?" "For Christ's sake, be smart about it. Ask if you can speak to the chief of security. Tell him that you want to leave with the next group of prisoners, because you're afraid. He'll understand. You'll see." Because everyone knew that the leaders were looking to take advantage of the situation. You know, to make people disappear.

Disappear in what way?

They had these huge metal cauldrons, in the kitchen, that they used to cook the food. And they'd put people in them. They'd close the lid and cook them. And I mean, if you put someone in there, with all that heat and steam, there'd be almost nothing left. Because the prison was run by the prisoners, right? So if the president said that someone had to disappear, they had to disappear, understand?

You mean like the guys in the kitchen?

Exactly.

And the authorities?

The authorities would say that they escaped. And I was told that there used to be this doctor there, and that when someone was stabbed, you know, a hundred, two hundred times, he would write a report saying that he fell into a ditch [*laughter*]. Or that he climbed over a wall and ran away. I mean, this sort of thing happened all the time.

Was there a cemetery there?

There was a cemetery just outside the prison walls. But it was more for show than anything else, you know, in case anyone showed up. So they could say, "He died, but no one from his family came, so we buried him in this common grave." But no one could tell you what killed him, or how he died, understand? So anyway, the day before we were transferred, this guard came by and said, "Tomorrow, everyone's going to Aranha Filho." And I said to myself, "Holy shit, don't tell me I'm going back there again!" And when the next day came, the police showed up with their dogs. And they told us all to stand against the wall. And then they started beating us across the back of the legs. And you know what? I figured that something like this might happen. Because I said to the others, I said, "Prepare yourselves, okay? Because if they didn't punish us then, you can bet they will now." Because that's the way things are in prison. Because if you do something wrong, the director will punish you. And if it's something small, he'll punish you by the book and make a note of it in your file. But if it's something big, something serious, like trying to escape, then he'll find a way to punish you more severely, understand? And you know what? As soon as I said this, they went and told the police. The guards said, "You see those guys over there—they're the ones who tried to escape." So then this policeman picked up this piece of paper, and he called out our names. And then he called out the names of all the other prisoners who tried to escape. And then this one policeman hit me hard across the back of the shoulders. And then there was this other guy, and the guards starting pushing him around and telling him to keep his head down. But he said that he wouldn't. So they hit him, and he hit them back. And then they really laid into him. And so then we laid into them. Because in those days, if a policeman or a guard hit a prisoner, all hell would break loose. So everyone else joined in until the chief of police arrived and ordered everyone to calm down. "Stop! Stop everyone! Put them all in handcuffs!" And because there weren't enough handcuffs to go around, they tied us all up with tape and put us in the back of these trucks, in these three big army trucks, together with all our things. And they bundled everyone's things together in these big white sheets. And then they tied them down on top of the trucks, so it looked like the sort of thing you see in Africa. You know, like we were refugees fleeing a war or something.

What about the prison staff?

They all left there too. In fact, many of them left before us. And it was a good thing they closed that prison down, because of all the corruption and the killings. But you know what? There were prisoners there who didn't understand, who were really attached to that place. But in my opinion, it had to be closed down, because that prison was an affront. You know, in terms of human rights. Because the government has to make some effort to rehabilitate its prisoners, before they are sent back into this world. But when they are way the hell out there, where they are basically abandoned, what chance do they have? And I mean, look at how badly they were treated! So one way or another, that prison had to be closed down.

But that's not why it was closed down, right?

No, because, like I said, it was closed down because of all the scandals that were written about in the press. And for security reasons. Because when Brizola was elected governor, in the early 1980s, he promised that there'd be no more mistreatment of the residents of the favelas.[4] And it was this approach that allowed these factions to become established, factions that we still have to this day. And it created generations of criminals, and they armed themselves, and took over the prisons. And then they took over the favelas too. And when Moreira Franco was made governor, after Brizola, he tried to undo all this by coming down hard, and by building new prisons. But you know what? By that time it was already too late. By that time the situation was already out of control. And so anyway, on the day that we were transferred, we were all taken to Vila do Abraão, where we were put on board this boat to the mainland. And then there was the two-hour drive to Rio, tied up in the back of this truck. And then some of the prisoners were sent to Carvalho Troiano, because that was near where Afonso Costa was being built. But the more dangerous prisoners, the ones who were troublemakers, they were sent to Aranha Filho. Because Carvalho Troiano could never have held me. Because if they sent me there one day, I would have escaped the next [*laughter*]. And they knew that, so they sent me to Aranha Filho.

THE BANGU PRISON COMPLEX

If 1979 marked the year that the Comando Vermelho consolidated its hold over the Vila de Dois Rios prison, it was not until much later that it succeeded in gaining control of the other prisons in the system. The organization's ability to spread its message, however, was greatly enhanced by the authorities' long-standing policy of transferring those they identified as leaders. Dispersed to other locations, these leaders then proselytized and recruited other inmates until a critical mass was formed. This process, which was not without bloodshed, continued throughout the 1980s, until the authorities were forced to deal with the situation by embarking on a program of prison building and reform.

The attempt to establish control over the prison system was paralleled by an equally protracted and bloody war for control of Rio's favelas. In the late 1970s and early 1980s, the CV played to its traditional strengths by robbing banks and financial institutions as a means to finance fellow prisoners' escapes. Over time, however, this strategy took its toll in terms of the death and arrest of many of its founding members.[5] And it was these deaths and arrests that caused the leadership, in 1982, to fund the CV's activities via the drug trade.[6]

Controlling the drug trade meant, in effect, controlling the favelas, which were the perfect places from which to operate. Many of the leaders of the CV were from such areas, and given the fact that favela neighborhoods had suffered from decades of neglect, there was no public authority to contest them. There were, however, local gangs and interested parties that had to be persuaded to relinquish control, and it was the struggle between these various groups and the CV that provoked what amounted, in places, to a civil war.[7] The most well-known and well-publicized of these conflicts was the battle for the favela of Santa Marta, in August 1987. After months of planning and preparation, the CV invaded Santa Marta with a contingent of fifty heavily armed young men. The battle, which lasted a week, left eight dead and forty wounded and was conducted in full view of the press and the police, who refused to intervene.

As the CV's power grew, the authorities in Rio were forced to react. Brizola, who began his first term of office with the intention of reforming the police and humanizing the prison system, ended it by being defeated, in no small part, because of the increase in violence.[8] His successor, Moreira Franco, ran his campaign on this very issue and took steps early on to attempt to deal with what was a growing public security crisis. Apart from giving the police free rein to go after and kill suspected criminal elements, he also oversaw the inauguration of the Laércio da Costa Pellegrino maximum-security prison in the neighborhood of Bangu.[9]

The prison in Bangu was, at the time, the most modern facility in all of Brazil. It consisted of four wings, or cell blocks, each of which held twelve men. The walls of each individual prisoner's cell were eight meters high and made of steel-reinforced concrete, and the entire facility was monitored via closed-circuit television. In addition, visitors to the prison could not meet prisoners face-to-face. Instead, they had to communicate by telephone on either side of a sheet of bulletproof glass. Finally, the roof of the prison was designed to prevent the landing of helicopters, a means of escape that had been used by the CV twice in the past.[10]

The transfer of the CV's leaders to the prison in Bangu took place during the last week of August 1988, and resulted, as planned, in their almost complete isolation. In response, the CV ordered their three thousand or so members to go on hunger strike and, when that didn't work, to kill a prisoner a day until the leaders of the organization were removed.[11] In the end, neither of these tactics persuaded the governor to reverse his decision. Nor did it stop the process of prison building and reform that resulted in the inauguration of the maximum-security facilities of Alfredo Tranjan (Bangu II) in 1995, and Dr. Serrano Neves (Bangu III) in 1997.[12] Nor did it stop the demolition, on April 2, 1994, of the birthplace of the CV, the Vila de Dois Rios Prison.[13]

When we reached the prison of Aranha Filho, I thought to myself, "This is going to be hard for me." Because I had nothing with me, because everyone's things were mixed together. And some of us were sent to Carvalho Troiano and some of us were sent to Aranha Filho. So how was I supposed to know which things were mine? And so I arrived there with just my clothes, because that's all I had on me. And it's interesting, because when you have things, you know, a photo or a letter, it makes you feel like you're someone, even though you're in prison. Because a prisoner spends so much time by himself that he becomes attached to things, so imagine what it's like when you have nothing, and you know you're not going to be given anything by the authorities. And that's where the family comes in, understand? And that's where they sent me, to a cell block that was just for the cv.

What about the others, the other three?

They were sent there as well. But to different cells, because I didn't know anyone in the one I was in. And the cell was about eight meters square. But I mean, some things had improved. Because before, everyone slept on the floor, right? But now there were bunk beds. Because they were building new prisons. And so the conditions there were better. I mean, there were no longer forty, fifty guys to a cell. So it was better than before.

And the food?

The food was better too, because now it was subcontracted out. And it was fresh, and hot, and there were decent-size portions. Only the meat was horrible. So I always gave mine away, because I was more used to fish, right? And then there was always someone there who had money, who could pay for things to be brought in. Because it was the same old story. I mean, it was like I was reliving it all over again. And then one morning, after I'd been there for about fifteen days, one of the guards said, "You have a visitor." And do you know who it was? It was the husband of my aunt. You know, the one who lived in Rio. Because I wrote my aunt a letter, and the letter said, "I'm no longer on Ilha Grande. I'm in Aranha Filho. And visiting day is Tuesday, but you can drop stuff off anytime." So when they called me, I went down, because the visiting area was below ground. And so then I sat there waiting.

What were you thinking?

I was thinking, "Hey, this is great!" Because like I said, I'd sent my aunt a letter. And her husband knew someone who worked at the prison. He said, "Look, my nephew's in Aranha Filho but I can't get a visitor's pass. I can't get in there." And the guy said, "Don't worry, I'll get you in." Because it's difficult, understand? Because you have to go downtown with all your papers, and you have to have your photo taken, and you have to explain who you are, you know, in terms of your relationship with the prisoner. Because it's much easier for family than for friends, understand? So when he got there I said, "Hey, it's great that you've come." And he said, "So, son, how are you?" "Well, I'm in prison!" "Son, I know you're in prison, but how are you?"

You mean psychologically?

That's right. But I didn't want him to know that I had all these problems. Because there were rumors flying around that something was about to happen, because I was no longer just a prisoner, understand? Because I had a reputation as someone who liked to hang out with the leaders, and who liked to try and escape. But I didn't want him to know about any of this. So I tried to convince him that everything was okay, that the years I'd spent in prison hadn't been that bad. And then he said, "So where do you go from here?" And I said, "From here, God only knows."

But you already knew, right?

I knew, but I didn't want to tell him. And then he said, "Okay then, I'm going to get a pass, so I can visit you. Oh, and by the way, I've brought you some things. And here's twenty reais. I know it's not much, but money's really tight right now. And another thing—the guard who let me in lives on our street, and I've known him since he was a boy." So I said, "Well, if you see him, point him out, okay? I mean, at least let me see his face." Because I thought that if this guard let him in, with all these things, then he's someone I should know, right? Because some guards get to work all angry, all stressed out, and they take it out on the prisoners. You know, they open up the cells and start beating people.

Does this sort of thing still happen?

These days not as much, because the guards are better educated. But I mean, it wasn't like that before. Because in those days, being a guard was a risky business. I mean, you almost had to be as stupid as the prisoners, right? So anyway, after he pointed the guard out, he left. And then, after someone visits you, you're searched before you can go back to your cell.

Why?

To humiliate you, to have you sit out there in the open with no clothes on. And I remember the first time I saw this happen, because I said to myself, "Jesus Christ, what's this all about?" And the guard standing next to me said, "This is what we do here. And if you don't like it, you'll be beaten, okay?" So I stayed there in Aranha Filho until they'd finished building Afonso Costa.

How long was that?

About six months. And during these six months I had very few visitors. I mean, my aunt's husband came to see me two, three times at the most. And Jandira continued to write me, saying, "Look, I'm coming to visit you, because now you're a lot closer." And I always wrote back to her saying, "No, no, don't come, because I'm about to be transferred." I mean, I always said something to stop her from coming. But even so I kept her letters. I kept all my letters. I kept them in this plastic bag. And every now and then I'd take them out, because I liked to imagine what the person was thinking when they wrote them. Because if someone writes you a letter, they're thinking of you, right? So I'd take them out and I'd say to myself, "I'm going to read this one again." And then someone in my cell would say, "You're reading that letter again? But you've read it so many times!" "Yes, I know, but it makes me feel like someone cares about me." Because on Ilha Grande, you could get out and run around. But in Aranha Filho, you were in lock-down mode. And at the side of each cell there was this little space, this little corridor where the sun shone in. And the authorities claimed that this counted as our time in the sun. [*Laughter.*] But the nights there were the worst, because there was all this talk about revenge, all this talk about settling scores. But only when we got to Afonso Costa. Because the leaders from Ilha Grande were there as well, but they were spread out all over the place. But everyone was going to be together in Afonso Costa. And so then the day came when we were to be transferred. Because this guard came by and said, "Afonso Costa's now ready. So get your things together, because everyone's going there."

And what were you thinking, when you were waiting to be transferred?

I was thinking that Afonso Costa would be the death of me. That's what I was thinking.

When we reached Afonso Costa, we were taken to this huge room, all two hundred of us. And then the guards started sorting us into groups. Because there were eight cell blocks in that prison, and each cell block had thirty-six cells, with one prisoner in each. And it was very much a first-world prison, because at six o'clock at night, all of the prisoners were locked inside their cells. And they weren't allowed out until six o'clock the next morning, and even then they had to stay inside their cell blocks. And they started with Cell Block 2, and they continued until they got to the end. And I noticed that they didn't send anyone to Cell Block 1, and I was wondering why that was. And you know what? Out of the two hundred prisoners that arrived that day, I was the only one left. I was the only one left waiting in that room. I mean, can you believe it?

But why?

I had no idea. But then the director came over to me and said, "You're the one who was in the navy, right?" And I said, "Right." "And you were on Ilha Grande?" "That's right." "And do you have anyone to visit you?" "Yes sir, yes I do." Because I didn't want to give the impression that I was there all alone. "And who is this person?" And so then I told him about Jandira. I told him that she was my woman. Because I was beginning to wonder what was going to happen to me, because they'd already dealt with everyone else. And I thought to myself, "Could it be that I'm being punished?" And then the director said to me, "You're going to Cell Block 1."

You and who else?

No one. So there I was, at one o'clock in the morning, all alone in Cell Block 1. And I kept thinking, "So what happens to me now? Who else are they going to put in here?" Because there were thirty-six cells, right? And they put me in cell number eighteen, which was right down the end. But then I thought, "Well, at least I'm alive, right?" Because my biggest fear was that they'd put me in with the leaders. You know, the leaders from Ilha Grande. So then I just sat there and waited. I waited for the next day, to see what would happen.

What about conditions there? Your cell, for example.

My cell was about two meters square. And there was this concrete platform for a bed, and a place to go to the bathroom, and a small area to take a shower. And then there was a lamp outside the cell that was kept on all night. Because you didn't have access to anything in that place. And it was freezing cold because it was winter. And all I brought with me were my letters. And when I got there, they gave me a blue pen and a plastic spoon and they said, "These are your things and these are the rules. You're not on Ilha Grande anymore, so get used to it." Because on Ilha Grande we had everything. And that's why the prisoners were so shocked when they were transferred, because in Afonso Costa we had nothing. And so anyway, the next day the other prisoners arrived. And what they did was, they emptied out a cell block from another prison, an older prison in the city. And there were twelve of them.

Who were they?

Well, there was Rodrigo Santos, otherwise known as Pingo, who was this big-time bank robber. And Edmilson de Souza, who was involved in all the kidnappings, in the 1980s.[1] And Ezechias of Bonsuccesso, and Dedão, who was leader of the favela of Alto das Queimadas, together with his brother Rubinho. And Washington, who was one of the founding members of the cv, who spent many years on Ilha Grande. And Pato, this huge guy who was also from Bonsuccesso, who died while he was there. And then there was also this guy Fernandinho, from Campos, who also took part in the kidnappings. And Humberto André, or Chiquito, as he was known back then. And I only knew these leaders by name—you know, by reputation—because they'd already been transferred by the time I got to Ilha Grande. And they'd spent the past six years together. And you know what? They were completely out of it. I mean, it was as if we'd met on the street or something. "Hey, brother, how's it going? Where are you coming from? Ilha Grande? Which cell block were you in?" And little by little, I got to know them. And little by little they got to know me. And I mean, it was great, because these guys were the real deal, these were the real leaders of the organization. And I thought to myself, "If I ever get out of here, I'm going to stick close to these guys, because they're all friends, and maybe it'll work to my advantage."

So you were still thinking of sticking with crime?

At that point I was, yes. And I'd be lying if I said that I wasn't. Because I thought to myself, "Maybe they'll come in useful. And who knows? Maybe I'll come in useful to them. Because maybe I can do their books or something." Because in those days there were no cell phones. But even so, their ability to manage their affairs was impressive. I mean, there were favelas out there that were bringing in two, three hundred thousand reais a month. And there were leaders in there that received three or four visits a day, from their lawyers. Nowadays no, because the situation has changed. But before, I mean, it was incredible!

And these visits were supervised?

No, no, they weren't. Because the guard would take the prisoner to this little area at the front of the cell block, and then he'd leave. And the lawyer would slide all the paperwork underneath. You know, the accounts from the favela. And a lot of lawyers were involved. And a lot of them ended up dead, because they double-crossed the leaders in prison. Because they'd say that they'd arranged for an escape. Or that such-and-such a judge had agreed to their release. But they were lying. So the next time they went to the favela they were killed. Because these leaders had authority, these leaders had the power to decide what went on out on the street. And that's why I was going to watch them very closely—because maybe I'd discover that they operated on the basis of some kind of principle, on the basis of some kind of ideology.

You mean as an organization?

That's right. But you know what? All I saw was them counting money, because it was all about crime.[2] I mean, they'd get together with their lawyers, and they'd decide which favelas to invade, and how many men it would take. And while they were all sitting there, you know, talking, someone said, "What about Bruno? Should he be listening to all of this?" And then someone else said, "It's okay, Bruno can stay, because he's one of us."

So they accepted you then?

That's right. Because I'd spent two years on Ilha Grande, right? And I'd tried to escape. And both of those things gave me a certain amount of prestige. But I mean, we were very different, them and me. Because I was a prisoner and they weren't, if you know what I mean. Because they had all these other things going on, out on the street. And they had the best clothes, and gold chains, and shit like that.

Even though it was a maximum-security prison?

It was in the beginning. But like I said, it didn't stay that way very long. And they tried, I mean, they really tried. And after two days the director came by, and he called us all to the front of the cell block. And he said, "You guys, I want you to listen up! Because this is the way it's going to be. You're all going to wear uniforms and, depending on how you behave, your women can come and visit you. And another thing—the water will be turned on at six o'clock in the morning and off again at six o'clock at night. And that's when everyone will be locked in their cells, understand?" So then the director said, "Any questions?" And I said, "Excuse me, sir." Because no one else said anything. I mean, there were all these big-time leaders there, and no one said anything. "Excuse me, with all due respect, sir, but it was my understanding that we had both duties and rights. So I'd like to know about our rights."

So you knew something about prisoners' rights?

Yes, because on Ilha Grande there was this library, and the prisoner who ran it let me take out books. Because it was a long time between when I tried to escape, and when the prison was shut down. And I read everything by Sidney Sheldon. You know, *If Tomorrow Comes*, *The Other Side of Midnight*, *Bloodline*, *Memories of Midnight*. I mean, I read all of his stuff. And I also read parts of the Bible, parts that I found interesting. Because Jesus was a revolutionary, right? So I wanted to know more about his life. So I spent all those cold dark nights on Ilha Grande studying. And when the prison was about to be shut down, I said to myself, "So now it's my turn to travel the road to Damascus!" Because I believe that me being sent to that cell block, and the arrival of all those other prisoners, was part of my journey along that road. That's what I was thinking.

And who were the other prisoners, the twelve disciples?

Yes, and what disciples! [*Laughter.*] And so anyway, getting back to the story, in the library on Ilha Grande, there was this book called *The Handbook of Penal Laws*. And I started to read it. So when the director showed up, I said to myself, "I'm going to ask him what this prison has to offer." I mean, it wasn't like I was trying to challenge him or anything. But I mean, a prison that size and that new had to have something to offer the prisoners, you know, in terms of rehabilitation. So I said, "Sir, you're talking a lot about our duties, but what about our rights? Because we want to study. We want to go to school." And he said, "That's not a problem, because we have a school here. And we'll figure out later on who's going to go, okay? I'll send someone around to ask who wants to study, okay?"

So he accepted what you said in good faith?

That's right. But when he said that someone would be coming around to take the names of prisoners who wanted to study, one of the leaders said to me, "Put my name on that list." But you know what? He wasn't interested in studying. He was just interested in finding ways of making contact with the other prisoners. So I said to him, "Look, we've got to be smart about this, okay?" Because it was almost impossible to make contact with the prisoners in other cell blocks, and so how were they going to deal with the leaders from Ilha Grande? Because they were already trying to figure out ways of killing them. And there I was, trying to convince them that they should be thinking about improving themselves, and that if they absolutely had to kill someone, why not wait until they got out? Because when they got to Afonso Costa, they thought they'd be able to move around. You know, inside the prison. So then the oldest guy, this guy Washington, he got the group together and he said, "By what the director's told us, it's going to be hard for us to communicate with our friends in other cell blocks. So how are we going to get ourselves out of here?"

You mean out of the cell block, or out of the prison?

Both. Because there was a group there that was interested in escaping. Because there always is, right? And this guy Dedão, from Alto das Queimadas, he said to me that if I could figure out a way of digging a tunnel, he'd finance it. Because he told me that they'd all heard about the spectacular escape I'd organized on Ilha Grande. And I said, "No, no, no, it was nothing. I just happened to have a friend who had a boat, that's all. But whatever, let's think about it, okay? And who knows, maybe we can find a way." And so he said, "All right then, you think about it."

So then I spent the night thinking about how I could organize an escape. Because there were thirty-six cells, right? And at the end of each cell block there was a water tank, so you could wash your clothes. And there was this channel that ran down the middle of the cell block to a drain, and the cover to the drain was secured by a metal strip that was padlocked at one end. So I said to Pingo, I said, "Pingo, why don't we open up the drain to see what's underneath?" Because they'd put us all in Cell Block 1, right? And Cell Block 1 was closest to the wall of the prison. So it was simply a matter of opening up the drain and following the course of the water. So I said to Dedão that if he could get someone to bring us in a padlock, we could use it to replace the one that was there. Except that the drain was in the middle of the cell block, down toward the front end, and the guards came by all the time to keep an eye on us, until we were locked inside our cells at night.

Wait a minute. You'd tried to escape once and failed. Now you were thinking of escaping again?

Yes, because these guys had money, and they were willing to pay for everything. And another thing—the prison was about to explode. And I didn't want to be there when it did. So I tried my hardest to get the guys to think about escaping, instead of killing each other. Because it was better that they focused on escaping, right? So then Dedão said, "I'm going to ask the guard for a padlock." And it cost him a thousand reais.

So it was easy then?

It was easy except that there was this metal detector at the entrance to the prison. So Dedão asked me, he said, "How's he going to get it in?" And I said, "Tell him to bring it in with the food at lunchtime." Because the food was subcontracted out, right? And they turned the metal detector off when the food truck came in. So all we had to do was get it to the guys in the kitchen. Because lunch was always served to the prisoners in Cell Block 1 first. And when lunch arrived, the guy from the kitchen said, "I've got it! It's in here!" So then he brought out the plates and he started to serve. And he covered the padlock with rice and beans and gave it to Pingo. Then Pingo took it out, cleaned it, and hid it inside his cell. So then I said to Pingo, "Okay, let's break off the old padlock and lift up the cover." Because the cover had two holes in it, a slot on either side. And it was held in place by this metal strip. So we had to break off the old padlock to remove it.

How?

Well, first we made a length of rope from an old pair of jeans. Then we took two metal bars from the casing of the light fixture, outside of one of the cells, a cell where there was no prisoner, so the guards wouldn't notice. Because there were thirty-six cells in our cell block, right? And there were thirteen of us. So there were a lot of cells that were empty.

How did you get them out?

That's an interesting question. Because Pingo paid a visitor to bring a hacksaw in. And what she did was, she broke the blade of the hacksaw into three pieces and hid them in her vagina. Because visitors there were watched very closely. And so when she came in, she went straight to the bathroom. And then she handed the blades to someone, who handed them to someone else, who handed them to me. Because there are people who make a living this way. You know, they get themselves a visitor's pass, as someone's friend or a member of their family, and then they're paid to bring things in, like drugs and cell phones.[3] And the guys with all the money were the guys with me, in Cell Block 1. So everybody wanted to work for them, understand?

Did they pay well?

They paid really well. I mean, they were extremely generous. And it was around this time that Dedão arranged a girlfriend for me [laughter]. He said, "Bruno, don't you have anyone to visit you? And I said, "No, no I don't." "Okay then, I'm going to find you a girlfriend. And I'll make sure she's really pretty." So then he sent a message to this girl in Alto das Queimadas. He said, "Look, you're going to visit this friend of mine, okay? And he's really smart and you're really pretty. So off you go."

In the understanding that she was going to have sex with you?

That's right. And that's why I wanted to be friends with these guys— because, I mean, Jesus Christ, a woman! Because it had been months since I'd been with a woman. So I figured I'd do anything for them. Anything. I mean, I'd dig a hole, I'd do anything to help get them out! [*Laughter.*] So I said to Dedão, "You'd do this for me?" And he said, "I'm going to send you a woman who's so pretty!" So then he sent for her, and she came and visited me for a few days.

Was there a ratão there as well?

Yes, because, like I said, the prison was new, but the guards were all the same! [*Laughter.*] But anyway, getting back to the story, when the pieces of the saw arrived, we took these three plastic razors and we broke off their heads. Then we cut a notch in the top of each of the razor's handles, and we attached a piece of the saw with dental floss. And then we hid them. Because there was a hole in the wall at the entrance to each cell, because the cell doors were supposed to be automatic. They were supposed to open electronically, but the equipment was never installed. But the holes for the equipment were still there, on the right side of each cell door. So we dropped the razor handles and blades into the holes so we could fish them out later. And then, when we had the chance, we cut away the bars from the casing of one of the light fixtures, and we attached them to the ends of the length of rope we'd made. You know, from a pair of jeans. And then we inserted the pieces of metal into the slots on either side of the drain cover and lifted. And it was really heavy, because it was made of iron. So then I said, "Let's move the TV to the middle of the cell block, so we can all crowd around. So when a guard comes by, he'll think we're watching TV." When in fact, what we were doing was seeing if we could lift off the drain cover. And you know what? We managed to lift it off! And then we replaced the old padlock with the new one understand? Except that the new one was all shiny and the old one was covered in rust. So what we did was, we took a two-liter bottle of Coke and we cut it in half. And then we filled the bottom half with piss, because the piss would make the new padlock rusty, so it wouldn't look like it was new. And then, when we lifted up the cover, we saw that there was a way out.

You mean you saw that you could dig a tunnel?

That's right, because the concrete underneath was all soft. I mean, it just crumbled in our hands. Because the prison was built in a hurry, and they didn't use the right amount of cement. Because we chipped away at it and underneath there was all this red dirt. And the idea was to dig until we reached the wall. But it was going to take time. I mean, it wasn't something that was going to happen overnight. And so I told everyone, I told them that we were going to have to dig the tunnel bit by bit.

And what were you going to do with the dirt?

That's an excellent question. Because when there was water, we could wash the dirt down the drain. But you had to do it slowly, so the drain wouldn't clog. And you know what? The other prisoners were really into it. They were into it more than anything else. And I mean, I had no idea if the tunnel was going to work. But in any case, we started digging. And I told them, I said, "Look, when you're free on the outside, you can kill anyone you want. But until then, let's concentrate on the tunnel, okay? Because it's the smart thing to do."

So everyone was on board?

Everyone. But even so, life in prison carried on as usual. I mean, it's not as if the tunnel was the only thing we had to think about. Because there were other things, like the school, and how we were going to communicate with our friends in other cell blocks. Because like I said, the guys in my cell block wanted to be able to move around. But there was just no way. And so look at the situation I was in, because, I mean, I barely knew them. Yet I was the one who was responsible for getting them out, and I was the one who was responsible for getting them in touch with the guys in other cell blocks, guys they hadn't seen in years.

So anyway, then I remembered what the director had said. So when this guard came by, I said to him, "The director mentioned the possibility of opening up a school. But I've heard nothing since. So I'm giving you my name, so you can pass it along, okay?" And later on that day the director sent for me. And when I reached his office, he asked me to explain what it was I had in mind. So I told him that on Ilha Grande, I was one of a small group of prisoners who was allowed out. But now that I was in Afonso Costa, I had nothing to do. So I wanted the opportunity to teach, because there were a lot of prisoners there who couldn't read or write. And do you know what he said? He said, "Well, we have this project sponsored by a foundation. And a group of professors is going to be coming by, and they're going to be training five prisoners as monitors. Now do you know anyone who might be up for this, I mean besides you?" And

I said, "Well, I'm sure if we look we'll find someone." Except that the funny thing was that no one in my cell block was up to it, not a single one! [Laughter.]

What did you think of this idea, this project?

I thought that it was an excellent idea. But you know what? It never caught on, I mean, in prison. Because the prisoners weren't interested, and neither were the guards. Because for them, their job was to watch over the prisoners and then to get the hell out of there, alive! And now the government wanted to send the prisoners to school? I mean, come on! But for me at least it was a great opportunity. And I mean, I threw myself into it. I threw myself into it heart and soul.

Even though you knew it wasn't going anywhere?

Yes, because I learned so much from the time I spent with those professors. Even though they were only there for fifteen days. Because it seemed like a lot longer to me. Because they'd get there in the morning and then they'd teach. And they'd use videos, and then they'd relate the information from the videos to things we read in books. And it was a great way to learn. But you know what? When I looked around at the other prisoners, I could see they weren't interested. One or two, maybe. But no matter, because the five of us who were trained to be monitors were going to take full advantage of the situation. So much so that I used to get anxious when the lessons were coming to an end. Because we had fifteen days of training, right? And each day was different. And I mean, it really opened my mind. And I realized then that I wasn't prepared to return to life on the outside, like so many other prisoners in there who were lost. Because I knew that if they were released, they'd return to a life of crime. And then they'd be killed, or they'd end up back inside again. Because in the eight years I was in prison, I saw a lot of guys do two, three years, and then be released. Then, after a few months, they'd be back inside again. And I'd say to myself, "Jesus Christ, you had this opportunity, and you're back inside again?" But you know what? The authorities knew what they were doing. They knew that they were releasing guys who were poor and uneducated and had no place to go. Not that I'm saying that it's all about being poor, mind you. Because it's true that there are very few opportunities out there, and the lack of opportunities is certainly a factor, right? But it's often the case that a family member's involved. You know, an uncle or a father, and so crime is all they know. Because if you look closely, each family has its own history, and it's often a history of crime, understand?

So there's more to it than just poverty?

There's much, much more. I mean, can you imagine if someone in your family is arrested and ends up in prison? Then, when they get there, nobody comes to visit, because nobody has any money? Then after a while, they're released, and they can't go back home, because another faction has invaded and taken over. So they have to go somewhere else. And the guys in this other community take them in and they say, "Here, take these clothes. Take this gun."

So a prisoner who is released has few options?

That's right, because crime is the easy option, right? Because the guy's going to go hungry, and he's going to want something to eat. So he's going to go out and steal a car or something, and then maybe he'll kill the driver, because when he was in prison he was beaten. You know, he was abused by the system. Because it's the system that produces these people. And in response, what do the authorities do? They come down hard, that's what they do. And then we end up with the situation we're in today, which is guerilla warfare. And why? Because there's no plan, there's no plan in place. So instead they use force. And force sometimes gets things done, I understand that, but only in the long run. And a lot of governments have tried using force. And it's always against the poor, always against the favelas. And that's what people in these communities fear the most. I mean, imagine living in such a place. Imagine trying to raise a family—because you're a nobody, and you know it. Because out there in the real world it's a completely different situation. Because out there you have rights. Out there are things like warrants and procedures that have to be abided by, that have to be respected. But not if you live in a favela, because in a favela they come in shooting.⁴ And they break down people's doors and they say that such-and-such a person's involved, that such-and-such a person's a criminal. And then they take them away. And to survive you have to be an artist. You have to be a magician. And so anyway, what was it we were talking about? We were talking about the course, right? And this big opportunity to work with the professors. Because I think you have to keep moving forward, you have to take advantage of every opportunity in life.

Even if they are few and far between?

Even if they are few and far between. And so when this opportunity presented itself, I said, "So this is how it's going to be?" Because these teachers changed everything, because they opened my mind and I started thinking of other ways of leading my life. But the other prisoners, no. Because the other prisoners were more interested in escaping, because otherwise they were going to be in there for a long, long time. So when they heard that I was going to be a teacher, they said, "But Bruno, what about the tunnel?" And I said, "Don't worry about the tunnel, because it's going to go ahead, okay? It's just that we need more guys to help us dig. Because you guys are no good." Because the guys in my cell block may have had all the money, but as workers they were useless. So I had to get other people in.

But how?

Through the school. So Dedão said to me, "There's this guy in Cell Block 7. And I've got to get him out of here, because I want him to take over this favela." And I said, "Put his name on the list then." Because only forty prisoners were allowed out to go to school, and ten of them were to be chosen by the leaders. And this guy's name was Ratinho, because he was about five feet tall and he looked like a rat. So he was perfect for digging tunnels. But when the chief of security saw his name he said, "Look, there's no way I'm going to let this guy live with you because he's a troublemaker. So I'm going to put him in Cell Block 2, which is right next to you, okay?" Because Ratinho was a born criminal, and he was always causing trouble. So then the chief of security asked me, he said, "Why him?" And I said, "Because he's my student." But of course he wasn't my student, because he was one of the ones who were chosen by the leaders. But you know what? He told me that he wanted to study, and so his name had to be on that list. Because otherwise, the whole school thing would have been a joke, right? So the chief of security agreed. But he wouldn't let him live with me. Only in Cell Block 2. And so then we started school.

Where?

In this classroom they had there. And classes were from eight in the morning until noon. And at the same time, we were starting to dig the tunnel. And we had the keys to the padlock and everything, except that we couldn't work every day. Only on days when there was enough water to wash away the dirt, and when the guard shift on duty was the kind that didn't spend the whole time watching over us. And we worked on weekends as well. Because Saturdays and Sundays were for visitors, and so everyone who had a visitor went outside to hang out on the patio. And so the cell block was left empty, except for those who didn't have anyone to come visit.

And Ratinho?

Above each cell block, there was this metal grate that ran all the way to the end, like we were in a cage or something. So we cut out a section of the grate above Cell Block 1, and Cell Block 2, so Ratinho could come on over. Because he'd climb over in the morning, and then, at around six o'clock at night, he'd climb back. And since the grates in the prison were all painted blue, we used bars of blue soap to glue the sections of grate back up. And we did this in the morning, and we did it again at night. And it was his idea, because he came up with it one day while we were in school.

So who knew about the tunnel?

The guys in Cell Block 1, obviously, and a few others. People we could trust, because it had to be kept a secret. And like I said, in the beginning, the guys in my cell block had all these ideas about how they were going to kill the leaders from Ilha Grande. And the leaders from Ilha Grande could see that they were all hanging out together in the school. And so I tried to get some of them to join us, to be students as well.

Why, to start a fight?

No, no, quite the opposite. To make it more difficult. To get them to talk to each other. Because if they started killing each other we'd lose the school. I mean, we'd lose everything, right? And then the authorities would say, "See, I told you so," which is what ended up happening anyway. Because the guys in my cell block would say, "Can't you get so-and-so into the school, so we can hang him?" And I'd say, "You can't go hanging a guy in the classroom!" [Laughter.] And then they'd say, "Okay then, how about we open up the back of the TV and hide a gun in there, so when the director comes, we can take him hostage and demand a helicopter." And I'd say, "Come on, guys! I mean, it's a great idea, but you can't go around doing things like that!" [Laughter.] Because I'd spent almost two years on Ilha Grande, right? And now I was in Afonso Costa, in the midst of all these problems. So I said to myself, "I'm going to do everything I can to prevent them from killing each other." And so I said to them, "Look, let's focus on the tunnel. And then when you guys get out, you can do whatever you want, okay?" Because otherwise, a lot of innocent people were going to be killed. Because when shit goes down inside a prison, there's not a lot of attention paid to the rights of the accused. Because they are tried, sentenced, and executed all in one go. And only afterward is it discovered that they were innocent. I mean, someone will say, "Go and kill the guy in the red shirt." So then they go there and there are four guys in red shirts, so they kill all of them. And so when it came time for the leaders of Ilha Grande to die, other people were going to die too.

You mean, people like you?

That's right, because I was there with them. So I had to be careful. Even though I knew that things on Ilha Grande were being done the wrong way, and that sooner or later they would be punished. And you know what? The authorities knew that something was going on. And the last thing they wanted was reports of a massacre in the press. Because they'd taken all those prisoners from Ilha Grande, where there was room to run around, and they'd locked them all up in Afonso Costa. So they knew there was going to be trouble. And they thought to themselves, "Maybe if we give them this school." But they only allowed forty prisoners out. And in the beginning, they only wanted to allow thirty, but I persuaded them to give me ten more. And at first, they wanted them all to be from Cell Block 1. But it was my idea to take them from different cell blocks. And then there were the ones that the leaders wanted—because in reality, they were the ones who made all of the decisions.

On the first day of classes there were forty passes for us, so we could be identified. And then we passed through this metal detector and went down to the classroom. And the interesting thing was that they all sat there like they were ready to study. But in reality, they weren't paying attention to anything I said. Because they weren't there to learn—they were there to talk business. And I remember the first class, because I showed them this video. And it was a video about slavery. And one of them said, "So there was trafficking back then?" And I tried to explain to him that it wasn't drug trafficking, that it was trafficking in men. And so then someone said, "So we're not so bad then!" And it was then that I realized that teaching them wasn't going to be easy. But then I had an idea. Because I thought to myself, "What if I try and talk to them in their own language, in ways that they can understand?" So when we started talking about math, I asked one of them, "What are you in for?" And he said, "Robbing banks." "And how much did you make, the last time you robbed a bank?" "You mean the last time, before I was arrested? I made fifty thousand reais." "And what if you'd invested that fifty thousand reais at 5 percent?" So I got him interested in his money. Because he was going to spend a lot of time in prison because of his money, so he might as well learn from it. You know, he might as well learn from his mistakes. And you know what? I was also learning from my mistakes. I was learning from spending time with those professors, and I was learning from spending time with those other prisoners. And after a while, I got to know all of them, and I got to know how they thought. And as a result, the class worked, I mean, it really worked. But do you know what was going on, what was going on out on the street? This guy Uë was becoming more and more powerful. And he pretty much controlled all of the favelas that belonged to this other guy, Escadinha. Because Uë had all the connections, you know, in terms of supplying drugs. And so Escadinha came to depend on him.

This guy Uë was CV, right?

He was a leader. He was a leader within the CV whose power was growing. So then Escadinha introduced Uë to other leaders, so he could supply them too. Because the guy who knows the most leaders is the guy who supplies the most drugs. And the guy who supplies the most drugs is the most powerful of everyone, understand? So it became a competition between suppliers. Because they were no longer supplying one or two favelas, like me. They were supplying twenty or thirty of them. And so they were becoming more powerful than the leaders of the favelas themselves, because the leaders of the favelas depended on them. And the leaders of the favelas who were in prison, you know, the older guys, they could see all of this happening. What I mean is, they could see all of this going on.

You mean they could see their power diminishing?

That's right. And because they were going to be in prison for a long time, they had to make sure that they were friends with these suppliers on the outside, so that when they got out, they'd have money and a place to go.

So there was a shift in the balance of power within the CV, from the leaders on the inside to a new generation of suppliers on the outside?

That's right. But then something bad happened. Because this guy Uë I was talking about, he killed this other guy, Orlando Jogador. He killed his entire gang. Because Orlando Jogador had been sent by the leaders of the CV to take over this favela, in Zona Norte. So when he was killed, things on the inside got a whole lot more complicated. Because it resulted in a split. And when this split happened, I was in another prison. I was in Carvalho Troiano. But everyone knew that it was about to happen. And the dispute between the different suppliers on the outside was beginning to affect things on the inside, including inside the classroom.

What do you mean?

What I mean is that people were no longer getting along. And so for me, the only solution was to get myself out of there. So I convinced the guys in my cell block to focus all their attention on the tunnel.

Who did most of the digging?

Me and Ratinho. Because I really wanted the tunnel to work. Because it was great that I got to go to school, but on the other hand, I knew that the whole thing was a joke. Because you could see that it was only a matter of time before they all started fighting, before they started killing each other. And I mean, it was one thing if a fight broke out during a game of soccer or something, you know, on the outside. But when people start killing each other at night, you know, in their cells, that's when the situation becomes more complicated.

How do you mean?

Well, say there's this cell block, right? With thirty-six prisoners. And twenty of them have sided with one side, and sixteen with the other. And suppose a message is sent by a leader, a leader with authority, that three of the sixteen have to be killed. And then they are killed. So what happens to the other thirteen? I'll tell you what happens. They go over to the other side. Because they see that the guys on the other side are serious, that they have the authority to kill the three prisoners. Now imagine living in a place where this kind of thing could happen at any time. And so I decided that we needed to work faster. And so I said to Ratinho, "Hey, Ratinho, let's get on with it and dig this tunnel!" Except that we no longer had anywhere to put the dirt. Because digging a tunnel is complicated. Because first you have to dig a hole, right? And then you have to pass the dirt to someone who is behind you. And then you have to shore up the tunnel with supports, to prevent it from collapsing.

Supports made of what?

Well, because we didn't have anything made of wood, we used these two-liter Coke bottles. We'd fill them up with dirt, and we'd place them where the tunnel was weakest. Because the tunnel was pretty small, because the bigger the tunnel, the more vulnerable it becomes, understand? And we put fans in there too. We had to, because the prison was built on top of a garbage dump, and so the fumes were really awful and a lot of the guys came up coughing and complaining. But we didn't use the whole fan, just the part with the motor and the fan itself. We'd wrap the motor in plastic, so it wouldn't get wet, and we'd take it down into the tunnel and clear a spot for it. You know, on a ledge. Then we'd feed the wire back out and plug it into an outlet. Because all the cells had outlets. Then we'd cover the wire with a mat or a newspaper so the guards wouldn't see. Then someone would sit there all day reading. And after a while they'd say, "Hey, are you guys done yet? I've read this newspaper fifteen times!" And there'd be days when I'd come up from digging, and there'd be a prisoner there holding the newspaper upside down. And I'd say to him, "You moron, do you want the guard to see you reading it upside down?" [Laughter.] But like I said, the real problem was that we no longer had anywhere to put the dirt. Because the guards were beginning to suspect, because they opened up one of the drains on the outside, and they saw all this red dirt. So they knew someone was digging a tunnel, so they searched all of the cell blocks. And so we stopped digging for a while. And we were wondering how we were going to continue.

You mean, what you were going to do with all the dirt.

That's right. Then one day, while I was exercising, I pulled myself up to the bars on my window. And while I was up there I noticed that there was this soffit, that ran along the top of the exterior cell wall. So then I got down and I broke off a piece of the antenna on the TV. And then I pulled myself back up and started digging around. And I discovered that the soffit was made of concrete blocks, and that if you poked around and removed one of them, there was this big hole inside. And so I figured that we could hide the dirt in there. But I mean, we had to be smart about it, so the police on the outside wouldn't notice. So one of us had to stand guard while the other one worked. And when the guy who was standing guard shouted, "Goal," it was okay to work. And when he shouted, "No goal," we had to stop, understand? So then we started removing the blocks. And everyone's families brought in pillowcases, so we could fill them with dirt.

And no one suspected anything?

No. Then one day, when we were getting close to the wall, we decided that Ratinho should come over on Fridays, as well as on weekends. And it was on one of these Fridays that the guard suspected something and sounded the alarm. So then Ratinho had to get out of there. Because he had to be back in his cell when his cell block was inspected. But because he had to go back so fast, we didn't have time to glue the sections of grate back up properly. Because it took four guys. You know, two guys standing on the other two guys' shoulders. But we just didn't have the time, because when they searched the prison, they always started with Cell Block 1 first. So when they sounded the alarm, it was like, "Quick, everybody out! Come on, move it!" Then, when everyone had climbed back down and gone back inside their cells, "Clang!" the section of grate came crashing down. And the guard heard it, and he came running. And he opened the cell block door and saw it lying there in the middle of the floor. But he couldn't figure out what had happened. Because he figured that someone was trying to escape, right? But escape how, and to where? It just didn't make sense. Because Ratinho was already back inside his cell. And so the guard locked us all in.

So then they called this older guy. And when he came in, he went down the line and looked each one of us in the eye. And when he came to me he said, "Where's the hole? Where's the tunnel?" And I said, "What tunnel? The only thing I know about is the school." "You may know about the school, Bruno, but you also know about the tunnel. Now why was this section of grate cut out?" "I don't know. I don't know anything about it. Maybe the wind knocked it down." "The wind, huh? Okay then."

Did you know him?

Of course, because he was on Ilha Grande. And I liked him, I liked him a lot. Because he was smart, and he didn't mess with people. So then he said, "There's no need to tell me where the tunnel is, because I'll find it myself." Then he walked across the cover to the drain. Because he figured that the grate had something to do with the tunnel. He just didn't know what. But you know what? When he came in, I knew that there was a 99 percent chance that we were finished.

You mean that he'd figure it out?

That's right. So then he looked inside all the cells, but he couldn't find any dirt. So then he climbed up through the hole above the cell block, and while he was up there, he noticed something. Because when we finished filling up one of the holes inside the soffit, we put the blocks back up and sealed them with paste that we made out of soil and water. Then we let them dry in the sun. But he must have noticed some new paste from the day before, because it was still wet. So then he did the same thing I did. He took a piece of metal and started poking around. And that's when he figured it out. So then he got down and said, "There's a tunnel and you're hiding the dirt up there. So where is it?" And you know what? He always came back to me! And I told him that if I escaped, I wouldn't escape by digging a tunnel. I'd escape through the school or the front gate. So then he started pacing back and forth. And he started asking everyone questions. And no one said anything. So then he stopped on top of the drain. And when he stopped on top of the drain, I prayed that no one would look at each other. Because this guard was smart, and he always tried to figure things out on the basis of psychology. So he stood there, watching the prisoners, to see if anyone did anything. Then Dedão looked at Pingo, and Pingo looked at me. But I didn't look back at him because I knew he was looking at me. So I just kept staring straight ahead. And I said to myself, "He's found it. He saw what Pingo and Dedão just did and he's found it." Then he said, "It's inside here. Open it up. Where's the key?" Then they brought the key, and of course it didn't fit. Because it wouldn't, right?

Because it wasn't the right key!

That's right. So then he said to the other two guards who were there, "They've switched the padlock on you. Now open it up!" So then they sent for the cutters. You know, the big metal cutters. And they broke open the padlock, and lifted up the cover and saw the tunnel. Then the guard said, "Who's responsible for this?" And there was silence. "So no one's responsible, huh? Okay, you guys are for it!"

Meaning what?

Meaning they'd punish us, by sending us to different cell blocks. Then the cell block was locked down for three days while there was an investigation. And all I could think about was the school. And I kept asking the guards if they thought the school would be closed down. And they said, "Don't worry, Bruno, this will pass." But then about three days after the tunnel was discovered, this guard showed up around six o'clock at night. And he said, "You, out!" And I said, "Where are we going?" "To see the director." "The director, at this time of night?" Then, when we got there, the director said to me, "I'm transferring you to Aranha Filho." And I said, "But sir, why are you sending me there?" "I'm going to redistribute everyone in your cell block." "But can't you just send me to another cell block? I mean, for Christ's sake, Aranha Filho?" Then they put me on my own in this cell. And they said to me, "Now you'll see about your rights, because you don't have any!" And I said, "Whatever. What the fuck."

So the director suspected you were behind the tunnel?

Yes.

Even though he didn't have any evidence.

That's right. And so then I was transferred. And the worst thing was that on the night I was transferred, I said to the guard, "I need to get my things." And the guard said, "The director said you're to go as you are." So then they put me in this van. And as I was getting in, the director made a sign that I was to be beaten. So then we left Afonso Costa, and on the way we stopped at another prison to pick up two more men. But when we got there, there was this guard there who knew me. And he said, "Naval, is that you? Is everything okay?" And I said, "Yeah, everything's okay." Then he turned to the driver and said, "This is Naval. He's one of the good guys." And the driver said, "You know him?" "Of course. He was with me on Ilha Grande. He's one of the good guys, okay?"

In other words, don't beat him.

That's right. So then the other two prisoners were put in the back of the van. And when the van turned onto the main road, they started talking. "So how's business? How are things in the favela?"

PRISON EDUCATION

In November 1994, the Brazilian National Council on Criminal and Prison Policy adopted the Standard Minimum Rules for the Treatment of Prisoners, which were approved in 1957 by the UN. These rules state clearly that provisions should be made for the education of all inmates, that the education of illiterates and the young should be compulsory, and that recreational and cultural activities should be provided for the physical and psychological enjoyment and well-being of all.[5]

As of December 2010, only 40,014, or approximately 9 percent, of prisoners in Brazil were receiving some form of instruction, despite the fact that 60 percent of them were under the age of thirty, 8 percent were illiterate, and 70 percent had failed to complete the first nine years of school, otherwise known as the *ensino fundamental*.[6] Furthermore, the absence of any national plan or policy means that the availability of educational opportunities varies tremendously by state, according to the level of financial support, local political conditions, and the size of the prison population itself. In fact, in comparative terms, a relatively high percentage of prisoners in the state of Rio de Janeiro receive an education (16.44 percent), compared, for example, to Rio Grande do Norte (3.62 percent), Alagoas (3.22 percent), Goiás (3.24 percent), and Maranhão (0.85 percent).[7]

According to data gathered by a national survey in 2009, wherever educational opportunities do exist for inmates, they tend to be both inadequate and extremely vulnerable.[8] They tend to be inadequate because they serve only a small number of prisoners when there is a substantial and unmet demand, and because they suffer grave problems in terms of a lack of qualified personnel, infrastructure, and teaching materials. They are vulnerable because the physical environment of most prisons is sufficiently intimidating to make teaching in them an unattractive proposition, because the education of prisoners is still seen by the authorities as a privilege rather than a right, because access to educational opportunities is often used as a means to punish prisoners and enforce discipline, and, finally, because day-to-day life in prison is subject to constant disruption by searches, lockdowns, rebellions, and fights, to say nothing of the restrictions imposed by conditions of severe overcrowding.

Prisoners, the survey revealed, greatly valued the time they spent in school each day, where they felt they were listened to and their ideas and opinions respected. This differed greatly from the way they were treated in prison in general, and led to feelings of suspicion, tension and conflict between prison officials, who often are not on board, and educators who are unaware of the broader context and dynamics of prison life.

If the absence of any national plan or directive has, in the past, been an obstacle to the provision of educational opportunities for inmates, there has been significant progress in this regard. Since 2005, the Brazilian ministries of justice and education have been working in conjunction with groups in civil society to push for the recognition of education as a constitutionally guaranteed right for everyone, including those behind bars. While there is, obviously, a long way to go, this effort has been bolstered by other measures adopted by the federal government. The first of these is the Programa Nacional de Segurança Pública com Cidadania, or Pronasci, which was introduced in 2007. Pronasci, which represented an admission by the federal government that something had to be done about the issue of violence, called for the investment of 3.3 billion reais over five years in the area of public security. The program, which supported ninety-four different initiatives, included funding for the construction of new prisons, which would include instructional spaces, and the professionalization of prison workers and guards.[9]

The second initiative was the passing of the so-called Lei de Remição, which allows inmates to have their sentences reduced by one day for every three that they are in school.[10] Both Pronasci and the Lei de Remição were designed, in part, to improve the quality of prisoners' lives and to better prepare them for their eventual return to life on the outside. The hope is that programs such as these will reduce what are, in comparative terms, extremely high rates of recidivism, especially among poor, dark-skinned youth.[11]

Of course, Brazil is not the only country struggling with the issue of educating and rehabilitating its prisoners. The U.S. Department of Corrections, for instance, spends a mere 6 percent of its seventy-billion-dollar budget on educating the almost two and a half million prisoners in the system, despite the fact that there is robust and fairly incontrovertible evidence to suggest that it saves taxpayers money in the long run.[12] One of the problems is that the taxpaying public doesn't support such programs, despite the projected savings, and despite the increased chance for inmates to embark on a new life.[13]

By the time we got to Aranha Filho, it was already midnight. And when the guard who drove us there opened up the back of the van, he said, "These guys are troublemakers." So then these other guards started coming toward us. And one of them hit the guy next to me across the face with a piece of wood. And then he kicked the other prisoner in the stomach. And when he came toward me, someone said, "No, not him, because so-and-so said he's okay." So then the guard who was about to hit me said, "Okay then, we'll leave this one alone. But these two here, we're going to beat the shit out of these two." And when they were finished, one of them turned to me and said, "You lucked out this time." I said, "Lucked out? What do you mean I lucked out? Did you know that you're breaking the law? Did you know that you could be arrested?" Because I couldn't just stand there, right? Without saying anything. So then one of the other guards said, "Come on, that's enough. We'll put him in with all the other troublemakers." So there I was, back inside Aranha Filho again.

Had anything changed?

It was different because there were different people there, and because there were no leaders. And everyone was talking about how the faction was about to split apart. And when I got to my cell, I could see that I was the oldest one there. Because the rest of them were really young. You know, guys in their late teens and early twenties. And they were all poor and uneducated, and there were thirty or forty of us in that one cell. And it was filthy, and it was disgusting, and the six months that I spent there were the worst, because I was back inside that hellhole again.

What about the leaders?

Like I said, there were no leaders. I mean, there were leaders there, but they were weak, and they couldn't control the place. And then, a couple of months after I arrived, this guy Césinha showed up. And it was Césinha who brought us news about Orlando Jogador. About how he'd been killed. And about how Uë was on the run, and how he was the most wanted person in Rio.

By whom? By the CV?

By the police. Because the CV would deal with him when he got to prison, because that's the way they did things. Because everything's resolved inside of prison, understand? So anyway, they sent this guy Césinha to Cell Block 3, Wing 5, because that's where they sent all the leaders, you know, to isolate them.

And you?

I was sent to Cell Block 3, Wing 1, thank God! And as soon as this guy Césinha arrived, he started causing trouble. Because do you know what he did? He picked up this vat of coffee and he threw it in this guard's face.

But why?

To cause trouble. To start a fight. And then, everyone else joined in. I mean, everyone started screaming and yelling and throwing things at the guards. And then the guards started unlocking all the doors, so they could take the prisoners out and beat them—except that when they unlocked the first cell door, the prisoners grabbed them, and pulled them in. And I was standing there watching all this happen. And I could see that it was going to end in disaster. So I shouted out, "Stop! Everyone stop!" And then the guards picked themselves up off the floor and they left. And when they left, I said to the other prisoners, "What the fuck do you think you're doing? Don't you know that there'll be hell to pay?" Then the chief of security arrived. And he said, "We're going to take everyone out. And you're all going to be beaten. And we're going to do it five prisoners at a time, even if it takes all night." So then they took us all to this place, this enormous hall that held more than a thousand people. And before they threw us in there, they poured soap and disinfectant on the floor. Because the guards all wore boots, right? And we had nothing on our feet, so we couldn't stand up when we were being beaten. And when the guard came by to get us, he said, "You five, out!" And then, when we got to this place, there was blood all over the floor, because they were beating everyone. And there were these ex-policemen there too, you know, policemen who'd been arrested and expelled from the force. And they were beating the prisoners too. And they were shouting, "You CV motherfuckers, we'll show you!" And I mean, they beat us across the shoulders, and they broke people's arms, and they smashed open people's heads. And there was this one guy there whose head was split wide open. And there was all this blood spurting out. And then they made out that it was the prisoners who had started it, that it was the prisoners' fault.

Which wasn't true, right?

Of course it wasn't! And there were these big containers there that they used to bring in the food. And when they went to beat me, I jumped on top of one of them, and I grabbed a lid, and I held it out in front of me. But they still managed to beat me, because they cut open my hand. So then I shouted out, "I'm going to denounce all of you, if it's the last thing I do!" So then they all stopped, and they took us, five at a time, to the doctor. And when I got there, I showed him my hand and I said to him, "You're a doctor, right? So tell me, how can you allow such a thing to happen?" And when he didn't answer, I said, "I demand that you take me to a hospital so I can have stitches in my hand. Otherwise I'm going to denounce you to the regional medical board. Because I have a lawyer, and you guys are breaking the law." And I was the only one who said anything, because all the other guys there were quiet.

Why, because they were scared?

Because they didn't know any better. So then the doctor said, "All right, all right, take this one to the hospital." And I said, "Oh no, oh no. I'm not going there alone. I'm going with all these other guys." So then we all went. But when we got there, the doctor said that it was too late to put stitches in my hand. So instead he wrapped it in a bandage. And then the police who were taking us back showed up. And they started threatening us, and saying that we were troublemakers. And I tried to explain to them what had happened, that one of the prisoners had gotten upset, and so had one of the guards. Because when things get out of hand, it's hard to talk to the guards. You know, to get them to calm down. Because everyone's shouting at each other, and you have to figure out which one of them will listen. Then you have to say to them, "Excuse me, Mr. Guard? With all due respect sir, this was never meant to happen. But now that it has, can you help my friends here?" Then the guard will say, "Who do you think you are, a leader?" "No sir, but I'll do what I can to make sure this never happens again, okay?" "Okay, but if it does, we'll kill the lot of you, understand?" "Okay, I understand. I mean, I get it, okay?"

You mean you have to be diplomatic.

That's right. Now, I'm not saying you have to kiss up to the guards. But the reality of the situation is that they're the guards and you're the prisoners, right? So when I got back to the prison, I went to talk to the leaders. And I said to them, "You know what? You really fucked up today. Because real leaders wouldn't have allowed this to happen." And I mean, there I was, standing in front of everyone. And you know what? Everyone was listening. And I mean everyone!

So you became a leader.

That's right, I became a leader, right there, that day! And when I got back to my cell block from the hospital, everybody clapped their hands. Because I was the only one to speak out, the only one to say that they were wrong. So then I said, "Who here has a lawyer?" And one of the prisoners said, "I do." "Then call him tomorrow. And tell him to come talk to me, okay?" Because some of the prisoners had lawyers, because they had money. And then we demanded that the director open up an investigation. But you know what? They're smart. They're really smart. Because they put out a report, in the press, that there had been this incident. That some of the prisoners had tried to escape, and that they'd started fighting among themselves. And then they didn't allow anyone from the outside to visit for fifteen days, so the prisoners' wounds would heal, so they wouldn't ask to be examined.

So they made it difficult for you to press for an inquiry?

Exactly. And I mean, I would have been an idiot to take them on, knowing everything that they'd done. So then the director called me in and he said,

"Look, I know something happened that shouldn't have happened, right? And I want you to know that we've already disciplined some of the guards, that we've let some of them go." But you know what? I knew that he was lying, because no one is let go without an investigation. And so that's what I told him. And then I showed him my hand, and he said, "I assure you this won't happen again. And you know what? I'm going to have you transferred to another prison, to a much nicer prison, so you can play soccer and run around."

Just to get you out of the way?

Of course! But I mean, look at the situation I was in! I mean, do you honestly believe that I wasn't going to accept? [*Laughter.*] Because I just wanted to get out of there. So the director said, "All right then, I'm sending you to this other prison. But in return, I want you to forget about this report, okay?" Because he already knew about it, because someone had told him.

And you accepted his offer?

Of course! I told him that for the love of Christ, get me out of there! Because I knew the report would go nowhere. Because what good would my word have been? After sixteen, seventeen days had gone by?

So you mean you fled, and left everyone there without a leader.

No, no, it's not like that. Because the whole thing started with them, with the leaders. It's just that it ended up affecting me, so it became my responsibility, understand? So anyway, when I got back to my cell, they told me that I was being transferred. And they called a lot of other prisoners' names as well. Because after this incident, they were transferring lots of prisoners to other places. I mean, they weren't stupid, right?

You mean the leaders?

No, no, the ones who were hurt the most. Because if they complained about what had happened when they reached these other prisons, nothing would come of it. So they got rid of the ones who were hurt the most, or they sent them to the hospital, where some of them ended up dead. Because some of them suffered from trauma, from being hit in the head. But in the report it said that they had fallen down. You know, playing soccer or something. Because the authorities had the power to do this, they had the power to change what was written in the report. So anyway, then they called my name. And the guard said, "Bruno, get your things together because you're being transferred." And I said to him, "Can you tell me where I'm going, to which prison?" "No, you'll find out when you get there." Because they never tell you where you're going. And I was thinking to myself, "Am I really going to the prison the director told me about, or are they sending me back to Afonso Costa?" And so imagine my relief when we arrived at Carvalho Troiano, a prison that was open, that had a lot of space—except that when we got there, it turned out that the chief of security was from Ilha Grande. And he looked at me and said, "Not this one. You can send him back, because I don't want him in my prison."

But why?

Because he knew about all the things I'd done, on Ilha Grande and in Afonso Costa. So he didn't want to be responsible for me. But you know what? I was sick of being in prison. And there I was, all of a sudden, in a prison where there was open space, where there were trees. Because it had been a long time since I had been around trees. Because Aranha Filho was a hellhole, a fucking hole in the ground, understand?

So you saw this as an opportunity?

Absolutely, I saw this as my salvation! So then he separated me from the others. And all of my things were lying there on the ground. You know, my flip-flops, my jeans, my sneakers. So I said to the chief of security, "Are you serious? Are you really not going to let me in?" And he said, "That's right. I'm going to send you back to Aranha Filho." "But I can't go back there. And besides, you know that when I was in Afonso Costa, I organized a school, right? And taught other prisoners." "Yeah, I know all about that. Just like I know about the tunnel."

So he knew?

Of course he knew. Everybody knew. So I said, "That wasn't me. I had nothing to do with it. It's just that the director didn't like me, and blamed me for everything. And there's another thing you should know. This prison of yours is extremely vulnerable. And you know what's happening on the outside, right?" Because the prison was in lockdown mode, and no one was allowed out. They only let out prisoners one cell block at a time, to eat. And then they put them all back in again. And the guy who was in charge there, the leader, was terrified, because there were people there from both sides, and when the killing began, it was going to be a bloodbath. So the chief of security said, "If I let you stay here, you're going to have to take over." And I said, "But I can't. I can't make that decision, because it's not up to me, understand? Now, if you were to give me fifteen days . . ." So then he said, "Okay, let me talk to the director." So a little while later, I was called to the director's office. And when I got there, I said to him, "Sir, director, sir, you know that the situation in your prison is extremely precarious, right? And that if I wanted to, I could escape."

Why did you say that?

Because I wanted him to want me to stay. So I wouldn't try and escape.

So you were promising that you wouldn't?

No, no, because no prisoner's going to make that kind of promise, because that would be bullshit, right? But I had to make it clear that I was looking for an opportunity. Because I was nearing the end of my sentence, and I was exhausted. So then he said, "Okay then, you can stay for fifteen days. But we'll be watching you, okay?" So I said, "Okay, okay." And then I went in.

So I had fifteen days to see how things were in that prison, because there were rumors that the faction was about to split apart, because of what happened to Orlando Jogador.

Because he was a leader, right?

But that's what's interesting—because he wasn't. He was a guy who was humble, who served his time quietly and was released. And when he was released he was told by the CV to take over this favela in Zona Norte. So that's what he did. And everyone there liked him, because he was a good guy, a good leader. And because he was a good leader, lots of people went to him for help. Like if they needed money to visit someone, or if they needed a tank of cooking gas. Because he'd give them money. I mean, he'd go out of his way to help them, understand?

So he was a leader in the old style.

That's right, because he wasn't interested in making money, or having a good time. He was interested in supporting his community. So when Orlando Jogador was killed, it created a huge rift within the organization. And when I got there, to Carvalho Troiano, all of these problems were already in play. And that's why I couldn't just take over, even if I wanted to, because it would have been a huge risk.

Did you know a lot of the prisoners there?

I knew tons. And when I was taken to my cell block, everybody shouted out, "Hey look, it's Bruno! Bruno's here!" And then they all clapped their hands. And there were a lot of prisoners there who were looking for someone to take over, you know, as leader. And there were a lot of prisoners there who were afraid. Because not everyone is involved with the organization, understand? Only around 25, 30 percent. The rest of them are just there to serve out their sentence and don't want to be involved. So what happens to them when there are all these killings, when there's a massacre? And so a lot of them were looking for someone to prevent this from happening. And when I got there, I quickly figured this out. And another thing I noticed was that there were no mattresses. There were these raised concrete platforms for beds, but no mattresses. And I mean, they'd been there for four, five months already, but still had nothing to sleep on.

Was it a new prison?

Yes, yes, it was. So then I called the leader. I called the president of the prison and I said, "What the fuck's going on?" And he said, "I've asked the director for the mattresses, but they still haven't come." "And what about the cell blocks? Why is no one allowed out?" And you know what? I could tell just by talking to him that I was going to have no problem, that he wasn't going to resist. Because he was overwhelmed, and most of the prisoners didn't like him, so he wanted to hand the leadership over to me. And people came up to me all the time and said, "Hey, Bruno, we hear you're taking over. Is that true? Because we're with you." And I noticed that they were mainly young guys, you know, eighteen, nineteen years old, who wanted to join my group. But I couldn't just go ahead and take over, because then the leaders in the other prisons would find out. So I said to myself, "I'm going to have to write them a letter, asking their permission. I'm going to have to tell them what's been happening in this prison." But I had to be careful. I mean, I had to be smart, so they'd understand. So I wrote the letter, and the letter said, "Dear friends, first of all, greetings to all of you. And here's hoping that you'll all regain your freedom soon. I am writing this letter for the following reason. I didn't come here, to this prison, with the intention of taking over anything. And, as you well know, wherever it is I've been, I've always tried to do my best. One way or another, I've always tried to make sure that everyone has a chance to regain their freedom, whether by conditional release, working, studying, or any other means available," which I wasn't going to talk about, right?

You mean the tunnel?

That's right. "It just so happens that in this new prison, which they've made available to our family, there are eight hundred prisoners, most of whom are very young. And apart from being very young, they are very divided, due to problems you are all aware of."

You mean outside on the street?

That's right. "And there are no mattresses in this prison. So everyone is sleeping on concrete. And no one's playing soccer, because no one's allowed out. In fact, there's a shortage of everything here. And there are none of our old friends here, because the prison is for prisoners who have been sentenced to less than six years. So I was wondering what you'd think about a friend of yours taking over? Because there's a group of us here who are more or less the same age." Then I signed it, and folded it, and put it away. And I thought to myself, "What's the best way to get the letter to them?"

Did you show it to the leader of the prison, of Carvalho Troiano?

Yes, yes, I did. I called him in and I said, "What do think of this letter?" And he began to read it and he said, "It's excellent!" Because he wanted out. So I said, "Okay then, I'm going to send it to Afonso Costa."

Why there?

Because more people knew me there, and because the leaders there were much more in tune with what was going on in the other prisons. So then I got Pingo to get his lawyer to visit me, in Carvalho Troiano. And when she got there, she said, "So, Bruno, how's it going?" And I said, "Fine, everything's fine. Now I want you to take this letter to the guys in Afonso Costa." Because she was a messenger for the CV. Because the CV paid her bills, her car, her everything, understand? So then she took the letter. But before she left, I asked her to make me a copy. So she made me a copy and took the letter with her. Then they sent a letter back, which was signed by all the leaders.

What did it say?

It said, "Dear friend and brother Bruno, we leave everything to you. Whatever you decide to do is fine."

So they supported you?

That's right. And I kept the letter, because it saved my life, later on. I mean it literally saved my life. So then I said to myself, "I'm going to have to get everyone together, to tell them I'm the new leader. But before I do, I'm going to have to put together my group." Because I needed a group of forty or so guys, you know, for security. And there were four cell blocks in that prison: A, B, C, and D. And there were more being built, because there were more prisoners being brought there every day, because they were emptying all the police precincts, and pretty soon there was going to be more than thirteen hundred men.

So the prison was built, in part, so they could empty out the police precincts?

That's right, because they were so overcrowded. And I thought to myself, "How on earth am I going to take control of this prison, if the prisoners are so divided?" Because there were prisoners from everywhere there, including the favela where Orlando Jogador was killed.

Was there anyone there who took part in the killing?

There were two, and I knew that it was inevitable that they were going to die.

Did they know that?

Of course! So then I asked to speak to the chief of security. And I said to him, "The prisoners are asking to be allowed out, to play soccer." And he said, "Bruno, I can let them out one cell block at a time, a different one each day, but that's all, okay? Because everyone knows what's going to happen." So then I told him, I said, "Then the situation's only going to get worse. Because you were on Ilha Grande, right? So you know that when someone has to die, they have to die, right? And there's nothing you can do about it. So why don't you let me talk to everyone, so I can explain what's going on? Or, if you like, you can do what you said you were going to do, and send me away from this place. Because you said I had fifteen days, right? And fifteen days are almost up. Because you know what? If this is the way it's going to be, then I don't want to be here. I'd rather be somewhere else, understand?"

What did he say?

He said okay. I mean, he agreed to the meeting. But before I did anything, I went to talk to the guy in charge of the kitchen. Because in a prison, the kitchen's key. And the prisoner who was in charge of the kitchen had been put there by the guards. So I talked to him, and I tried to make him understand that being in charge of the kitchen was a big responsibility. Because I didn't want the kitchen to be like the one on Ilha Grande, you know, where people were stealing food. But you know what? It was already heading that way, because there was less and less food at mealtimes, and the prisoners were beginning to notice. I mean, they'd give you a spoonful of rice. Then you'd head to the salad and there'd be none. And then there'd be this tiny piece of meat.

Who was taking the food?

The guards, because they were always in the kitchen. And they were taking everything and loading it into their cars.

And the guy in charge of the kitchen didn't say anything?

He couldn't, because the guards told him, they said, "If you complain, we'll find someone else. Then you'll be locked up all day." Because at least in the kitchen he could move around, right? So I told the guy in the kitchen that from now on he was my guy. And he said, "Okay." Then I asked him about the knives. I said, "And the knives, where are all the knives?" And he said, "The knives are kept in that drawer over there, next to where the guard sits, because I have to ask his permission to use them." "Okay, from now on, pay close attention to the knives, okay?" Because these weren't just any knives. These were knives that were used for slicing meat. And a prisoner who has a knife in prison has a tremendous amount of power—except that sometimes he doesn't.

What do you mean?

What I mean is someone might say to me, "Hey, take this knife and go kill so-and-so." But I won't, because he has friends, he has leaders who like him.

Like the guy in the kitchen on Ilha Grande.

That's right. So even if someone tells me to, I still won't, understand? Not unless the order is signed by everyone. Because if I kill him, and it turns out that he's a guy who's done a lot of good, then I'm in trouble, right?

So who had this kind of power, this kind of authority?

The old leaders, the old guard, because they commanded respect. But like I told you, a new generation of leaders was emerging. And they were waiting for the old guard to fuck up so they could take over—like if Escadinha didn't kill Uë when he arrived in prison. Because Escadinha was one of the old guard, he was one of the founders of the organization. But Uë was supplying his community with drugs. He was supplying a lot of the leaders' communities with drugs.

So even though he betrayed the organization, a lot of the leaders depended on him?
That's right.

But before you said that a lot of people supplied drugs. People like you, for example.
But that was before, that was in the 1980s. Now the leaders made sure they had direct contacts with the suppliers, so they could do away with intermediaries.

So the supply of drugs was becoming centralized.
Precisely, because they started organizing these big shipments. And that was the deal with Uë. He organized these big shipments, and so he had a tremendous amount of power.

But was he a leader of a favela?
No, no, no, he was a supplier. And he was an important guy within the CV, until he killed Orlando Jogador. And some people say that it was a betrayal, and some people say that it was an act of revenge, because Orlando Jogador put Uë's brother in a wheelchair. But I mean, who knows? Because nobody really knows. All I know is that war was about to break out. And I mean, I failed to escape from Ilha Grande, right? And I failed to escape from Afonso Costa. And I'd lost all chance of a conditional release. So I was going to have to take the leadership of that prison to its conclusion. I was going to have to take it to its very end, understand? So that's what I was thinking.

So then I said to the chief of security, "When are you going to allow me to have this meeting?" And he said, "Whenever you'd like." "Okay, let's make it a Friday then." Because the day after Friday was Saturday, and Saturday was visiting day. And since we'd be talking a lot about improving conditions for visitors, everyone would be thinking about what I said, when they went back inside for dinner that evening. So the chief of security said, "Okay then, we'll make it a Friday." So then I started thinking about writing up an announcement. And I asked around if anyone could write, if there was anyone whose writing people could easily understand. And one of the guys in the kitchen said, "There's this friend of mine, in Cell Block C." So I said, "What's his name?" "His name's Tiago." So then I went to Cell Block C. And when I found him I said, "Hey, Tiago, come with me, because you've got work to do." And he said, "Work, what work?" "Don't worry. You're going to be doing some writing for me, okay? Now I need help with this announcement. I'll need four copies, one for each cell block, okay?" So then he said, "Well, what do you want me to say?" And I said, "At the top of each sheet of paper write 'Rio de Janeiro' and today's date. Then write, 'Dear friends, I would like to announce that on Friday, at two o'clock in the afternoon, all the cell blocks will be opened so we can all come together for a meeting on the soccer field, where our brother and friend Bruno and his group . . .'"

So you had already formed your group.

No, because at this point, I was still on my own. But I knew that pretty soon I was going to have to appoint some lieutenants, including some who were really mean. Because that's the way it is, understand? Because I'd say to a guy, "You're going to be the bad guy, okay? You know, the one who does all the killing." [*Laughter.*]

Because you had to have someone like that?

That's right. And there were guys who came up to me and said, "Bruno, if you need someone to rip off someone's head . . ." And there were a lot of guys there who wanted war. So I got them to come and work for me, so I could keep my eye on them. And when they said all this shit about starting a war, I said, "Look, if there's a war, there's a war, okay? But in the meantime, let's get this place organized. So don't do anything until I say, okay?" So then they'd say, "But there are guys here who were there when they killed Orlando Jogador! And look, I have this knife . . ." So you see how the prison was? You see the situation I was in?

You mean they were ready for war.

That's right. And that's why the authorities wouldn't let anyone out. And the thing was that the guys who were pressuring me thought that I'd been sent there to have this war. But in reality, that was the last thing I wanted. But I couldn't say anything, because I needed them. I needed all of them. I mean, a bunch of them came up to me and said, "You know there's going to be a war, right?" And I said, "I know, I know. Don't worry, okay?" And you know what? I could see that Uë's guys were in the minority. And I could see that they were afraid.

And when they looked at you, what did they think?

They thought, "My life's in this guy's hands!" And they came up to me. And they gave me presents, because they wanted to be my friend. And so anyway, when the big day came, everyone was allowed out.

Were the prisoners searched?

That's an excellent question. Because the chief of security asked me, he said, "Can we post a guard at the entrance to each cell block, and have people searched?" And I said, "But sir, if you do that, you'll undermine my authority. Because it will be a sign that you don't trust me." "But what guarantees can you give me that there won't be trouble?" "I can't, because there are no guarantees. But I've done everything I could, okay?" And he said, "Okay."

Were you nervous?

A little, because I'd never done anything like this before. And because there were a few older guys there, guys with more experience than me. But they weren't leaders or anything. They were there because the authorities thought that they were okay, that they weren't dangerous. It just so happened that they were from areas that were controlled by the CV, that's all.

So they weren't really CV then?

They weren't drug dealers if that's what you mean. But they were still associated with the faction. Because a lot of them were robbers. And they'd sell the stuff they robbed to pay for their drugs. And perhaps a drug gang would owe someone money, like a supplier. So the guys who robbed would lend it to them. So it was all connected in one way or another. But most of the guys in that prison were there because they lived in an area that was dominated by the CV. Because they couldn't be sent anywhere else, understand? But anyway, getting back to the meeting. Once everyone was allowed out, they all went over to the soccer field and stood there waiting. So then I picked up my agenda, which was written on a piece of paper, and I climbed up onto the stage.

What about your group?

They were on stage with me. Because before the meeting I went around and I said, "You and you and you, get yourselves up there."

How many people were there, in the crowd?

There were about a thousand. And the guards took up their positions around the perimeter, and the chief of security and the director stood together at one side. And then I stepped forward on the stage and I said, "First of all, faith in God." And everyone else said, "Faith in God." "Now I want you guys to listen. Because as you know, our family has taken control of this prison. And I know that this is meant to be an open prison, but that it isn't. But if we all work together, it will be, okay? Because there are things that I want you to do. But first, I'm going to ask the director for something. I'm going to ask him for the mattresses. Because it's been six months already, and I reckon he'll spend less on mattresses than he will on sending our sick brothers to the hospital. Isn't that right, Mr. Director, sir?" And you know what? I could see that he was nervous, because he was the one who should have been making the announcement, not me. So then I said, "Mr. Director, sir, why don't you come over here? How about it, everyone? This is Doctor Bradzinski. This is the director of the prison, who's going to help us get things done. Isn't that right, sir?" So then he made his way through all the prisoners. And like I said, he was extremely nervous. And when he got to the stage, he said, "About the mattresses. I've already put in the request. It's just that these things take time." Then someone in the crowd shouted out, "Lies, it's all lies!" Then everyone else started shouting. So then I shouted out, "Be quiet! Pay attention, you motherfuckers, because I'm the one in charge here!" So then there was this silence. And I could see that the director was startled, because he looked over at me [*laughter*]. And then I said to him, "It's okay, sir, you can go ahead."

What did he say?

He said, "From now on, if there's anything you need, write it down on a piece of paper and hand it to Bruno, okay? Because then he can hand it to me." And then I said, "Whoa, hold on a minute. Whatever it is, we'll write it out and everyone will read it and sign it. And then we'll hand it to you, okay?" Because in his innocence, he was making me out to be his representative, to be his intermediary. And I couldn't let that happen. So then he said, "Okay, okay, whatever you feel is best." So then he left, and all the guards left with him. And so then there were just us prisoners, from two in the afternoon until eight o'clock at night. And we all had dinner together. And I talked to everyone about opening up a school, and about playing soccer. I said, "We're going to get together some teams.

And if anyone knows anyone who wants to donate shirts, we'll organize a league."

Like on Ilha Grande?

That's right. I was going to do everything like it was on Ilha Grande, except for the leadership, of course. And then I said, "Does anyone else have anything to say?" And then this one guy raised his hand and said, "Yeah, about the kitchen, there's hardly any food. I mean, the guy in the kitchen gives us nothing." And the guy who was in charge of the kitchen, who was part of my group, said, "Look, I give you whatever the guards give me, okay?" And you know what? The guard from the kitchen was standing right there. So I said to him, "From now on this guard here is going to give us the right amount. We're going to figure out how much it is and he's going to give it to us. Isn't that right, sir?" And the guard said, "If you tell me how much it is, I'll give it to you."

Just like that?

Just like that, because he had no choice.

So the meeting put pressure on everybody.

That's right. And that's why it was such a good meeting, because everyone left there happy.

A few days after the meeting, this group of new prisoners arrived. And usually I'd go to meet them. And I'd give them the same speech I gave all the others. And I'd get them to write down their names, nicknames, and where they were from on a piece of paper. Except that this time, I couldn't get over there right away, because there were too many things to do. I mean, I was planning on getting to them, but only after they'd spent time in the cela de espera.

Which was how long, in this case?

Three days. But you know what? One of them sent the director a letter. And the letter said, "Mr. Director, sir, we've been here since Monday and no one's been to see us. So I was wondering about our rights." And he sent the letter via a messenger. And this messenger was part of my group, because I made sure to include some of them. So then the messenger came to see me. And he said, "Hey, Bruno, there's this guy in the cela de espera who's acting like he's a leader or something. Do you want me to kill him?"

What did he do wrong?

He went to the director instead of coming to me!

Did he do that on purpose?

Well, that's what I had to find out. And when the letter reached me, I looked at it, and I said, "This is a work of art! I've got to meet this guy!" So then I went to the cela de espera, in Cell Block D, and I asked the guard to let me in. And after I went in I said, "Which one of you is Jorge?" Because that was his name, Jorge. And when he came up to me I said, "Are you the guy who sent the letter to the director?" And he said, "That's right, it was me, because I needed to speak to someone, because no one came to meet us when we came in. And there are no mattresses, and some of my guys are getting sick." So I said to him, "Look, from now on you and me are going to work on this together, okay? Because I'm Bruno, and I'm the leader of this prison, and I'm trying to improve conditions here. But you know what? You should have sent that letter to me first, before sending it to the director. But perhaps you weren't aware of all these rules. So anyway, where are you from?" And he said, "Copacabana."

You mean a favela in Copacabana?

No, no, no, he was a journalist. And he was into drugs.

Was he a dealer?

No, no, he was an addict. Because I said to him, "What are you in here for?" And he said, "I was arrested with some marijuana, and sentenced to three years." Then I looked at his arms, and they were covered with needle marks.

So he was a heroin addict?

That's right, because he loved to get high. And he ended up doing all my writing for me, as my personal secretary. And I managed to make him quit. I managed to make him give up drugs, like I was his therapist or something. I said to him, "Don't even think about it, okay?" And he said, "Don't worry, because I'm mainly into marijuana these days." "Okay then, let's keep it that way, because you have a lot of work to do before you're released." And he was granted a conditional release, you know, toward the end of his sentence. And he helped me a lot. Because I already had this other guy, right? This friend of a friend who worked in the kitchen. But I told him I didn't need him anymore. And I put him in charge of the finances. Because I set up this fund. You know, for emergencies.

Where did the money for this fund come from?

From the favelas. Because sometimes a prisoner would be released and he'd have no money. Or a family would come to visit, and they wouldn't bring anything with them. So I started to help people out, and I started to make improvements. And the first thing that I did was to improve conditions for visitors. Because visiting days were Saturday and Sunday, but Saturdays were for Cell Blocks A and B, and Sundays for Cell Blocks C and D. So in reality, there was only one visiting day. So I managed to make Wednesdays and Thursdays visiting days too. I presented the idea to the director. And you know what? He agreed.

Did he agree to everything you suggested?

Pretty much. The only thing he didn't agree to was this barbecue I was going to have. Because when the grills and the charcoal arrived at the main gate, he told them to take it all away. But in the end I turned the prison into a pretty okay place, I mean for a prison. But you know what? I encountered a lot of resistance.

From whom?

From the guards. From the police. Because there was this military police battalion stationed nearby. And they did everything they could to intimidate the prisoners, like waking them up in the middle of the night by setting off firecrackers. Because the military police were supposed to take care of the outside of the prison, and the guards the inside. So if the military police were running around inside the prison setting off firecrackers, someone must be letting them in, right? Because a lot of them wanted the prison to go up in smoke, so they could come in and kill everyone.[1] And things got so bad that I had to go talk to the chief of security. And I told him that if the battalion commander refused to do anything, we'd send our lawyer to the Department of Corrections, downtown, and that we'd bypass the director. And the chief of security said, "You'd do that? You'd bypass the director?" And I said, "What I'm saying is that we can either go through the director, or not. It's up to you."

So it was an ultimatum?

It had to be, because otherwise I wouldn't be able to run that prison. Because you can't run a prison by dealing only with the director. Because he'll see that you're weak, understand? No, you have to know about the law. You have to know about the prison system, and how to get in contact with the authorities directly. So anyway, after I spoke with the chief of security, it all stopped. But you know what? The mattresses still hadn't come. So I asked the director for a meeting. And before I went to see him, I got the journalist to draft a letter saying that we'd appeal to the Catholic Church, to the Pope if necessary, because some of our guys were getting sick and coming down with tuberculosis.

And the mattresses were something you'd promised, right?

That's right. So I said to him, "What's going on?" And he said, "Look, I've sent in the request, and they should be arriving by Friday." "Okay then, I'm going to hold another meeting." So then the next day, everyone was allowed out. And I took my position in front of my group and I said, "Welcome everyone. The director has told me that the mattresses will be here by Friday. Now, I'm not promising you anything, understand? But the director told me that they won't be here any later than that, because that's what's written on this piece of paper." And I showed them the invoice, because I made a copy of it beforehand. Then, the next week, the truck arrived with all the mattresses. And I got a bunch of guys to help unload them. And it was this big party. And everyone put the mattresses on their beds, with the plastic covers still on them.

So it was a big deal.

It was a huge deal. And the next thing I did was to do away with the cell that they used to punish prisoners. Because I heard that they were putting people in there for no reason. And it was a small cell, about three meters square, and sometimes they'd put fifteen people in there at a time. So during one of my meetings, I said to everyone, "The next thing we're going to do is to get rid of that cell, and we're going to turn it into a library. And I'm going to ask everyone who has a family to donate one book. And I'm going to tell the director we want to study. Okay?" So then everyone raised their hands and said, "Okay." So then I wrote a proposal, and I sent it to the director. And the director called me into his office and said, "I think we can do this. And I'm thinking of donating some books myself, because I've been discussing it with my daughter." So then I said, "I also need a space to teach, to hold classes." And he said he'd put me in touch with the secretary for prisoner education. And then this woman showed up, who I knew from Ilha Grande. And when she saw me she said, "Bruno! So you're here, huh?" And I said, "Yeah, I'm here. Now will you help me with this classroom?" Because there were four classrooms in that prison, but they were outside the prison walls, and so the authorities were afraid to use them. But I told her that everyone wanted to study. So she said she'd ask the director to open the school.

So there used to be a school there?

That's right, but then it was shut down. And everything was all broken— you know, all the tables and chairs. But I figured it wouldn't take much to get it going again. So this woman said to me, she said, "Find out who can read and write, and who's illiterate, okay?" And I said, "Okay, I'll get the information to you within a few days." So then we put together a department of education, to work in parallel with the administration. And I managed to get computers installed. I managed to get ten of them, and a printer, so everything could be done by computer, instead of by hand. And then I got the journalist to record every prisoner's name, and the date that they were sentenced, and for how long, so no one would be there longer than they should. So prisoners were being sent home from there every week. And another thing I did was to set up a lottery and a numbers game. And I got televisions installed and VCRs so we could watch movies. And we got hold of this transmitter device from Paraguay, so all the TVs could show movies at the same time. Because there was this guy who worked there who brought in things we wanted.

You mean, you paid him to bring things in?

That's right, and if something cost sixty reais, then that was his price for bringing it in. But you know what? This whole time there were rumors that Uë had been arrested in Fortaleza, and that he was about to be transferred to Bangu. So everyone was waiting to see what would happen. But until then, everything had to stay the same, understand?

So then I just went about my business. You know, the business of running the prison. And I put everyone to work. I said, "Let's organize a soccer league. You! You can be in charge of the uniforms, okay? And you! You can be in charge of the players. Here, write all their names down in this book. And you! You can be in charge of getting information to our friends on the outside." Because there were all these parties, and the first party was for the Day of the Child. And I asked the director if we could go ahead and open up all the cell blocks.

What did he say?

He said yes. He said that I could have everything I wanted. And then, the next day, this group of prisoners arrived from Zona Sul, a group of young guys. So I went over to Cell Block B to meet them and I said, "Listen up! This is the way it's going to be, okay? Now where are you guys from?" And they all said, "Vila de Deus." And afterward, one of them came up to me and said, "Do you know what's going on, on the outside?" Because what had happened was that Uë was now supplying Vila de Deus.

And Vila de Deus was CV, right?

That's right. And whether they liked it or not, it was going to affect the guys who had just arrived. What I mean is, it was going to put their lives in danger. So I said to them, "Listen, there's no need to be afraid, because as long as I'm in charge here, things are going to be okay." Because there was this power struggle going on, and these guys were in the middle. And you know when you make friends with someone for the first time, when you hit it off right away? Well, one of them was this guy Marcelinho. And I said to him, "You're going to work for me in the kitchen. Now do you practice any kind of martial art?" Because he was this great big guy. And he said, "Yeah, I do *capoeira*.[2] But the guy who is really good at capoeira is my friend here, Nelsinho." "So you're good at capoeira, eh? Okay, Mr. *Capoeirista*, you're going to work for me in the kitchen as well. And if there's a problem, I want you to take out the guard who's been stealing our food, okay?" And he said, "Okay."

Were the guards still stealing food?

Yes, because we still didn't have control of the kitchen, because I was waiting for the chief of administration to return from leave. And you know what? This Nelsinho guy, he was interesting because he used to work for a bus company during the day. I mean, he was the guy who collected the fares at the back of the bus. And at night he worked for the drug gang, doing their books. And I mean, he wasn't into drugs or anything. He just wanted to make some extra money. It's just that he had no idea of the danger he was in, no idea at all.

So he wasn't, you know, a trafficker?

No, no, no, and I could see that right away. So anyway, like I said, when the guys from Zona Sul arrived, I went to meet them. Because that's what I always did, because first impressions are important, right? And the guys who were smart, who were more in tune with the situation, I took them aside and I said, "You know what's about to happen, right? But don't worry. Just stick with me, okay? Because I know you're not interested in being involved." And I said this to as many people as possible. But there was this one guy, Jesus Christ, this one guy who was an assassin. I mean, he wanted to kill as many of Uë's people as he could.

You mean in prison?

That's right. And he liked me, because he was my friend. And despite the fact that he was really angry about the situation, he never showed any anger toward me. All he showed me was his desire to get on with it. He'd come up to me and say, "Come on, Bruno, let's kill all of these motherfuckers. Let's rip their heads off!" And I'd say, "Look, we can't do anything until the situation's resolved in Bangu. Because what if we make the wrong decision? So nothing's going to happen, and no one's going to die. Because you know what? We're actually getting somewhere. We're actually making progress. And if anything happens, we'll lose everything, okay?"

So the prison really was about to explode?

Absolutely. And there was this one guard there who was pure evil, who wanted the prisoners to fight. Because as every prisoner knows, there are good guards and there are bad guards, right? What I mean is, there are guards who've been there a long time, who know the prisoners and their families. And they're the good guys. And then there are those who have just arrived, who've just started their careers, and who want to see the place go up in smoke. And one day, when a group of prisoners was out working with me on the field, this guard I was telling you about got into a fight, with one of the prisoners. So then one of the other prisoners came running up to me and he said, "Bruno, there's a problem with one of the guards." Then, when I got there, there were all these other guards there, because the guard who got into the fight had blown his whistle. So I said to him, "Hey, Mr. Guard, sir, what's going on here?" And he said, "I'll tell you what's going on. This motherfucker hit me. So now I'm going to beat the shit out of him." So then I called all the guys who were working with me on the field. And there were thirty of them, and they all stood around with their shovels and their scythes. And I said to the guard, "Either you and your guys get out now, or I can't be responsible for what happens to you." Then the chief of security arrived. And he said, "Bruno, what's going on here?" And I said, "This guard here is having a hard time controlling this one prisoner. I mean, who the hell knows why? Maybe he's having a bad day. But if he can't control this one prisoner, how the hell's he going to control the rest of these guys?" Because that's why I called them over. So then the chief of security said, "Okay, Bruno, get everyone back to work." And I said, "You heard the man, get back to work!"

And the guard?

The guard understood what had happened. He understood that he had no authority inside of that prison. And from then on we didn't have a problem with him. And I told the chief of security that since the prison was about to explode, he should choose his guards more carefully. Or, you know what? Take them all out of there. And do you know what he said? He said, "You mean I can pull all of the guards?" And I said, "Sure. Pull them all out and leave things with me." And so that's what he did. And that was another thing I managed to achieve.

Jesus Christ, he really trusted you.

Yes, he did. In fact, he trusted me too much, because at the same time we were digging a tunnel.

Another one!

Yes, because there are always prisoners trying to escape. And as the leader of the prison, I couldn't say no, right? But I told them they had to be smart about it. I told them that everything had to appear normal. Because we'd already won over the police, and now we'd won over the guards and the administration. And so the prison was completely under our control, right? So I left it up to them. I told them that if they thought they could dig a tunnel from inside one of the cell blocks, then it was up to them.

But you weren't going to be held responsible.

That's right.

But you weren't thinking of escaping, right?

No, no, I wasn't. But I mean, things can change very quickly. Because someone might decide to kill this guy and this guy and this guy. So then what happens to you? So if there's a way to escape, you escape! You know, you go and you let someone else take over. Because who knows? Because what if I was unprepared for what was about to happen? So I could never be against a group of prisoners digging a tunnel, understand?

And where was this group?

Cell Block B. And they told me about the tunnel because they trusted me. "Hey Bruno, we're digging a tunnel, okay? Because our cell block is closest to the wall. So what do you think?"[3] "From your cell block to the wall? Yeah, I think that will work. In fact, I was thinking about it myself!" So then, the next day, this other group from Zona Sul showed up, from the favela of Jakeira—including this guy Pato, who owed some money.

What do you mean?

He was an addict. And he owed some money, to someone inside the prison.

So you allowed drugs?

Some drugs I didn't allow, like heroin, because of the journalist, remember? But marijuana and cocaine were okay. Especially marijuana, because it kept the prisoners quiet. Because there are always drugs inside a prison. And I'd be a hypocrite if I said there weren't, because I made money off of them.

How do you mean?

I made money from drugs. I told the dealers, "You can sell drugs, but a percentage goes to us, okay? To pay for parties." Because there are prisoners who support their families this way. You know, someone brings them drugs and then they sell them.

You mean like José Carlos, on Ilha Grande.

Exactly. It's just that I wanted nothing to do with it, because it had caused me enough trouble. So anyway, this guy came up to me and said, "This guy from Jakeira's just arrived. And he's an addict, and he owes someone money." So I said, "Okay, okay, let me go talk to him." Because inside a prison no problem can be resolved without the leader. Nothing, understand? I mean, it's not like a guy can say, "So-and-so owes me money, so I'm going to kill him!" No, he has to talk to the leader first. Then he has to pay the leader to have the situation resolved. You know, "You go about your business, and give us our share, and we'll take care of the situation, okay?"

But if someone owes someone money, and they don't pay, aren't they always killed?

Sometimes. Or if they can't pay, they can be made into a slave. Or they figure out some other way of paying. I mean, in the past, you could even offer your sister. You know, you'd offer your sister, or something like that. But while I was in charge, I wouldn't let them kill anyone, because that wasn't my way, understand? So anyway, I went to talk to this guy Pato. And I said to him, "So what's the deal? I hear you owe someone money." And he said, "Yeah, but my sister's going to bring it when she comes to visit." "Okay then, when she gets here, do me a favor. Pay the guy and don't do it again, okay?"

You mean, don't run up debts for your family.

That's right. And then, when visiting day came, I was walking around outside on the patio, because I was waiting for this girl who was coming to see me. And I said to myself, "I have so many things to do today. But you know what? I'll see her anyway. I'll take her to the ratão." Because there was a ratão there in the boiler room, next to the kitchen, because I turned it into a little motel. You know, with a shower. I put in a shower and a bed, so I could take care of my women. Especially the pretty ones [*laughter*].

Was it for everyone, or just for you?

It was for me, because I was the leader, right? And for members of my group, but only those who were close to me.

What about the other prisoners?

There were rooms in the prison for conjugal visits. It was this separate building, with lots of small bedrooms, so people could fuck. But there were other places too, because people always found ways to create them. Like next to the library, for example. But the guards didn't like it. And on visiting days they'd sit there out front, to stop the prisoners from going in, unless of course you gave them money.

So the place wasn't that different then?

No, no, it wasn't. So anyway, while I was outside waiting, Pato came up to me and said, "I've paid the guy because my sister brought the money." "Okay, now do what I said." "You mean, don't do drugs?" "No, no, you can do drugs. Just don't overdo it. Because the next time I won't be so nice, understand? Now what are you in for?" "Trafficking." "And what about your family—is anyone else involved?" "No, no, just me." "And who visits you, your mother?" "No, my girlfriend. And my sister comes with her." "Okay, that's good. Now listen. Don't go running up debts, okay? Because your sister comes all this way to visit you, right? So don't make her go back home and tell your mother that you owe more money, okay?" "Okay, okay, I get it." And then the person I was waiting for didn't show. So I hung out there on the patio with everyone else. And then I saw Pato with his girlfriend and sister. And I went over to them, and Pato introduced me. He said, "Bruno, this is my sister Lucia. Lucia, this is Bruno."

Did she know you were the leader?

Yes, because he said, "This is the guy who's in charge of the prison." But she didn't say anything. She just said, "Hi, how's it going?" And I said, "You know what? You need to talk to your brother." "I know, I know. I've already spoken to him, because my mom's really worried." "I've spoken to him too. Because I mean, Jesus Christ, to have a sister like you visit him in prison, a sister who's so good looking!" [*Laughter.*] Then she said, "But what about you, what about your family?" "Well, I went out one day to fetch a loaf of bread and a meteor fell on my house. And when I tried to explain it to the police, they blamed me instead! So that's why I am here, with no family, no nothing." "Ah, come on, you're lying!" "No, no, no, I swear it's the truth." So then we stayed there talking and joking around. And then I said, "Excuse me, but I have to go." Because I had a lot of things to do, because it was getting close to the day of the party we were organizing for the children. And communities associated with the CV were sending in donations. You know, toys, cakes, soft drinks, and things like that. And I was keeping everything in the kitchen, in the pantry with all the food. It was just that I didn't have the key. But I'd promised the guy in charge of the kitchen that I'd get it for him once the chief of administration came back from leave. And he was back from leave. It was just that I hadn't met him.

How many months had you been there by then?

Six. About six months. And then, when it was time for all the visitors to leave, I went up to Lucia and I said, "Wait, wait here a second." And then I ran to the kitchen and I grabbed a doll, because she told me that she had a daughter. And I said to her, "Here, a doll for a doll." And she said, "Thanks!" And then she left. And you know what? She looked back at me three times. And when she looked back at me the third time, I waved. And I said to myself, "Do you think she'll come back? Or was I too . . . ?"

Was it the first time she'd been to visit?

Yes. So then I went back inside. And everyone was talking about their visit. And all I could think about was her. And I said to myself, "There's something about that woman. There's just something about her."

You'd already had other women, right? I mean, as leader.

Oh my God, yes, I'd had lots of women. Because they'd walk up to me and smile, and before I knew it, they'd be telling their brothers that they wanted to get to know me. And a lot of guys wanted their sisters to get to know me. Because, I mean, who wouldn't? Who wouldn't want to become the brother-in-law of a leader?[4] So yes, there were a lot of women. But Lucia, she was different.

You mean, you saw her as something more serious?

As something more serious, exactly. Because there was something about her that was attractive to me. And that Monday, when they opened up the cell blocks, I said to Pato, "Is your sister coming Wednesday?" And he said, "I don't know." And that's all I thought about all day while I was preparing for the party. And we ordered this enormous cake from a local store, and it was in the shape of a soccer field. And I thought to myself, "I'm going to need someone to help me with this party, I'm going to need a first lady" [*laughter*]. Because this party was going to be a huge deal. But even so, there was a group of prisoners that weren't happy, because they wanted to get on with all the killings. So they didn't want anything to do with the party. "A party, inside a prison? Fuck that. Let's take care of business instead. Because there are guys here who need to be killed, because they betrayed our friends." Because by then Uë had been arrested in Fortaleza. And we were all waiting to see what would happen when he arrived in Bangu, because that's where the leaders were. That's where the leaders would say, "Uë, you fucked up, so now you have to die." But then Uë would say, "Exactly how much money do you guys owe me? Because if you kill me, you know what will happen, right? Because my guys will take over."

So the situation was complicated.

It was extremely complicated. So anyway, that Wednesday, Lucia didn't come, because it was difficult for her, because it was so far away. Because you had to get there at four in the morning, and then you had to take a number, and then you had to stand for hours in line. I mean, a prisoner's family has to go through a lot. So then Pato said to me, "My sister's not coming today." So I thought to myself, "I wonder what happened. I wonder what she said when she got home." And I found out later that she said she wasn't going to visit him again, because of this crazy leader guy [laughter]. Because her mother told me afterward that she said, "Jesus Christ, Mom, I met this crazy guy, and I think he likes me!" And her mother said, "Oh my God, that's all I need. As if it's not enough that my son's in prison. Now my daughter's going to become involved with a leader!" And that's when she told her she wasn't going again. And when Pato's sister didn't show, that Wednesday, I asked him, "Is anyone coming Sunday?" And he said, "I don't know." So I said, "I'm going to write your sister a letter. Now, is there any way you can get it to her?" And he said, "Yes." So I called for the journalist, and I said to him, "I've got a job for you. I've got to write this letter, to this woman, and it's got to impress her, okay?" And he said, "Okay, let's think this through." So then he suggested some things that were really stupid. So I said, "Never mind, I'll write it myself." So then I sat down and wrote the letter. And the letter said, "Of all the stars shining in the sky, yours is the brightest. And just when I thought your star would be mine, it disappeared. So I wanted to send you this letter, to give me hope. Because your star is my hope. It's my light . . ." [laughter].

So you were showing your sensitive side!

I know! And I mean, can you imagine if the contents of that letter had gotten out, inside that prison? So that's why I wrote it myself, because it had to come from me. Because it was full of love and emotion. So I had to write it myself, understand?

So then I sent her the letter. And I know that she received it. But the next Sunday she didn't show. But you know who did? Her mother. And when she got there, I said, "Hi, Dona Maria?" And she said, "Are you Bruno? My daughter told me all about you. And then there's my son, who's given me so much trouble." "Don't worry about your son. He's going to be okay, because I've already spoken to him. And by the way, about your daughter, it was all a joke, okay? To make her feel comfortable. Because everything's cool, everything's okay." And in the end, everything was okay, because she spent the whole day with her son. But I didn't hang around.

You know, with them. And all that week I kept thinking, "I know she got the letter. What must she think of me?"

So you really fell for her?

Yes, yes, I did. But I knew that this sort of relationship was impossible, that it rarely ever works out, because I still had a lot of time left to serve. And there were times when I thought I'd end up dying there in that prison, even though I was the leader. But you know what? She was like a light to me. It was as if she was showing me the way. It was as if she was saying, "Come, follow me!" But I tried not to think about it, because I'd seen almost everything in my six, almost seven years in prison.

So you mean you had your feet firmly on the ground?

That's right, and I said to myself, "Forget about it, because she's not coming back." And so then I made arrangements to meet with the chief of administration, because he was the guy who was in charge of provisions— you know, food, toothpaste, and things like that. And you know who it was? It was Seu Jonas, from Ilha Grande [laughter]. I escaped from his house, remember?

I bet he was the last person you expected to see.

Absolutely, because when I knocked, he said, "Come on in." Then, when I went in, he said, "You, Naval?" Because it never occurred to him that it would be me. Not Naval who worked on his house. Not Naval who tried to escape. Because he never thought for one minute that I'd be in charge of a prison, because when he knew me, I wasn't in charge of anything. Because the guy he knew was quiet, and humble, and liked to fish.

And he was a good guy, right? I mean he liked you?

Of course! And so then I figured that if he was in charge of the provisions, he had nothing to do with the business of stealing food. Because I trusted him, because he was a man of integrity.

It must have felt good then, to know you had someone like him to work with.

It was excellent. So then he said, "So you're the leader of the prison, eh?" And I said, "Seu Jonas, if there are more than two people, then someone has to be in charge, right?" And that was what I always said, to convince people that I didn't really like being a leader. Because it was dangerous, because you had the power of life and death in your hands. But I preferred to use that power to get things done. You know, good things, understand?

And then I told him that we were going to have this party, for the children, and that the director had said that it was okay. And he said, "That's great." And I said, "There's one other thing I need to ask you, Seu Jonas." "What's that?" "I need to ask you if we can take control of the kitchen, like on Ilha Grande. And another thing, that guard with all the keys—leave us the keys, so if there's a problem, we can resolve it." And he said, "Let me think about it, okay?" Because he was the one with the authority to get the guard out of there. And then, a couple of days later, right before the party, he handed me the keys and said, "Here you go. They're all yours."

What about the guard?

He took the guard out of there. I mean, he disappeared. So then we unlocked the pantry. And from then on we knew exactly where everything was, understand?

So he trusted you, again!

That's right, because he understood, I mean about the escape. And then he said to me, "But Naval, I thought you'd be gone from here by now." And I said, "You know what? I could if I wanted to." But on the other hand, I had a tremendous amount of responsibility, because a lot of people depended on me. So there was no way I was going to walk away from the situation.

So then we started to prepare for the party. And I said to the guy in charge of the kitchen, I said, "Why don't we put together a menu for the weekend? How about *feijoada* on Saturday, and chicken baked in mayonnaise on Sunday?" Then, when there were only a couple days left before the party, Pato's grandmother arrived. Because Pato told me, he said, "Guess who's coming to visit? Not Lucia, not my mother, but my grandmother. And she wants to meet you!" So when she walked in, I went over to meet her. And I said, "Hi Vó, is everything okay?"[5] And she said, "You're Bruno, aren't you?" And then she said, "I have just one question for you. Aren't you afraid of being in charge of all these people? Aren't you afraid of what they'll do to you?"

She asked you that?

Yes, she did. And it was an excellent question. And I thought to myself, "Jesus Christ, this old woman came all this way to ask me a question I'm afraid to ask myself!" It was like she was saying, "What were you thinking? I mean, look at the situation you're in! Is this what you want?" But as I told you before, it wasn't by choice. I mean, things just happened. That's just where I ended up, understand?

But no one forced you to become a leader, right?

No, no, they did not.

So you know what? I think you liked it. I think you liked being a leader.

You know what? You're right. I did like it. I liked seeing things work out the way I wanted. So anyway, then Pato's grandmother said, "Now that I've met you, I'm going to go home and tell Lucia to come visit you, so that you're not here all alone." And so Lucia's grandmother gave me hope [*laughter*]. And I don't know what it was she said, when she got back home, but Lucia was there the next weekend. And I said to her, "Hey, how's it going? I didn't think you'd ever come back." And she said, "Well, here I am!" And I thought to myself, "I've got to get to know her better, because I bet she's not the saint she makes herself out to be!"

Did you have the chance to talk to her alone?

Not really, because she was always with her brother. But then one day I asked her if we could talk. You know, inside the boiler room [*laughter*]. I said, "Look, there's this boiler room. Don't worry, because it's nice and clean. And we can sit and talk." And to tell you the truth, I wanted her then. But in the end we just sat and talked, because I wanted to know more about her, about her family. But it was hard to get her to talk. And I kept thinking, "She's hiding something." Because her brother had a girlfriend, right? So for her to visit as well, she must have been either really close to him, or they were both involved. Because sometimes the whole family's involved. I mean, it's quite common.

But did you think that was the case with her?

No, no. I mean, her brother was involved because he was an addict. And his girlfriend had that same look about her too. But Lucia, I wasn't sure about Lucia. Because all she told me was that she had a daughter, and that her mother worked, and that sometimes she worked with her. But that was all. So then I told her how I got involved. I told her a little bit about my life. And she could see that I was different from the other guys.

You mean you weren't a vagabundo?

That's right. And I said to her, "Now look, I don't want to involve you in anything, but the Comando Vermelho is about to split apart. And it's going to affect you, because you live in a community that's under their control." But when I was telling her this, I never imagined that she had this past, that she'd been through what she'd been through, understand? And then she said, "Whatever I can do to help, okay? I mean, in terms of the party. Because my daughter really liked the doll." "Okay, then, I'm going to need this and this and this. Now, will you help me?" "Yes." So then she went to the store and ordered the cake. And I gave her money to buy clothes. Because we had this fund, right? And a lot of the prisoners didn't have anything. You know, shorts, flip-flops, or sneakers. So we started buying things for them.

From where?

From stores in the neighborhood. Because a lot of prisoners didn't have anyone to come visit. So I thought the clothes and the party, with all of the children running around, would make them feel included.

So that was another thing you got done?

That's right. And another thing—in the morning there was hardly ever any bread. And since Lucia had hired this bakery to bake the cake, I asked the owner to drop off twelve hundred French rolls the following morning. Because it's a prisoner's right to eat bread each morning. But they claimed that the machine that kneaded the dough was broken.

Was it?

It may well have been. But the longer they left it that way, the better it was for them, because all the flour and wheat that was delivered was stolen. I mean, tons and tons of the stuff. So when the guy came by to deliver the cake, I told him, "Tomorrow morning, bring twelve hundred French rolls, okay? And I'll tell the guards on duty to let you in."

But why?

To make a point, to put pressure on the administration. Because I'd been asking for the rolls for a long time. Because sometimes there were rolls and sometimes there weren't. And when there were, they'd arrive late, around lunchtime. And so a lot of prisoners would have nothing to eat until then, and they'd go hungry. And so when the bread arrived, the next morning, everyone said, "Jesus Christ, rolls! French bread!" And then on the fifth day—because we didn't just get them for one day, we got them for five—I grabbed the receipts and I went to see the director. And the director said, "Now you're buying bread?" And I said, "Yes." "But who's paying for it?" "Everyone. Everyone's families." Because I didn't want to tell him about the fund, right? "And here are the receipts." "Okay, from now on we'll provide the bread, okay?"

So he accepted your challenge?

That's right. Except that there was no investigation, no inquiry to see what had happened. It was like, "Hey, the assholes found out, so we'll have to give them their bread, okay?" Because that's the way things are in this country. Because as long as no one complains, nothing happens. But then, when someone does complain, it's like, "Okay then, we'll fix it for you." That's all. So then they started giving us bread.

But who did pay for the bread? I mean, the bread that you brought in.

That's an excellent question. Because I sent a letter to Jakeira, asking for help. And the leader of the favela said, "Tell Bruno I'm sending him five kilos of marijuana—except that he's going to have to find a way of getting it in" [laughter]. And it's interesting how we got it in. Because they were building another cell block, and the workers who were building it came in each day, because they worked for this firm. So I got someone from my group to find out which of the workers was from an area that was controlled by the cv. Then I went up to him and I said, "Where are you from?" And he said, "Vila Olímpia." So then I said, "When you get here in the morning, do they search you?" And he said, "Sometimes they do, but usually they don't, because there are too many of us."

So he was the one who was going to bring the marijuana in?

That's right. Because he was part of our community, and so he had to, understand? So then the marijuana was made ready. And we found someone to bring it to Vila Olímpia. So then I said, "This is what I want you to do. You're going to pick out five bags of whitewash, and you're going to put them aside, okay?" Because there was this place outside where they kept all the materials. "Then you're going to put the marijuana inside one of the five bags, okay?" And he said, "But how are you going to get the bags in?" "Don't you worry about it. Leave that to me, okay?"

But how were you going to get them in?

Well, I had this idea that we should paint one of the cell blocks, Cell Block B, where the guys were digging the tunnel. Because you know what? I was worried, because every time I went in, they acted all surprised and nervous. And I told them, I said, "Look, if a guard comes by and sees you like this, he's going to suspect. So you have to act more relaxed. You have to make it look as if everything's okay." And so I thought that painting the cell block would provide a distraction. So I asked the chief of security if I could have five bags of whitewash. Because there were dozens of bags of whitewash there already. And the chief of security said, "Let me talk to the foreman, okay? And I'll let you know later." Then, at the end of the day, I was called to the front office. And when I got there, the prison director was there, together with the chief of security, and a guard with a pair of handcuffs. And the five bags of whitewash were standing in the corner. And I thought to myself, "Holy shit, they've found out." Because I figured that the marijuana must be in one of them.

How did you know?

Because the prisoner who brought the bags in told me. Because the authorities thought that he was "their guy," but he wasn't—he was "my guy." But I mean, they took me by surprise. And it was almost six o'clock at night, and the prison was in lockdown mode. So I figured they must have found out.

And had they?

No, it's just that I imagined they had. Because when I got there, they were all standing there. And so I thought to myself, "They've found it and they're going to arrest me for trafficking." So when I got there I said, "What's the deal?" And the chief of security said, "You can take these five bags and brushes." But you know what? I refused to take them, because in the back of my mind I thought, "If I don't touch them, they can't arrest me, right?" Because I'd been in prison for six years already, and so I wasn't about to do anything stupid. So then the chief of security said, "Go on then, take them!" And I said, "No, no, not right now. If it's okay with you, I'll send someone to pick them up in the morning." "Whatever. Just get them out of my office, okay?" And let me tell you, I wanted those bags out of there right away. It's just that I was afraid to touch them! So anyway, the next day I asked my guy to go get them and to bring them over to Cell Block B. And he said, "Are you sure? Are you sure the chief of security said it was okay?" And I said, "Yes, yes, he already said that it was okay." So then I told this friend of mine, Tostão, who was from the favela of Jakeira, to take the marijuana and to sell it. And to put all the money he made in the central fund. Because I wanted nothing to do with it. I wanted nothing at all to do with drugs.

So you left it up to the others to sell.
That's right. I left it up to Tostão, Nelsinho, and Marcelinho. You know, the guys from Zona Sul.

So everyone liked the way I ran the prison, except for this one group of guys that didn't. And then there was this soccer match, and a fight broke out between the two teams. Because the guys who played for one of the teams were from a favela that was controlled by Uë. And the guys who played for the other team were from a favela controlled by Escadinha. Because that's how teams were organized. And the guys who played for Escadinha's team said, "Bruno, if you're not going to let us kill them, then we'll take care of them on the soccer field. Because it's time for war, okay?" And I said, "For Christ's sake, guys, you don't know what you're doing! You know we can't do anything until . . ." "No, Bruno, the waiting's over. Everyone knows what's going to happen." And then, a few days later, it did happen, because Uë was transferred to Bangu. But when he got there, do you know what they did? They gave him a gun. Escadinha and the other leaders who were supplied by him gave him a gun. They sent him to a cell block that was all CV, because that's where the issue was supposed to be resolved. Except that it wasn't, because instead of killing him, they gave him a gun. And then he went and killed these two other guys. And when he killed these two other guys, Escadinha went over to his side. And so did a bunch of others. And when the leaders in Afonso Costa found out, they decided to kill all of Escadinha and Uë's men.

So the split was really between Bangu and Afonso Costa.
That's right. So then they started killing people. And about fourteen or fifteen were killed right away. And then Escadinha and Uë were transferred to another cell block, you know, to get them out of there.

What about in your prison?
Every day, guys in my group would come up to me and say, "So, Bruno, has the order arrived?" And I'd say, "Look, as soon as it does, we'll make a decision, okay? But in the meantime we're going to continue doing what we're doing." Then the guys who were associated with Uë would come

up to me and say, "So, Bruno, what's going on?" And I would say, "Look, stop worrying, because we're all friends here, okay?" And when I told them this, that they weren't going to be punished, a bunch of guys in my group said they wanted out, because they were afraid of what might happen to them when they were transferred to another prison.

You mean, like the guys from Ilha Grande?
Except that the guys from Ilha Grande were doing everything wrong. And we were doing everything right. Then, a few days later, a message arrived. And it was a list of prisoners who were to be killed. But you know what? The guys who signed the letter meant nothing to me. And most of the guys on the list had nothing to do with Orlando Jogador's death. They were just guys that the leaders in Afonso Costa didn't like.

You mean, they were taking advantage of the situation to take out their enemies.
Precisely. And one of the guys who signed the letter was Edmilson de Souza. And the first time I met him was in Afonso Costa, because he was transferred to my cell block with all the other prisoners, remember? And on his first day, we got into a fight because I used this bucket of water when it wasn't my turn.

So you mean he signed it to get back at you?
That's right, because then I'd have to kill all these people, and then I'd be in prison for a long, long time, because I'd be held responsible. But you know what? The document was signed by six people, by Edmilson de Souza and by five others I barely knew. So it wasn't something that was signed by the leaders, you know, the ones with authority.

So you were thinking of ignoring it?
Yes, yes, I was. So then I went to see the director. And when I went in, he said, "So Bruno, what are you going to do?" And I said, "With your permission, sir, I'll get the guys who need to leave out of here." "Okay, I'll give you four days." So then I gave the list of names to the chief of security, and he arranged for their transfer.

How many were there?
There were twelve. And some of them were sent to Afonso Costa and the others to Aranha Filho. And only two of the guys who were sent to Afonso Costa ended up dead, because the leaders there figured that the others had nothing to do with it.

You mean they figured that it was more personal?

That's right. So anyway, once the guys in Afonso Costa found out what had happened, they sent a message telling their friends to take over, because I couldn't be in charge anymore. Because there were guys in Afonso Costa who were really mad at me. And they were saying, "Get Bruno out of there." Whereas others were saying, "No, no, no, leave him be."

So you had friends there?

I had lots of friends there. Because they knew how I ran the prison. So then I called another meeting. And I got everyone together on the patio. And I explained to them what was going on in all the other prisons. And I told them that my leadership had to be respected, and that I couldn't be responsible for the safety of anyone who didn't, because my group was 100 percent behind me. But you know what? It made people even more mad. It made them even more determined to get on with the killings. But from my point of view, it was all wrong, because it wasn't their problem, it was the leaders' problem. And I mean, after all the good things I'd done, after all I'd accomplished, how the hell was I going to do that? I would have to be a real Judas, a real Machiavellian, right? Because all the prisoners there liked me, and so did their families. And so if I changed from being a really good guy to being a really bad guy, they'd say, "Jesus Christ, what happened to him?" So it was important for me to continue doing what I was doing. Even if it meant I had to be killed. Because at least I'd die in peace, right? And I wouldn't feel guilty or anything. Because by then I figured that all the good things I'd done had made up for all the bad things, understand?

So you figured you'd earned your redemption?

That's right. Then one night, while I was sleeping, this group of guys came into my cell. And there were about ten of them, and they told me that they'd been told to take over. And I looked at them, and I said, "What took you so long? I mean, every time I held a meeting, I asked if there was anyone out there who was interested in taking over. I mean, all you had to do was raise your hand! And another thing—if I'm going to step down, I'm going to do it on my terms, when I'm ready. Otherwise I'm not going to, understand? And let me tell you something—you'd better be prepared, because running a prison isn't easy!" And you know what? I could see that some of them were nervous. I could see that some of them were really scared.

You mean to take over?

That's right. So then I called another meeting, of everyone. And I said, "Whoever's Amigos dos Amigos, over there." So then seventy guys moved to one side. And then I said to them, "God be with you, because you're no longer part of the Comando Vermelho family."

So you gave everyone a choice?

I gave them the choice to stay or to leave that prison, because that was what was happening in other prisons. And the government was having to find a place to put them. Because they used to be Comando Vermelho, and now what were they? So then they were taken to this cell block that had been emptied out. And you know what? As they left, they all clapped their hands.

You mean as a way of saying thank you?

That's right. And the next day, the prisoners who had left the CV began to be transferred. And so then I got the rest of my group together. And there were ten of us. And I asked for all of us to be transferred to Lemos da Silva, in the city. Because there was no way I could stay there, because I'd divided up the prison and I'd handed over the leadership. So now I had to get out. Because if they hadn't killed me by then, it was only a matter of time, because the guys who signed the letter in Afonso Costa would put pressure on them.

So you mean you were vulnerable.

I was extremely vulnerable. Because one day you're the leader, right? And the next day? And I mean, you're powerless in that situation. And not only could they kill me, they could kill everyone else in my group. So I had to get out of there. I had to get out of there with my friends because, I mean, they saved my life. And even today, after all this time, we talk about this adventure, this adventure that we were on together.

What about Lucia? Was she still visiting you?

By this time we were together. What I mean is, we were involved. But I warned her that something could happen, so she wouldn't be surprised if she found out one day that I was dead. Besides, by then she'd already told me about her life, about how her boyfriend was involved, and how he'd been murdered. So I thought to myself, "Is it possible she's a black widow?"

Graffiti demonstrating a change in command in a Rio favela. Photograph by author, 2007.

THE FACTION FALLS APART

On June 13, 1994, Orlando da Conceição, otherwise known as Orlando Jogador, was murdered along with eleven of his men by Ernaldo Pinto de Medeiros, otherwise known as Uë, in the favela of Grota in the Complexo do Alemão. The assassination of Orlando Jogador caused Uë to be expelled from the CV, following which he founded the Amigos dos Amigos. Uë himself was on the run for two years until he was captured in 1996 and sentenced to 209 years in prison for his part in the killing. He was held in Cell Block D in Bangu until his spectacular death at the hands of Fernandinho Beira-Mar.

Fernandinho Beira-Mar had become, by the late 1990s, the CV's main supplier of drugs, making multiple arms-for-cocaine deals with the Forças Armadas Revolucionárias da Colômbia (FARC), which generated millions of dollars in revenue and got him onto the U.S. Drug Enforcement Administration's list of the world's most wanted terrorists and drug traffickers. And it was in the jungles of Colombia, in the company of FARC officials, that Beira-Mar was finally tracked down by the Colombian Armed Forces in April 2001.

On his return to Rio, Beira-Mar was imprisoned in Cell Block A in Bangu with other leaders of the CV. Then, on the morning of September 11, 2002, he and his men overcame two guards and made their way through six steel doors until they reached Cell Block D, where the leaders of the Amigos dos Amigos were being held. They then proceeded to kill four of them, including Uë, who was shot, had his jaws and skull smashed in, and was set on fire inside a funeral pyre of mattresses. Beira-Mar's men were armed with three pistols and a shotgun despite the fact that a search had been conducted forty-eight hours earlier. On completing his mission, Beira-Mar announced via cell phone, "It's under control. Everything's under control."[6]

The Bangu massacre was a huge embarrassment for the authorities in that it demonstrated, once again, the power of criminal factions in Rio and the extent to which the public security forces had been corrupted. By way of response, the authorities made a concerted effort to break the power of criminal factions at their point of origin by placing their leaders in strict isolation, by cutting back on visitation rights and other such privileges, and by transferring the most powerful of them to specially built federal prisons out of state.[7] While these measures failed to rid the system of warring factions, they did make it more difficult for the leaders in prison to exercise control of the drug trade. As a consequence, the measures themselves were met with fierce resistance in the form of widespread prison riots; waves of coordinated attacks on public buses, government buildings, and the police; and the assassination of prison officials and employees.[8]

So then we were sent to Lemos da Silva, in the city, because this friend of mine, Falcão, was there. And he was part of the old guard from Ilha Grande. And he'd done what I'd done. He'd told everyone that they could leave.

So you knew him then?

I knew him from Afonso Costa, because he was a student there, in my school. And right before we were transferred, we heard a rumor that the leaders who let the prisoners from the Amigos dos Amigos go were to be killed, because they didn't do what they were told, and they weakened the CV. Because the leaders of the CV didn't want the ADA [Amigos dos Amigos] to become established, and so now they wanted a show of force. So I said to my group, "I'm going to get us out of here. And the only place we can go is Lemos da Silva, to be with Falcão."

Because you figured he'd protect you?

That's right. Because I knew that if I was sent to Afonso Costa I'd be killed. And if I asked for protection, then, when I got out, and went to visit Lucia . . .

So you already figured that out? You were already thinking about the fact that she lived in an area that was controlled by the CV?

Of course! So I knew that the situation had to be resolved one way or another. Otherwise, when I left prison, I was going to have to go somewhere like Recife, or the frontier. And I didn't know if Lucia would go with me, because I wasn't sure of her feelings for me. Because on the one hand, I was thinking that she could be the love of my life. But on the other, I wasn't sure how far she'd go. Because when she visited me in prison, she was the girlfriend of the leader, right? So everyone treated her well, even the guards. But now the situation was different. And I wasn't sure what was going to happen. Because there were guys in my group who were desperate to kill me, any way that they could.

You mean in Carvalho Troiano?

That's right. Because everyone who was there with me was going to be judged the same way. Because if I didn't kill anyone, neither did they, understand? So they were all wondering, "What's going to happen when I go back to my community?" And so they were thinking, "Maybe it's best if we kill him now, to show the guys in Afonso Costa that we know how to follow orders."

So you placed all of your faith in Falcão?

I placed all my faith in Falcão. Because he'd been in prison for a long time. And he was sick of it, and all he wanted was to get out. And if all someone wants is to get out, then they won't want to cause any trouble, right? So they try to resolve things peacefully. And the fact that he was trying to resolve things peacefully, and there hadn't been any killings in his prison, made me want to go there.

And it helped that you had a good relationship with the authorities, right?

Of course. Because I told the director that I needed to be transferred, me and my friends, because someone else was now in charge. And he said, "Who? Who's in charge?" And I said, "I'm not going to tell you. You're the one who should know. It's your prison!" Because if I had told him who was in charge, when I got to Lemos da Silva, I could have been accused of being a traitor. And that wouldn't have been good, because it would have been one more reason for Falcão not to trust me. So then the director said again, "I'll send you there if you tell me who's the new leader." And I said,

"But I can't. All I know is that I was the leader, and now I'm not, okay?"
"So who is?" "I don't know."

But he let you go anyway?

He let me go anyway. He wrote down my name and number and then the next week I was transferred.

And what were you thinking, when you left that place?

When they called me, I thought, "Thank Christ I'm out of here." Because the situation was intolerable. Because one day you're the leader, right? And the next day you're not. So it was difficult. And I mean, I could have been killed at any moment. So I couldn't sleep, because I had to be on my guard twenty-four hours a day.

And you were transferred along with how many?

There were sixteen of us.

But I thought there were only ten left in your group.

There were. But we took along some others, including two who wanted to kill me.

But why?

So they could tell everyone the truth about what happened. Because the director asked me, he said, "Who do you want to go with you?" And there was this guy who'd threatened to kill me with a knife. He cornered me this one time, and he took out his knife, and he held it against my throat and said, "Do you have any doubt that I can kill you?" And you know what? I was the one who invited him to join my group, when he first arrived. And now he was trying to kill me? So I said to him, "Hey, if that's what you want. If you think you can get away with it, go ahead." Again he said, "Do you have any doubt that I can kill you?" "Like I said, if you can get away with it, go ahead." Because I'd already given up control of the prison. But some of them still wanted me dead. But you know what? They didn't have the power. They didn't have the authority. So they were thinking, "Hey, I could kill Bruno right now, but what happens if he has friends in other places? What happens then?" Because it's tricky to kill someone who has a reputation. I mean, there has to be an order or something. And it has to come from the top. But nobody said, "Go ahead and kill Bruno." They just said, "Get him out of there." Because there was never any order to kill me. And that's what I was thinking when this guy said, "Do you have any doubt that I can kill you?" So I said, "Go ahead. If that's what you want, go ahead." So then, when we got Lemos da Silva, there was this business of the cela de espera.

How many days?

Fourteen, with everyone together in the same cell. And my God, it was horrible. I mean, it was a shit hole. Because the cell was about six meters square, with a hole for a toilet in the corner. And it was dark and damp and everyone slept on the floor. Because Lemos da Silva was an old prison. And when we got there I said to myself, "Jesus Christ, now I'm really screwed." Because I'd given up the leadership, right? And I was no longer in Carvalho Troiano, a prison I thought I'd walk out of one day.

So in comparison, Carvalho Troiano was a five-star prison?

Compared to Lemos da Silva, yes it was. So we all stayed there, in this one cell. And no one said anything. But you know what? I was already feeling relieved because guys would come by and say, "Hey Bruno, what's happening?"

You mean other prisoners?

That's right. Prisoners who knew me, who'd been in prison for a long time.

And what about Falcão?

He came by too, because he was the leader. Because he used to walk around with his guards. And he said to me, "When you're done with this we'll talk, okay?" And I said, "Okay."

What about the guys you brought with you, the ones who were planning to kill you? What were they thinking?

They were thinking, "Thank Christ we didn't lay a hand on him!" [*Laughter.*]

So then after two weeks we were allowed out. And Falcão came up to me and hugged me. And he said, "So, Bruno, tell me what happened in that other prison? Because there were these rumors." And I told him that they were all lies, and that everything was fine until the order came through from Afonso Costa. Because I told him about it, even though I hadn't told anyone else.

You mean, no one knew the order came through?

No. I kept it to myself. But then, when I got to Lemos da Silva, I told Falcão. Because he received an order too. So what did he do? He told the guys in Afonso Costa that he gave the orders, and not them.

The same as you then?

Except that I never told them that. I never sent them a message. Because Falcão was old school. He was one of the founding members of the CV. And so look at the situation I was in! [*Laughter.*] Because I'd managed to get myself transferred to a prison where the leader was a good guy, right? But now he was acting like a fool! Because when I gave up the leadership of Carvalho Troiano, I said to the guys, "Look, you're welcome to take over. But you should know that the guys you want have already been transferred. And the other guys, well, they had nothing to do with it."

So you claimed that you did what you were supposed to?

That's right. And even then, I told the guys who were there when Orlando Jogador was killed, I said to them, "You can either go or you can stay here. It's up to you." And they decided to go, because they figured they could convince the leaders in Afonso Costa that they had nothing to do with it— except that when they got there, there were witnesses who said they were there. So they were killed. And it was when these two guys showed up that the leaders in Afonso Costa said, "Let's get Bruno out of there." And I knew that if I stayed there any longer, I'd end up dead. And that's why I tried to get out. Except that I couldn't go to Afonso Costa, right? And I couldn't just ask to leave. After all those years in the CV, it just wasn't possible. So I had to explain to someone what I'd been doing. And that's why all of us went to Lemos da Silva, to be with Falcão, understand?

You mean you needed to clear your name before you got out?

That's right. So it wouldn't be an issue on the outside. And so anyway, then Falcão said, "Don't worry, because I'm the leader here. So nothing's going to happen to you, okay? And these guys in Afonso Costa, they can go fuck themselves. This Edmilson de Souza and these other guys, they can go fuck themselves. Because I've been at this since the sixties. So don't you worry, okay?" So then I said, "Okay, but be careful, okay?"

You mean watch your back?

And the guys who are closest to you, the guys in your group. Because I mean, I had to watch my back too, even with Falcão. Because I thought to myself, "Is it possible that he'd welcome me with open arms, and then turn on me? Was he really telling the truth?" Because he was the leader of a favela, right? And he'd been part of the organization for years. So was he really going to turn his back on them, on this new generation of leaders? I mean, you had to be really tough to do that.

Or really stupid.

Or really stupid. Because I had nothing. And if I wanted to, I could get out of there and run, to Recife, or somewhere like that. Except that I couldn't, because I was in love.

But couldn't Lucia do something? Couldn't she say, "Look, this guy Bruno, he's my boy-friend?"

No, no, no, she could never do that. And after talking to her, I realized that she needed someone to give her life direction. Because she was drifting, and she needed someone who was responsible, who would take care of her.

But didn't she have a thing for vagabundos?

Yes, yes, she did. And I realized that she was a little bit stupid that way, in that she exposed herself to way too much risk. So I figured something must have happened, in terms of her family. But when I met them, when I met her mother and grandmother, I could see that they were good people, that they were a real family. So I started to pay more attention to her, and she started to pay more attention to me. And the fact that she visited me, and brought me food and clothing when things were so difficult for me was huge. So I said to myself, "If she's gone through all of this, and she came to visit me in Carvalho Troiano, and now she's visiting me here in Lemos da Silva, she must like me, right?"

Right.

So like I said, after two weeks together in this cell, we were allowed out. And after I'd spoken with Falcão, I said to myself, "I think I'll be safe in this place." Because they sent me to Cell Block 5, with Falcão, because he arranged it that way. And Cell Block 5 was the only cell block where women were allowed to visit on the weekend. They stayed from nine in the morning until five in the afternoon. And there was a shower there, and a place to take a bath. And Lucia came to visit me the first weekend I was there. You know, she filled out some forms and got a visitor's pass. So I stayed there with her.

How many months were you there?

I was there for almost a year. And the atmosphere in that prison was really tense, because everyone knew that, at any moment, the leaders in Afonso Costa were going to send out orders to have the other leaders killed. But at the same time, Saraiva Neto was being built. And the government was going to send everyone there, because the government was going to take everyone from Afonso Costa and Lemos da Silva and transfer them to Saraiva Neto. Because it was a new prison that was much more secure.

What about Afonso Costa?

The CV was losing that space, because it was being given over to the ADA.

So everyone was being sent to the new prison?

That's right. And they were waiting for everyone to get there, so they could resolve things. So then they inaugurated Saraiva Neto, and a lot of the prisoners from Carvalho Troiano and Lemos da Silva were transferred there—except not the ones they wanted, because Falcão didn't go.

Why not?

Because his time was almost up. So the authorities decided to release him from there, in the city. And you know what? A lot of the guys who were in my group in Carvalho Troiano were in his group. And he asked me to join his group too. But I didn't want to. He said, "Bruno, why don't you join us?" And I said, "I've had enough of this leadership bullshit. All I want to do is work. I want to be able to do something." So he gave my name to the person in charge of prisoner education. And she called me in and I got to teach computing. You know, the basics.

But weren't you worried, because Falcão was so weak?

He was weak but he was acting like he was strong. Because there was this one time that I went by his cell, and he was talking to the guys in Afonso Costa, because we had cell phones by then.[1] And he was talking to this guy Gordão. And they started arguing. And he told this guy Gordão that he was part of the old guard, and that he was the one who gave the orders. Then he hung up. He said, "Who do these motherfuckers think they are? They can all go fuck themselves, because I'm Falcão!" And I thought to myself, "Oh my God, he's going to die. And when they come to get him,

I'm going to die too!" Because even though I wasn't part of his group, I was with him, understand? So I said to him, "Calm down. You know you're right, because you are the leader. But try and calm down." Because I wasn't going to go against him, right? Even though I knew he was being stupid. Because the guys in Saraiva Neto didn't give a shit, because they were going to be in prison for a long, long time. So all they were interested in was being in charge. You know, being in control. So I told Falcão that I didn't want anything to do with his group, because the last group I was in brought me nothing but trouble. I told him that all I wanted was to serve out my sentence. Except that given everything that was going on, I knew I had to find a way out of there. So when I went to teach computing, I asked the woman in charge if I could arrange a meeting with the director, because that was every prisoner's right. And she said, "But why, Bruno? Didn't you say you were going to be out of here in a few months?" And I said yes, but it didn't matter, because there was something I had to do. So she set up a meeting with the director and then they called me. "Bruno. Meeting up front with the director!" So I put on some clothes, some long pants and a shirt, and then off I went.

When I reached the director's office, I said, "Excuse me, sir?" And the director said, "What is it, Bruno?" "I came here to ask to be transferred." "Where do you want to go?" "Saraiva Neto." Then he sat there, looking at my file, without saying anything. "You want to be transferred to Saraiva Neto?"

Did he know about the split?

Of course. And then he said, "But Bruno, why there?" And I said, "Because that's where I want to go. Because I don't want to stay here. So the first chance you get, I want you to send me to Saraiva Neto." "But you know that . . ." "Look, that's where I want to go, because it's my right." "Okay, okay, I'll get to it as soon as I can." Because there was already a group of prisoners who were planning on killing Falcão, who were being told what to do by the leaders in Saraiva Neto. But you know what? Even though his life was in danger, Falcão did nothing, because he didn't know how to deal with the situation. Then one night, a friend of mine gave me his cell phone, and I called Saraiva Neto. And Pingo answered the phone, and he said to me, "Bruno, get yourself over here, okay? Because they're going to kill Falcão. I haven't heard anything said about you, but I know they're going to kill Falcão."

So it was a warning.

That's right, it was a warning from a friend. So I told him, I said, "I've already asked to be transferred. So I'll be there soon, so don't worry, okay?" And that night I couldn't sleep. And I kept thinking, "Fuck! I got myself out of one bad situation, and now I'm in another. So I've got to get to Saraiva Neto and I've got to resolve this situation once and for all." Then the next day, this guard came by and said, "Bruno, get your things together. You're being transferred."

Did you tell Lucia what was going on?

Of course. I left a message on her pager. And it said, "I'm being transferred to Saraiva Neto." And boy, was she upset, because she knew that if I went there, there was a good chance that I'd be killed.

So you told her everything.

Everything. Because we spent every Saturday and Sunday together. From nine in the morning until five in the afternoon.

So she knew what it meant to be transferred there?

She knew that it would be dangerous. And when I got there, after waiting outside in the sun for four hours, guess who I saw? Dr. Bradzinski, the director of Carvalho Troiano. And when he saw me, sitting there in handcuffs, he said, "Bruno, you're coming here? But everyone here wants to kill you!" And do you know what I said? I said, "But if they do kill me, sir, could you do me a favor? Could you play the number of holes in my body on the lottery?" So then he laughed and said, "Okay, okay, but first you're going to have to sign this form, to say that you're responsible for your own safety. Because I don't want you in there, okay?"[2]

You mean if something happens, it's your responsibility?

That's right. And I said, "That's fine. Just give it to me and I'll sign it, okay?" And at that point I really didn't care. Because I mean, I was already there, right? So I might as well find out what all these guys wanted.

But you had friends there as well, right?

Yes, yes, I did. And I mean, I'd pretty much figured it out. You know, before I left. I'd pretty much figured out that I had more guys on my side. You know, like it was a vote in congress or something.

So who was there that you knew?

Pingo, Dedão, a bunch of guys. And when I was being taken to my cell block, guess who I ran into? My old friend Edmilson de Souza. You know, the guy I got into a fight with, the guy who signed the order to have the twelve guys killed. And when he saw me, he said, "Bruno, is that really you? I've been meaning to talk to you." And I said, "Look, the only reason I'm here is because I asked to be transferred, okay?" "That's good. Because I'm looking forward to seeing you get out of this one." Because he'd hated me for a long time, and he'd like nothing more than to see me dead. So then I went into my cell block, which was Cell Block 5. And the leaders were all in Cell Block 1, on the other side of the prison. Because the prison was divided into two sections, A and B. And there were ten cell blocks: 1A, 2A, 3A, 4A, and 5A. And 1B, 2B, 3B, and so on.

How many cells were in each cell block?

Sixteen.

So it was a bit like Afonso Costa?

Except that there were four prisoners to each cell. And in Afonso Costa there was only one, right?

Who was in Cell Block 5 with you? Anyone you knew?

Yes, there were these two older guys. And one of them was a real asshole. I mean, I couldn't trust him at all. And I knew that he'd kill me if someone told him to. But the other guy was okay. I figured I could trust him, because he wasn't the type to follow orders, understand? Because it happens a lot in prison. You know, a leader will give an order, and someone else will carry it out.

But that's not what happened, right? I mean, no one gave the order to kill you?

No, because there were a lot of people in that prison who liked me, who were glad to see me there. So then they invited me over, to see what I had to say.

You mean, like an audience?

It was more like a trial. So then they sent me a message, to go over to where the leaders were. Except that the guard wanted ten reais to let me out. So I told him, I said, "Tell the guys in Cell Block 1 that I won't pay to come over and see them." Except that that's not what they were told. Because they were told that I said I'd go over when I was ready. So the next day, a guard I knew from Ilha Grande came by. And he said, "Bruno, you're still here, in prison?" And I said, "Yeah, I'm still here. Now is there any way you can get me over to Cell Block 1, so I can talk to my friends?" And he said, "Sure." So then he unlocked the cell block door and let me out. Then, when we got to Cell Block 1, he unlocked the cell block door and let me in.

So then the guys in Cell Block 1 looked up and said, "It's him—it's Bruno!" And everyone came out of their cells to see me. Then one of them said, "What's going on? Because we sent you a message, and we heard that you said you weren't coming." And I said, "Listen, if a message can get confused between one cell block and another, imagine what can happen between two prisons."

You mean Afonso Costa and Carvalho Troiano.

That's right. Then Edmilson de Souza said, "Look, we sent you a message to kill someone, and then we heard back that you said you didn't have to." Because he had to make it look as if I'd betrayed the organization, that I was a traitor. And then he said, "You know that Falcão's going to die, right? And that if you don't explain yourself, you'll die too?" So then this guy Gordão took out this knife, this great big knife, and he started walking toward me. And I thought to myself, "This is it. He's going to kill me!" And then he said, "Come on, you motherfucker, explain yourself. Explain what happened!" So then I took off my shirt, and I said, "I've got nothing to explain, okay? All I've got is my life. So if you want it, take it!"

Why did you do that?

To show them I was defenseless, that my life was in their hands. And I told them that I only had a few months left to serve, and that I wanted them to know everything that had happened in that prison, and that if someone was saying bad things about me, they were lying. They were lying because they wanted something. You know, from them. So then this guy Gordão said, "Go and get so-and-so, because he can tell us what happened. He can tell us what was said." So then they brought this guy in. And after he said what he had to say, I hit him. I punched him in the mouth and he fell to the ground. And I said, "This guy knows nothing. He's an asshole."

Did you know him?

Of course, because he was with me in Carvalho Troiano, because he was in my group. And he told them that I'd said that the guys who signed the letter meant nothing, you know, to me, and that they had no authority. Except that when I hit him, everyone in the cell block joined in. I mean, the whole place went up in smoke. Then after a while, Pingo shouted out, "Let him speak, for Christ's sake, let him have his say!" So then, after everyone had calmed down, I said, "Here's the deal. I've been with this woman for a while now, and she's from an area that's controlled by the CV. But if I can't go there after I'm released, after all the years I've spent with you guys in prison, then you might as well kill me now. I'd rather die here, right now, than be hunted down on the street. So if you're going to do it, do it now. But before you do, let me show you a letter—a letter written by you guys, giving me permission to take over the prison." So then Edmilson de Souza said, "What letter?"

Did you have it with you?

I had it hidden in the sole of my shoe. So then I said, "And another thing. It was never my intention to take over as leader, because that's not what I do. All I wanted was to improve conditions there, for everyone. Because when I got there, there were no mattresses, and no one was allowed out, because the place was about to explode. So now you're giving me all this shit about not following orders, about not doing what I was told? Well, let me tell you something. I didn't come all this way from the frontier to involve myself in your silly little problems, okay? Because they're your problems, for you to resolve. So don't go putting me in the middle, okay?" Then Gordão said, "But you were the leader. And as the leader you . . ." "Now listen! Every time I held a meeting, I asked if there was anyone out there who wanted to take over. You know, as leader. And no one said anything, because no one knew how to run the prison. And one more thing. If you think I'm afraid of you, you're wrong. Because if I was afraid of you, do you think I would have asked to be transferred?" So then I put my hand in my sneaker and took out the letter. And Pingo took it from me and said, "He's right! He's telling the truth!" And then they all stood there, looking down at the floor, without saying anything.

And what about Gordão? Had he signed the letter?

No, no, because he wasn't one of the leaders back then. So then Gordão grabbed the letter and read it. And he said, "Brother Bruno, everything's cool. Everything's okay."

Even though the letter was signed by a bunch of older guys?

That's right.

So he couldn't kill you.

That's right, because the letter was signed by people who were important, who still commanded respect within the CV. So he realized he couldn't go through with it. So then he said, "Everything's okay then." And I said, "Everything's okay." Then we all stood around talking. And we had a glass of whisky together. And all the time I was thinking, "Jesus Christ, that was close!" And you know what? It was close—it was really close. And another thing. There was this guy there whose job was to assume responsibility for crimes that were committed inside of prison. And he was sitting by the cell block door when I came in, like he was waiting for me. So I tapped him on the shoulder and I said, "You're not assuming responsibility for my crime. Oh no, you're not!" Because I knew what he was there for.

And he made money this way?

They gave him cocaine, and sneakers, and shit like that.

And he never got out, right?

That's right, because that was his job. It was what he was there for. And when I entered the cell block he looked up at me. And he had this scruffy beard, and dry skin, and all these rotten teeth. He looked up at me with this look of death in his eyes, and I said to him, "You're not assuming responsibility for my crime." And he said, "What do you mean? What are you talking about?" "You're not assuming responsibility for my crime because I'm going to get myself out of it, you'll see!" And so then I went in. And what happened happened. And then, like I said, I ended up standing around talking to everyone.

But weren't you afraid that they'd still come after you? You know, at night?

No, because they couldn't.

And by then you knew that Falcão was about to die, right?

That's right.

And you couldn't say anything to him?

No because I had no way of contacting him, because I didn't have a phone. And besides, I was there to save my own life. So then they killed him, and three other members of his group. They killed him with knives.

And after all this, how long were you there?

I was there for three months. And everything was cool. Everything was fine, because my life was getting back to normal. Because I was no longer a leader. I was just another prisoner, understand? And during those last three months I managed to get hold of some pens and pencils, and I gave them to the guys who couldn't read or write. And I got everyone in my cell block to exercise. You know, I'd get them up early in the morning, and I'd say, "Come on, guys. Let's get some exercise, so we don't get out of shape!" Then, just as they were getting used to me, they called me out. "Bruno, you're free to go!" And I thought to myself, "Could this be it? Could this really be it?" Because I'd already been in prison for longer than I should. I mean, I'd been there for an extra eight days already.

What was the problem?

It was an administrative problem, some sort of oversight. So I told Lucia, "Go find Dr. Regina," who was my lawyer. "Go find Dr. Regina and go with her downtown and find out what's happened to my case." So they went downtown. And after they resolved the situation they came all the way out to the prison. And it was eleven o'clock at night when they got there. Because Sérgio, Lucia's brother-in-law, drove them there in his car. And then when they got there, they called for me. And I heard the noise of doors being unlocked from far away. Because at night, a prisoner can hear everything, right? So then they unlocked the door to my cell block and came in.

And what were you thinking?

I was thinking that they had to release me, because I'd been there for such a long time. And then they said, "Are you Bruno?" And I said, "Yes, yes, I am." "Then come on then!"

Were they guards you knew?

These two, no, because they were new. But when I got to the place where they filled out all the paperwork, there were two there that I knew, because they were both from Ilha Grande. So when I saw them, I thought to myself, "These two, at this time of night? Maybe they're going to stick me in the trunk of a car and drive me around!" But then one of them said, "So, Bruno, you're finally getting out, eh?" And I said, "Are you serious? Am I really getting out of here?" "Yeah, your girlfriend's outside, with your lawyer, and some other guy." And then, when I got outside, I got into the car and just sat there, looking around. Then we dropped my lawyer off at her house in Jacarepaguá. Then Lucia and I went to a motel in Barra. And when we went in I said, "Hey, this is great!" Because there was a bar there, and a hot tub. And while I was taking a shower, I wrote the word "freedom" on the inside of the glass door—because I was out, I was free. And I could hardly believe it. So then I said to Lucia, "I'm not going to live in that favela, okay? I mean, we can go there and visit, but I'm not living there, okay?" Then, when we went there the next day, I thought to myself, "Is it possible that someone sent a message, you know, to have me killed?" Because they'll do that. They'll give you a taste of freedom and then they'll take it away. But then I said to myself, "No, no, no, I don't think so, because there's no reason, there's no reason for anyone to do that to me."

Because you were clean, right?

That's right. I was clean and I had no enemies and I had no debts.

So who was in charge of Jakeira?

Tostão, who was with me in Carvalho Troiano. He was transferred with me to Lemos da Silva. And from there he was released, and he was told to take over.

So the favela was in good hands then.

Yes, for a while it was.

TURF WARS

When Fernandinho Beira-Mar murdered Uë, in September 2002, it was not only an act of revenge but also a manifestation of an increasingly bloody conflict between warring factions. Beginning in the late 1990s, the ADA started making inroads into CV territory in Rio's Zona Sul and, in particular, the favela of Rocinha, which had always been considered the crown jewel of the drug trade. In January 2001, the dono of Rocinha, Denir Leandro da Silva, was found hung to death in his prison cell in Bangu, the reason being that he refused to stop dealing with the ADA. Then, in April 2004, the CV attempted to regain control of the favela by invading it in broad daylight. The invasion failed and prompted the ADA to strengthen its hold and to further expand its field of influence and operations.[3]

One of the favelas that was affected by this process was Jakeira. When I

Members of the Amigos dos Amigos patrol an alley to prevent rival gangs and the police from entering Rocinha. Photograph by Q. Sakamaki, 2007. Used by permission.

first set foot in Jakeira, in the early 1990s, it was only partially under the CV's control. What this meant was that the upper part of the favela was where drugs were sold. The lower part, however, was run by a neighborhood association that was well organized, active, and engaged with members of the community and representatives of the local state. Over time, however, the drug gang's influence spread until, in November 1998, it forced the president of the neighborhood association out at gunpoint. From that point on, the drug gang exercised almost complete control over everyone and everything, including transportation, local commerce, government projects, and cultural events.[4] Of course, there were always the occasional internal disputes and rivalries to keep things interesting, to say nothing of the constant threat of invasions and shakedowns by the police. All in all, however, things were pretty calm until in the early 2000s, when the CV began to experience a challenge to its authority.

Paralleling what was going on in Rocinha, the favela of Jakeira also went through a period of instability until, in early 2006, the ADA seized control.[5] Once the ADA established its authority, life in Jakeira returned to something approaching normal. This meant that weekly deals were made between the gang-controlled neighborhood association and the police to keep conflict to a minimum. And the situation stayed that way until January 2010, when

Federal troops and the police occupy the favela of Rocinha, November 2011. Photo-graph by Governo do Estado Rio de Janeiro / Marino Azevedo, 2011. Licensed under CC BY 2.0 BR: https://creativecommons.org/licenses/by/2.0/legalcode.

Jakeira was occupied by the military and the police, in an attempt to clear out and secure the area in the buildup to the 2014 FIFA World Cup and the 2016 Olympics.

Beginning in 2008, the authorities changed the way they waged war against organized crime in Rio. Prior to that point, standard practice was to go into a favela, kill as many suspected criminal elements as possible, and then withdraw, a tactic known in military circles as "mowing the grass."[6] Now the idea was to occupy such areas and establish a permanent police presence in the form of Unidades de Polícia Pacificadora (UPP).[7] As of March 2014, there were thirty-six UPPs in Rio, most of them located in and around areas where World Cup and Olympic events are to be held.[8]

Talking to my friends in Jakeira, many of whom have lived there since the 1960s, it is obvious that the presence of a UPP has changed the mood and the day-to-day life of the place.[9] Gone is the threat of invasion by rival gangs or the police, and gone are the young men who used to patrol the streets at night with high-powered weaponry. In their place is a group of equally young policemen and women, many of whom are experiencing their first tour of duty. And while relations between the residents of Jakeira and the police have certainly improved, the police are still viewed with a degree of

The UPP of Rocinha. Photograph by Fernando Frazão / ABr, 2013. Licensed under CC BY 3.0 BR: http://creativecommons.org/licenses/by/3.0/br/legalcode.

suspicion, which is not surprising given how they used to operate and the short amount of time they have been there.[10]

Otherwise, the complaints that you hear are pretty much the same as those voiced in other communities, having to do with the poor quality of the schools, medical care, public transportation, and the built environment in general.[11] While literally millions of reais have been spent on public security, the long-promised investments in infrastructure and urban services have yet to come.[12] Yet it is clear that such investments are essential if the recently dispersed criminal elements are to be kept out, and if poor, predominantly dark-skinned young men are to be discouraged from joining them.[13] After all, the reason that criminal elements became established in the favelas in the first place is because they represent zones of long-term social abandonment.[14]

Since they first emerged on the hillsides of Rio in the late nineteenth century, the favelas have been home to a population that has essentially been denied citizenship—not citizenship in the sense of being Brazilian, but citizenship in the sense of acceptance and inclusion.[15] Most of my middle-class friends would never set foot in a favela. They would be terrified. And they get equally upset when people they assume live in a favela invade their territory, whether it be public universities, the beach, or the mall.[16] And until that

Police patrol the Complexo de Alemão, November 2010. Photograph by Marcello Casal Jr. / ABr. Licensed under CC BY 3.0 BR: http://creativecommons.org/licenses/by/3.0/br /legalcode.

attitude changes, and the walls of social apartheid come tumbling down, there will always be those who seek the recognition and respect they crave by illegal means.[17]

The other area in need of investment is the prison system, which exists primarily to punish those who come from nothing, and offers nothing in return in terms of personal security or rehabilitation. As a consequence, it is the various criminal gangs and factions and not the authorities that dominate the lives of inmates, both on the inside and after they are released.[18] And it is this relationship between criminal factions on the inside and communities on the outside that needs to be breached. And if I were to hazard a guess, I would say that it won't be breached by locking up more and more people for longer and longer periods of time in what can only be described as subhuman conditions. In fact, if Bruno's testimony tells us anything, it has the exact opposite effect.

Of course, the issue of gangs is by no means specific to Brazil. Throughout the region, there is evidence that the warehousing of ever-increasing numbers of the poor is serving to strengthen gang control both inside and outside the prison system.[19] And while public funding for prisons is always a tough sell, the consequences of not doing anything are potentially catastrophic. Which brings us back, finally, to the issue of drugs. Most countries in Latin America continue to follow the lead—and funding—of the United States to pursue a prohibitionist and criminalizing agenda, which drives up prices, makes drugs more attractive and profitable, and leads to more arrests.[20] Fortunately there are signs of progress, however, in terms of a growing disillusionment with the war on drugs model and increasing recognition of the damage it has done. In March 2009, the Latin American Commission on Drugs and Democracy, which included former presidents of Mexico, Colombia, and Brazil, called for drugs to be treated as a matter of public health and for repression to focus on organized crime.[21] In addition, there have also been experiments with legalization, most notably in Uruguay, where residents over the age of eighteen are allowed to buy forty grams of marijuana per month and to grow six plants per year in their own homes.[22] Of course, legalizing marijuana is one thing, cocaine and its bastard cousin crack cocaine quite another, to say nothing of the impending epidemic of prescription drug abuse.[23]

I picked Bruno up at the entrance to the favela of Jakeira at five o'clock on a Monday morning. We figured it would take us two hours to drive along the coast to Manguaratiba, where we would take the ferry to Ilha Grande. Two and a half hours later, we were sitting, waiting, in a café across from the docks. Most of our fellow travelers that day were tourists, a good number of them foreigners. The rest were carrying supplies for the various hotels, restaurants, and small businesses on the island. As we waited for the ferry to pull away, Bruno reflected on the moment, almost twenty years to the day, when he was handcuffed, together with eighteen others, in the hold of a prison transport boat. This time he got to make the journey up on deck, a privilege that was not lost on him as we slowly approached Vila do Abraão, an hour and fifteen minutes away from the mainland.

When we reached Vila do Abraão, we asked if there was any way of getting to Vila de Dois Rios, the site of the former prison. We were told that a state university truck made the journey a couple of times a day, but that if we weren't invited guests, we wouldn't be allowed to go along for the ride. After much pleading and begging, including a fairly pathetic attempt on my part to impress them with my credentials, we realized that we weren't getting anywhere and decided to rent bicycles instead.

The distance between Vila do Abraão and Vila de Dois Rios is about seven kilometers. The problem is that it's seven kilometers straight up and down a rather large hill. The climb up was hot, muddy, slow, and exhausting, and at one point Bruno turned to me and said, "You know what? She must have really loved me to make this trip. I mean, in the middle of the night, in the pouring rain?" He was referring, of course, to Jandira. Once we reached the top, the journey down was a lot faster, in large part because we were able to ride, as opposed to pushing our bikes. It was still difficult, however, because of the extremely poor condition of the road. Because if it wasn't potholes we were avoiding, it was rocks and boulders and other assorted debris.

Finally, about an hour and a half after we set out, we reached our destination. Vila de Dois Rios was a lot smaller and a lot more compact than I had imagined, consisting of thirty to forty single-story houses spread out across a grid-like pattern of roads. The first person we saw when we got there was a young military policewoman whose job was to orient and register guests. Bruno explained to her that he knew the place well, and started asking about who was around. "How about Seu Albinate? Do you know Seu Albinate? Is he still around? And what about Seu Jeferson? Is he still here?" "Seu Albinate passed away," came the reply, "a little more than two years ago. But Seu Jeferson's here. He lives at the end of that first road on the right." So off we went to find him, and as we rounded the corner, we saw a figure at the end of the road, standing next to a workbench. Bruno turned to me as he pedaled and said, "It's him. That's Seu Jeferson!" "Are you sure?" I replied. "Yes, yes, absolutely!" So then we cycled down the road until we came to within fifteen to twenty feet. Then we laid down our bikes and walked toward him.

"Seu Jeferson, do you remember me? Do you know who I am?" said Bruno. A little perplexed, Seu Jeferson stood there, behind his workbench, staring. "Seu Jeferson, it's me, Naval. Remember?" "Naval? Naval? Naval! Oh my God, is it really you?" "Yes, Seu Jeferson, it's me. I've come back! Did you ever think you'd see me again?" Then they hugged. Then they hugged again. And this time they didn't let go, and tears of joy began to roll down the old man's face.

For the next twenty minutes or so, I stood there, rather embarrassed, as they rekindled what was obviously a deep and meaningful friendship. Stories were told and photographs examined until Bruno introduced me as the author of a book about his life. "Well," said Seu Jeferson, "we must show him around. Let's take him to the museum." So then we walked toward the site of the old prison, stopping on the way for beer and cachaça at the bar in the middle of town. Sitting outside, on plastic chairs, we were soon introduced to three former prison guards who had worked there during the early 1990s and had returned to Vila de Dois Rios to retire.

With a little prompting, they remembered Bruno, and the cast of characters that were there with him, which prompted another round of drinks and storytelling. Central to that storytelling was Bruno's escape and the pursuit across the island that followed. Bruno tried to explain to them that as a prisoner it was his duty to escape, but that he didn't mean any harm. And it was obvious, from sitting there listening, that they liked Bruno, and that they respected him for the way he treated people, to say nothing of the fact that he had returned, after all these years, to visit. "No one comes back here," said one of the guards, "at least no one who was in prison!"

Then, when we left, we crossed over to the site of the old prison. The prison had been demolished in April 1994, and the small part that remained had been turned into a museum. As we walked around the exhibit, examining the photographs and artifacts, we came across a party of visitors who were accompanied by a guide. "Here's where they cooked the food," she said, pointing to a large round container. "No, no, no," interrupted Bruno. "This wasn't for cooking food; this was for baking bread, and it was really good bread." "But how do you know?" asked one of the members of the group. "How do I know? Because I lived here, for more than two years, in this prison." And that was it. And for the next twenty minutes or so Bruno had them eating out of his hand with tales of hardship, intrigue, and, of course, his attempted escape.

When we finally left there, close to an hour later, we headed off to the right toward the beach. And when we got there, Bruno showed me the shed with all the fishing equipment. Then, from there, we went by Seu Jonas's house. And there, in the middle of the road, was the drain they were pretending to unblock and the house where the sisters lived, just as Bruno had described it. Then we walked back toward the square to the bar, where the guards we had talked to earlier were still sitting drinking, which led to another round of beer and cachaça, and then another.

Then, as we were finishing up, this other guy walked in who recognized Bruno instantly—the chief of security at Carvalho Troiano, the one who told Bruno he could stay only if he took over the prison. And so then they stood there, reminiscing and explaining to everyone else what had happened. And it was clear to me then that Bruno was every bit a man of his word, and that

The prison museum, Vila de Dois Rios, Ilha Grande. Photograph by Tânia Rêgio / ABr, 2012. Licensed under CC BY 3.0 BR: http://creativecommons.org/licenses/by/3.0/br /legalcode.

if I ever had any doubts about the veracity of his testimony, they were completely unfounded.

Then, finally, when everyone was done talking, Bruno said his good-byes and we headed back up the hill with our bikes. Sitting at a bar across from the docks, I could see that Bruno was emotionally exhausted. "Are you glad we came?" I asked him. "Oh my God, yes," came the reply. "I've been wanting to do this for ages. Because even though I was a prisoner, the years that I spent here were really important. I mean, I met some really good people, like Seu Jeferson, and Seu Jonas, and Barbicha." "I can see that. I can see that now. But hey, who knows? Maybe next time we'll rent a car and drive to the frontier. Now would you be up for that?" "Sure, I'd be up for that. In fact I'd like that a lot."

Sixteen months later, Bruno and I flew to Campo Grande, where we rented a car and drove the four hundred or so kilometers across the Pantanal to Corumbá. We both had things we wanted to accomplish. I, for my part, wanted to get to know the place, and to visit the house and the hotel that Bruno bought after his first two trips to Rio. Bruno, for his part, wanted to

Photograph by author, 2014.

track down an old friend he hadn't seen or heard from in twenty-three years. Finally, there was the border, which both of us wanted to cross—Bruno because he wanted to buy a cell phone for his son, and me because, well, I just wanted to see how easy it was to get across.

Finding Bruno's hotel was not a problem, as it was located on the corner of one of the main squares downtown. His house, on the other hand, was a little more of a challenge, because the neighborhood where he lived had changed almost beyond recognition. We eventually found it, however, by driving around and asking questions of neighbors. As for Bruno's friend, we tracked him down at a local market, where he was managing a stall. His friend's name was Jorge. And it turned out that Jorge was not only a friend, but also a former associate who, after Bruno's arrest, continued to do business with Ademar, Bruno's original contact in Rio.

And it was Jorge who told us about Ademar's death from a cocaine overdose. And it was Jorge who told us about how Valdoberto, Bruno's partner, had been shot, execution style, in the back of the head for failing, one too many times, to deliver. And while I was sitting there, listening to them reminisce, I realized that when they were in their early twenties, drug dealing seemed like a game, a game with no real harm or consequences—until, that is, they were arrested. Jorge had been arrested in Curitiba, with drugs hidden in his car. And as a consequence, he spent two and a half years in a federal prison. So now, like Bruno, he wanted absolutely nothing to do with it, a fact that was made clear to me when he refused to answer questions about the nature of the drug dealing business today.

And so anyway, after we said our good-byes and left, we headed for the frontier, which was about five kilometers out of town. Given all the attention that had been paid to it in the press, I expected that the border would be closely monitored and controlled. But it wasn't, because we drove through a couple of times without being stopped or asked to show our documents. It was as if the border wasn't there, noticeable only by the unmanned checkpoints and by the change in the language of the signs. And that's where my journey with Bruno ended, where, for him, it all began, fifteen years after I first set eyes on him, and fifteen years after his release.

TIMELINE OF EVENTS

HISTORICAL EVENTS		BIOGRAPHICAL EVENTS
Military coup	1964	
	1967	Bruno born in Recife
CV takes over Ilha Grande prison	1979	
Brizola elected governor	1982	
	1983	Bruno enlists
Morreira Franco elected governor	1986	
TC splits from CV	1988	
Bangu Prison inaugurated		
	1991	Bruno arrested in Rio
Ilha Grande prison closed down	1994	
Uë kills Orlando Jogador		
ADA splits from CV	1998	
	1999	Bruno released
Beira-Mar kills Uë	2002	
	2007	Beginning of interviews
Establishment of UPP in Jakeira	2010	
FIFA World Cup	2014	

Introduction

1. Bruno's name and nickname have been changed, as have the names of all the individuals he comes into contact with.
2. For that conversation, see Gay, *Lucia*, 93–100.
3. Arias, *The Rigoberta Menchú Controversy*.

1. Trafficking

1. The navy is the oldest branch of the Brazilian military. Its origins can be traced to the transfer of the Portuguese crown to Brazil in 1808 in the wake of Napoleon Bonaparte's invasion of the Iberian peninsula.
2. The Brazilian military has recruited heavily from the Afro-Brazilian population, in no small part because all Brazilian men aged eighteen are required to register for military service. The problem is that few such recruits have progressed through the ranks. The leadership of the armed forces remains predominantly white and denies that race is a factor, arguing that the relative position of blacks and whites has more to do with social class than with discrimination and prejudice and that each candidate is judged solely on the basis of his or her merit (the armed forces began admitting women in the 1980s). For issues of recruitment, see Kuhlmann, "O serviço militar."
3. The Brazilian Institute of Geography and Statistics, which has administered the census since 1940, places Brazilians in five racial categories based on self-identification: *branco* (white), *pardo* (brown), *preto* (black), *amarelo* (yellow), and indigenous. In 2000, 91,298,042 Brazilians classified themselves as branco, 65,318,092 as pardo, 10,554,336 as preto, 761,583 as amarelo, and 734,127 as

indigenous. Unlike the United States, there is no "one drop of blood" rule, meaning that many, if not most, of those with African heritage consider themselves brown and not black. Those of African descent, whether pardo or preto, have historically been severely disadvantaged despite the image of Brazil as a racial democracy. In recent years, the Brazilian government has moved to address this issue by introducing racial quotas for admission to public universities.

4. The only so-called black admiral to date in the navy's 190-year history is João Cândido Felisberto. Born to slaves in June 1880, in a small town in the southernmost state of Rio Grande do Sul, João Cândido joined the navy at the behest of a family friend and benefactor, Alexandrinho de Alencar, who went on to become an admiral himself and minister of the navy. On November 22, 1910, after fourteen years of service, João Cândido led a revolt of 2,400 sailors in Rio de Janeiro to protest the use of flogging as a form of corporal punishment, despite the fact that it had been outlawed as a means to punish slaves as far back as 1886. João Cândido and his men took over four ships in the bay of Guanabara and threatened to bombard the city if the government didn't agree to their demands. After the sailors were granted amnesty a second revolt, a few days later, gave the government the excuse they were looking for to go after, expel, and, in some cases, kill the sailors who were involved. Although he played no part in the second revolt, João Cândido was thrown into a tiny cell on the Ilha das Cobras with seventeen others for three days without food and water. When the doors to the cell were opened, only João Cândido and one other sailor had survived. João Cândido died on December 8, 1969, after a life of persecution, and it wasn't until July 2008 that he was granted posthumous amnesty. See "João Cândido: A Luta pelos Direitos Humanos," Projeto Memória, 2008, http://www.dhnet.org.br/dados/livros/dh /livro_joao_candido_luta_dh.pdf; Love, *The Revolt of the Whip*.

5. The Pantanal is one of the world's largest tropical wetlands and is located mostly within the Brazilian state of Mato Grosso do Sul, but extends into Mato Grosso, Bolivia, and Paraguay. It covers an area of between 140,000 and 195,000 square kilometers.

6. The real was introduced in 1994 as part of the Plano Real, a reform package designed to end thirty years of high inflation. At the time, the real was meant to have an approximately fixed 1:1 exchange rate with the U.S. dollar. As of February 7, 2014, one U.S. dollar was worth 2.39 reais.

7. Literally "mouth of smoke," a boca de fumo is a place in a favela where drugs are sold.

8. The Paraguayan War (1864–1870) was fought between Paraguay and the combined forces of Argentina, Uruguay, and Brazil and resulted in the deaths of approximately 400,000 men. The only subsequent dispute was a relatively minor one between Brazil and Bolivia over the territory of Acre, which was ceded to Brazil in 1903.

9. This estimate by the Catholic Church–affiliated Pastoral dos Migrantes is

contested by the Brazilian government, which claims there are 180,000 illegal immigrants in the country.

10. Approximately four thousand Haitians made their way to Brazil in the aftermath of the 2010 earthquake, mainly via Peru. The Brazilian government has subsequently moved to restrict further migration by issuing one hundred temporary work visas per month from its embassy in Port-au-Prince. See Simon Romero and Andrea Zarate, "Influx of Haitians into the Amazon Prompts Immigration Debate in Brazil," *New York Times*, February 7, 2012.

11. The price of imported goods in Paraguay can be up to 80 percent cheaper than in Brazil.

12. For a media report on this issue, see "Fronteiras do Brasil (Drogas, armas e contrabando)," posted by Duranvideo, YouTube, June 30, 2011, https://www.youtube.com/watch?v=-DpnI8Tw4qg.

13. For the relationship between globalization and border control, see Andreas, "When Policies Collide." For the emergence of new drug routes, see Brune, "The Brazil–Africa Narco Nexus."

14. "Drug Control: Air Bridge Denial Program in Colombia Has Implemented New Safeguards, but Its Effect on Drug Trafficking Is Not Clear," U.S. Government Accountability Office Report to Congressional Requesters, September 2005.

15. Both Colombia and Peru introduced shoot-down laws in the early 1990s that were subsequently suspended in the aftermath of the accidental killing of an American missionary and her daughter in 2001. Colombia reintroduced its shoot-down law in 2003. See Feitosa and Pinheiro, "Lei do Abate."

16. SIVAM stands for Sistema de Vigilância da Amazônia. Critics claim that the system has never been fully operational and that a lack of air traffic controllers means that much of the airspace under eleven thousand feet is unmonitored, which is exactly the altitude used by small planes carrying drugs. See Monteiro, "O curto vôo da Lei do Abate"; and Wright, "Cocaine Traffickers Develop New Routes from Brazil."

17. "Maior parte de armas e drogas entram no País por 18 pontos," *Jornal do Brasil*, January 9, 2011.

18. "Brazil Launches Crack Cocaine Rehabilitation Program," *Huffington Post*, June 6, 2013.

19. Juliana Barbassa, "In Booming Brazil, Crack Strikes Late but Hard," Associated Press, July 17, 2011.

20. Paula Moura and Lourdes Garcia-Navarro, "Brazil Looks to Build a 10,000-Mile Virtual Fence," National Public Radio, *Parallels* (blog), May 16, 2013, http://www.npr.org/blogs/parallels/2013/05/16/184524306/brazil-looks-to-build-a-10-000-mile-virtual-fence.

21. SISFRON stands for Sistema Integrado de Monitoramento de Fronteiras.

22. Quoted in Brian Winter, "Brazil's 'Gringo' Problem: Its Borders," Reuters, April 13, 2012. See also "Brazil's Long Shadow Vexes Some Neighbors," *New York Times*, November 4, 2011.

2. Things Come Undone

1. The federal police force currently employs around 10,000 women and men, whereas 500,000 or so serve in the civil and military police.

2. The Centro de Informações de Marinha, or CENIMAR, was created by official decree on November 21, 1957. During the dictatorship it was considered the most efficient of the various military intelligence agencies and was involved with the hunting down and massacre of a group of guerillas in the region of Araguaia in north-central Brazil in 1972 that effectively broke the back of the armed resistance.

3. Bailes funk are dance events featuring funk carioca, a local hip-hop derivation of Miami bass that became popular in the 1980s. They are also vehicles for the sale of narcotics and demonstrations of drug gang power.

4. Brazil is party to the 1988 UN Convention against Illicit Traffic in Narcotic Drugs and Psychotropic Substances and introduced an initial chemical control law in 2001, with an updated 2003 decree, imposing strict controls on 146 substances that could be used in the production of narcotics.

5. The civil and military police in Brazil operate at the state level. The military police's function is to patrol the streets and respond to crimes in progress. During the dictatorship, they were incorporated into the armed forces and employed to hunt down enemies of the regime. In the absence of any meaningful reform since then, they continue to operate as a deadly, militarized force. The civil police, on the other hand, investigate crimes that have already been committed and staff the police precincts. The civil police, for their part, are notoriously corrupt and inefficient and are widely known for their use of torture to extract information from suspects in their custody. For rare, ethnographic, insight into the world of the civil police, see Willis, *Antagonistic Authorities and the Civil Police*.

6. The PCC is the Primeiro Comando da Capital, a São Paulo prison-based gang that, in May 2006, launched a series of coordinated attacks against police officers and prison staff that left approximately 450 people dead. The PCC, which was established in the early 1990s, currently claims to have 7,500 members, most of whom are behind bars, and is active in twenty other states. See "São Paulo Governor Fights Prison Crime Cell," *Rio Times*, November 20, 2013.

7. Archaeological evidence suggests that coca chewing emerged around 6000 BCE. Dillehay et al., "Early Holocene Coca Chewing in Northern Peru."

8. U.S. Drug Enforcement Administration Intelligence Division, "Coca Cultivation and Cocaine Processing: An Overview," September 1993.

9. De Acosta, *The Natural and Moral History of the Indies*.

10. In the United States, cocaine use was popularly associated with poor populations, in general, and African Americans, in particular, who were increasingly seen as a threat. See Spillane, *Cocaine*.

11. Gootenberg, *Cocaine*, 35.

12. Gootenberg, *Cocaine*, 40.

13. Everingham and Rydell, *Modeling the Demand for Cocaine.*

14. President Richard Nixon declared the war on drugs at a press conference in July 1971, arguing that drug addiction had "assumed the dimensions of a national emergency" and that drug abuse was "public enemy number one."

15. "Why Is Less Cocaine Coming from Colombia?," *Economist*, April 2, 2013.

16. "America's Drug War in Latin America Expanding," *Huffington Post*, February 3, 2013.

3. The Family

1. Literally, "vagabonds," a term that is often used to describe suspected criminal elements from the favelas.

2. The Terceiro Comando split from the Comando Vermelho in 1988.

3. Cela de espera literally means "waiting cell."

4. "Ministro Justiça José Eduardo Cardoso prefere morte a presidios no Brasil," posted by Sal Sal Sal, YouTube, November 14, 2012, www.youtube.com/watch?v =Su6cFwRZ9m8.

5. See, for example, Nigel S. Rodley, *Report of the Special Rapporteur, Sir Nigel Rodley, Submitted Pursuant to Commission on Human Rights Resolution 2000/43, Addendum: Visit to Brazil*, E/CN.4/2001/66/Add.2 (UN Commission on Human Rights, March 30, 2001); Human Rights Watch, "Behind Bars in Brazil," November 30, 1998, http:// www.hrw.org/reports/pdfs/b/brazil/brazl98d.pdf; Amnesty International, *Brazil: "No One Here Sleeps Safely": Human Rights Violations against Detainees*, AI Index: AMR 19/009/1999 (New York: Amnesty International, June 22, 1999). See also Brazilian Parliamentary Commission of Inquiry, *CPI do sistema carcerário*, June 2008, http:// msmidia.profissional.ws/moretto/pdf/RelatorioCPISistemaPenitenciario.pdf.

6. The Standard Minimum Rules for the Treatment of Prisoners was adopted by the First UN Congress on the Prevention of Crime and the Treatment of Offenders, in Geneva, in 1955. While not legally binding, the standards provide guidelines for international and domestic law for citizens held in prisons and other forms of custody.

7. International Centre for Prison Studies, "World Prison Brief: Brazil," http://www .prisonstudies.org/country/brazil.

8. Brazil has the fourth largest prison population in the world but ranks forty-fourth in terms of the prison population rate. The United States is the world leader in both categories.

9. In this sense, I argue that the spread of drug use in Brazil—which is itself a symptom of development—is a more powerful explanation for increasing incarceration rates than neoliberalism. For a different view, see Wacquant, "The Militarization of Urban Marginality"; and Godoy, *Popular Injustice.*

10. "Tráfico é motivo de 24% das prisões no país," *Folha de São Paulo*, May 12, 2012.

11. These conventions were the Single Convention on Narcotic Drugs (1961), the

Convention on Psychotropic Substances (1971), and the Convention against Illicit Traffic in Narcotic Drugs and Psychotropic Substances (1988).

12. Lei de Crimes Hediondos, https://www.planalto.gov.br/ccivil_03/leis/l8072.htm.

13. Lei Antidrogas, http://www.planalto.gov.br/ccivil_03/_ato2004-2006/2006/lei /l11343.htm. The same law also led to the creation of the Sistema Nacional de Políticas Públicas sobre Drogas (SISNAD).

14. The law appears to have had an even greater impact on women, since almost 60 percent of women in prison in Brazil have been arrested for drugs. "Mulheres presas: A Lei de Drogas fracassou?," *Banco de Injustiças*, July 2, 2013. See also Boiteux, "Drugs and Prisons."

15. As of 2010, there were close to four thousand public defenders in Brazil, compared to twelve thousand public prosecutors and almost sixteen thousand judges.

16. "One in Five: The Crisis in Brazil's Prisons and Criminal Justice System," International Bar Association Human Rights Institute Report, 2010.

17. In 1955, a law was passed that granted special privileges to those with a university degree or a government job. Despite being struck down in 1991, however, the law remains in effect. See, for example, "Até preso, rico leva vantage: O decreto da prisão especial é de 1955—e já foi revogado," *Veja*, January 17, 2001.

18. "Rio terá mais 8 casas de custódias até meados de 2011," *O Globo*, August 8, 2010.

19. There is even a move afoot by the Rio legislature to define overcrowding as a form of torture. See "Superlotação carcerária será tratada como tortura por comitê da Alerj," R7, July 17, 2013.

20. The Amigos dos Amigos split from the CV in 1998.

21. "Mapeamento inédito revela como as facções criminosas se distribuem nos presídios fluminenses," R7, October 18, 2010.

22. Caldeira, "Segurança pública e política penitenciária no Rio de Janeiro."

23. In some prisons there is a neutral wing for those with no link to criminal factions. In most, however, the prisoners are simply sorted according to the faction that dominates the neighborhood where they are from. See Philip Alston, *Preliminary Report by the Special Rapporteur on Extrajudicial, Summary or Arbitrary Executions, Philip Alston, Addendum: Mission to Brazil, 4–14 November 2007*, UN Doc. A/HRC/8/ 3/Add.4, May 14, 2008. See also Caldeira, "A Última Jabuticaba."

4. The Devil's Cauldron

1. For conditions at the prison on Ilha Grande, see "Presídio da Ilha Grande: Parte 1," posted by Impaktonatv, YouTube, April 20, 2012, www.youtube.com /watch?v=LkMQoadVnv8; and André Cypriano, The Devil's Cauldron, 1999, www.f8.com/FP/DC/index2.htm.

2. Seu is a less formal and more intimate form of address than Senhor.

3. An illegal numbers game prohibited by federal law since 1946. For an account, see Chazkel, *Laws of Chance*.

4. For an account of conditions for visitors at the prison through the eyes of a foreign ethnographer, see Goldstein, *Laughter Out of Place*.

5. Brazil was the last country in the Western world to abolish slavery, although it is estimated that 25,000–40,000 Brazilians continue to work, to this day, under slave-like conditions. By the time the institution was struck down, in 1888, an estimated four million slaves had been brought over from Africa, 40 percent of the total number of slaves brought to the Americas.

6. Dos Santos, *Os porões da república*, 91.

7. The prison was destroyed by explosives by order of Governor Carlos Lacerda in 1962.

8. The number of prisoners held in the Colônia Correcional de Dois Rios fluctuated considerably according to broader social and political conditions. In 1903, when the prison was first reopened, only eighty-one inmates were being held there. By 1917, however, there were 1,056, a number that declined to 197 in 1927, and increased again to 1,388 in 1937. In the early years of the institution's existence, almost as many women were held there as men.

9. Dos Santos, *Os porões da república*, 137.

10. Getúlio Vargas served two terms as president of Brazil, first as a dictator from 1930 to 1945, and then as a democratically elected head of state from 1951 until his suicide in 1954. He championed nationalism, industrialization, centralization, and social welfare. Despite his promotion of workers' rights, however, Vargas was a staunch anticommunist.

11. Ramos, *Memórias do cárcere*.

12. Rio served as the capital of Brazil from independence in 1822 until 1960, when it was moved to the purpose-built city of Brasília.

13. The decision to close the prison was influenced by the fact that, during World War II, Fernando de Noronha was used as a navy base under U.S. military command.

14. Dos Santos, *Os porões da república*, 295.

15. Following the coup in 1964, the Brazilian military introduced a series of institutional acts that effectively undermined the power of the national congress and state legislatures.

16. By this time, the Vila de Dois Rios prison had been renamed the Instituto Penal Cândido Mendes, a name it retained until it was demolished in 1994.

17. The most compelling account of the Comando Vermelho's early years is provided by one of its founding members, William da Silva, in his book *Quatrocentros contra um*. See also the documentary by Caco Souza, *Senhora Liberdade* (2004; http://www.youtube.com/watch?v=-lCHgA93XhQ), which is based on interviews with da Silva in prison, and the compelling and evocative film by Lúcia Murat, *Quase Dois Irmãos* (2004).

18. Political prisoners were granted amnesty in Brazil on August 29, 1979.

19. Amorim, cv_pcc, 131–140.

5. On the Run

1. Brazil recently passed legislation allowing conjugal visits for gay prisoners. Such privileges are increasingly rare in the United States, despite evidence that they reduce levels of recidivism. See "As Conjugal Visits Fade, a Lifeline to Inmates' Spouses Is Lost," *New York Times*, January 12, 2014.

2. The maximum allowable prison sentence in Brazil is thirty years. In normal circumstances, however, prisoners who commit common crimes serve 16.7 percent of their sentence before they are eligible for parole or progression to an open system or minimum-security facility. Prisoners who commit heinous crimes, on the other hand, are required to serve 40 percent of their sentence before they are eligible and 60 percent if they are repeat offenders.

3. Cachaça is a popular distilled spirit that is usually made from sugarcane.

4. Leonel Brizola was one of few leaders who resisted the overthrow of President João Goulart in April 1964. He spent the next fifteen years in exile in Uruguay, the United States, and Portugal.

5. Amorim, CV_PCC, 186.

6. Amorim, *Comando Vermelho.*

7. I witnessed this process in person in the favela of Vidigal in the mid- to late 1980s as the CV slowly but surely wrested control of the favela from civic-minded activists who had been in charge for more than a decade. See Gay, *Popular Organization and Democracy.*

8. When Brizola first took office, in January 1983, he made fundamental changes to the state's public security system. Instead of viewing the poor as a population to be repressed, he emphasized the need to respect citizens' rights, whether they were residents of the elite neighborhoods of Zona Sul or the densely packed favelas of Zona Norte. Thus it was Brizola who prevented the police from acting as rogue force, and it was Brizola who was subsequently blamed for allowing drug gangs to become established in the first place. For an account of this change in police culture, see Buarque de Hollanda, *Polícia e direitos humanos.*

9. Wellington Moreira Franco was elected governor in November 1986. Reversing the course set by his predecessor, he gave the police free rein to go after suspected criminal elements, broadly defined, which led the police to kill, on average, one thousand civilians per year. In most cases, civilian deaths at the hands of the police were classified as acts of self-defense that occurred during shootouts when, in fact, they were the result of the indiscriminate and arbitrary execution of individuals, many of whom had little or no involvement with crime. For homicide rates and issues of measurement, see Zdun, "Difficulties Measuring and Controlling Homicide." See also Soares e Souza, *Constituição.*

10. The first of these was the aforementioned escape of Escadinha from the Vila de Dois Rios prison on New Year's Eve in 1985 (chapter 4). The second was an attempt to rescue inmates from the Frei Caneca prison in downtown Rio in August 1987, which ended with the helicopter being shot down and bursting into

flames and the death of one of the leaders of the CV, Paulo Roberto de Moura, otherwise known as Meio-Quilo.

11. Amorim, CV_PCC, 309–316.

12. In 2004, the area that houses the now twenty-six different correctional facilities was renamed Gericinó, to reduce the stigma associated with the region.

13. There was considerable local resistance to the demolition because it threatened the livelihoods, both legal and illegal, of many of the local inhabitants. For footage, see "Implosão do presídio da Ilha Grande," posted by Manezinho da Implosão, YouTube, November 7, 2013, www.youtube.com/watch?v=5gM2mgXc2Io.

6. Paradise Lost

1. While drug trafficking remained the main source of the CV's revenue, the organization was involved in a series of high-profile kidnappings in the 1980s. For example, "At least 26 captives have been ransomed this year. A newspaper calls the city the 'hostage of organized crime,'" "$2.5 Million Ransom Paid to Free Brazilian in Kidnap-Plagued Rio," *Los Angeles Times*, June 23, 1990.

2. That is not to say that their discourse was not framed by a language of rights. For this issue, see Holston, *Insurgent Citizenship*, 300–309.

3. For a more recent example, see "Mulher é presa ao tentar entrar em cadeia com droga e celular na vagina," Globo.com, g1, July 2, 2014, http://g1.globo.com/rn /rio-grande-do-norte/noticia/2014/07/mulher-e-presa-ao-tentar-em-cadeia-de -natal-com-droga-e-celular-na-vagina.html.

4. For police violence, see Cano, *The Use of Lethal Force*; Amnesty International, *Brazil: "They Come in Shooting": Policing Socially Excluded Communities* (Amnesty International, 2005); and Americas Watch, "The Killings in Candelária and Vigário Geral: The Urgent Need to Police the Brazilian Police," *Human Rights Watch Short Report* 5(11) (1993).

5. See United Nations High Commissioner for Human Rights, "Standard Minimum Rules for the Treatment of Prisoners," 1955, unispal.un.org/UNISPAL.NSF/o /70D535E1E3DCA2B885256F010074C34D.

6. "Só 9% dos presos do país têm atividade educacional, diz governo," G7, June 30, 2011.

7. Despacho do Ministério da Educação, "Diretrizes Nacionais para a oferta de educação para jovens e adultos em situação de privação de liberdade nos estabelecimentos penais," July 5, 2010, section 1, p. 28.

8. The survey gathered information from the states of Pernambuco, São Paulo, Rio Grande do Sul, and Pará, and the Federal District of Brasília. See Carreira, *Relatoria Nacional para o Direito Humano à Educação*.

9. For the evolution of the Pronasci program, see "Governo Dilma prioriza cadeia e ações antidrogas e abandona Pronasci," *Rede Brasil Atual*, July 23, 2013.

10. For the Lei de Remição, see Presidência da República, Casa Civil, Law No. 12.433, June 29, 2011, www.planalto.gov.br/ccivil_03/_ato2011-2014/2011/lei/l12433

.htm. For complementary laws involving education inside prisons, see Presidência da República, Casa Civil, Law No. 12.245, May 24, 2010, www.planalto.gov.br /ccivil_03/_Ato2007-2010/2010/Lei/L12245.htm; and Presidência da República, Casa Civil, Decree No. 7.626, November 24, 2011, www.planalto.gov.br/ccivil_03 /_Ato2011-2014/2011/Decreto/D7626.htm.

11. It is estimated that seven out of every ten inmates in Brazil find their way back into prison, which is one of the highest rates of recidivism in the world. See, for example, "No Brasil, sete em cada dez ex-presidiários voltam ao crime, diz presidente do STF," ISTOÉ Online, September 5, 2011.

12. Lois M. Davis, Robert Bozick, Jennifer L. Steele, Jessica Saunders, and Jeremy N. V. Miles, "Evaluating the Effectiveness of Correctional Education: A Meta-analysis of Programs That Provide Education to Incarcerated Adults," Rand Corporation, 2013, http://www.rand.org/pubs/research_reports/RR266.html.

13. For a similar take on the situation in Brazil, see "Para melhorar sistema prisional é preciso enfrentar a sociedade, afirmam especialistas," Agência Brasil, August 24, 2010.

7. The Leader

1. A prison riot was the excuse for the Carandiru prison massacre on October 2, 1992, in São Paulo, which left 111 inmates dead.

2. Capoeira is a Brazilian martial art that was developed primarily by people of African descent with native Brazilian influences in the sixteenth century.

3. For more recent coverage of an escape from a prison in Rio, see "Presos fogem do Complexo de Gericinó, em Bangu, pela tubulação de esgoto," O Globo, February 3, 2013.

4. There are reports that in some prisons in Brazil, women are forced to have sex with the leaders. See, for example, "Líderes de facções exigem sexo para evitar execuções," Estadão, December 24, 2013.

5. Vó is a Portuguese term for grandmother.

6. "Tá tudo dominado," Veja, September 18, 2002. The incident is also dramatized in the opening sequences of the film Tropa de Elite 2: O Inimigo Agora e Outro, directed by José Padilha (Rio: Zazen Produções, 2007).

7. One of the consequences of the Bangu massacre and other prison riots in Rio and São Paulo was the introduction of the Regime Disciplinar Diferenciado, which enables the authorities to keep prisoners in isolation for twenty-two hours per day for up to 360 days. The law, which was passed on January 2, 2003, has been criticized as being unconstitutional and a violation of prisoners' rights. Despite its passing and implementation, however, there is evidence that the leaders of criminal factions still have the capacity to give orders to lieutenants on the outside. See, for example, "Beira-Mar pode ter ordenado ataques à ONG AfroReggae," Estadao.com.br, August 12, 2013.

8. Between 2001 and 2005, sixty-seven prison workers were assassinated in Rio.

Some were executed because they were responsible for imposing harsh measures. Others were executed because they refused to take bribes or because they backed out of agreements to facilitate escapes. See, for example, "Diretor de Bangu 3 é assassinado," *Estadao.com.br/Cidades*, August 5, 2003.

8. Judgment Day

1. The authorities have thus far failed in their attempts to block cell phone transmissions from inside Brazil's prisons. See, for example, "Brazil: São Paulo to Block Cellphones in Prison," *Infosurhoy.com*, October 1, 2013.
2. A common occurrence, despite what the penal code says. See, for example, "Presos são obrigados a assinar declaração responsabilizando-se por sua integridade física," *O Globo*, September 4, 2005.
3. "Clashes in Rio Slum Spur Plea for Help," *Los Angeles Times*, April 15, 2004.
4. For the relationship between gangs and the surrounding community, see Zaluar, *Condomínio do diablo*; and Zaluar, *Integração perversa*; Alvito, *As cores de Acari*; da Silva, *Vida sob Cerco*; Misse, "Malandros, marginais e vagabundos"; Dowdney, *Crianças do tráfico*; Arias, *Drugs and Democracy in Rio de Janeiro*; Penglase, "The Bastard Child of the Dictatorship"; Leeds, "Cocaine and Parallel Polities in the Brazilian Urban Periphery"; and Barcellos, *Abusado*.
5. This was the only time in the twenty-plus years I have been visiting the favela that I was told not to come.
6. This does not mean that there were no dissenting voices during this time, or attempts to move policy in a different direction. Of particular note in this regard is the political and intellectual work of Luiz Eduardo Soares, who served as secretary of public safety and security at both the state and national levels. For a personal account of his experiences in office, see Soares, *Meu casaco de general*.
7. The decision to use the police to clear out and occupy the favelas was influenced by a visit by Governor Sérgio Cabral to the city of Medellín, Colombia, in 2007. See Crandall and McDermott, "City on the Hill." For parallels with the war in Afghanistan, see "Afghan Offensive Is New War Model," *New York Times*, February 13, 2010.
8. The two most important UPPs to date are those located in the Complexo de Alemão and Rocinha, which, in recent years, have been the headquarters of the CV and ADA respectively.
9. The idea of a permanent police presence in the favelas is by no means new. In July 2000, for example, a new military police division, known as the Grupamento de Policiamento em Áreas Especiais, was established in the favelas of Pavão-Pavãozinho and Cantagalo in Rio's Zona Sul. The project was designed not only to reduce the level of violence in these communities but also to foster a close working relationship between residents and the police. Despite its success, however, the experiment was ultimately abandoned because of a lack of support by the state governor and, more importantly, the leadership of the police. For a description of the program, see da Silva and Cano, "The Case of Pavão-Pavãozinho-Cantagalo."

10. Not only are the police in Rio extremely violent, they are also notoriously corrupt. See, for example, "Entrevista com o Polícia," *Insight—Inteligência* (April–June 2010): 18–31.

11. A complaint that is fairly specific to the favelas of Zona Sul is the impact of outside investment on gentrification. See, for example, "Invasão estrangeira na favela: Procura por imóveis cresce, preços sobem e especialistas alertam para riscos," *O Globo Blogs*, November 24, 2012.

12. For the projected cost of the UPP program, see "Gasto com UPPs do Rio no ano da Copa será de R$ 720 milhões," *R7 Rio de Janeiro*, April 24, 2013. For the continued lack of urban services, see, for example, "Moradores do Alemão reclamam da falta de coleta de lixo e esgoto," *O Dia*, January 14, 2014.

13. For problems associated with the return of criminal elements, see "Tráfico volta a ostentar armas em áreas de favelas pacificadas," *O Dia*, March 10, 2014.

14. Although not used in quite the same context, this term is borrowed from the ethnography by Biehl, *Vita*.

15. For a historical perspective, see Fischer, *A Poverty of Rights*; McCann, *Hard Times in the Marvelous City*; and Perlman, *Favela*.

16. See, for example, "Mass Beach Robberies Prompt Brazil Police Crackdown," *InSight Crime*, November 29, 2013; and "Whose Mall Is It?," *New York Times*, January 15, 2014.

17. For a similar perspective, see Bourgois, *In Search of Respect*.

18. For this issue in other parts of Brazil, see "Prison Violence Brings Scrutiny to State in Brazil," *New York Times*, January 8, 2014; and "Presos iniciam uma greve de fome em penitenciária do Maranhão," *O Dia*, January 14, 2014.

19. See, for example, "Prisons in Latin America: A Journey into Hell," *Economist*, September 22, 2012; "Inside El Salvador's Secretive Prison Pits Where Notorious Gangs Are Crammed Together Like Livestock in Cells the Size of a Shed," *MailOnline*, August 29, 2013; and "Inmates Control 60% of Mexican Prisons: Report," *InSight Crime*, September 25, 2012. See also "How Imprisoned Mexican Mafia Leader Exerts Secret Control over L.A. Street Gangs," *KQED News*, September 19, 2013.

20. According to Argentina's Federal Penitentiary Service, the percentage of inmates incarcerated for drugs increased from 1 percent in 1985 to more than 27 percent in 2000. Metaal and Youngers, *Systems Overload*, 91.

21. Latin American Commission on Drugs and Democracy, "Drugs and Democracy: Toward a Paradigm Shift," accessed June 3, 2014, www.drogasedemocracia.org /Arquivos/declaracao_ingles_site.pdf.

22. "Uruguay Becomes First Country to Legalize Marijuana," *NBCNews.com*, December 10, 2013.

23. "2013 UN Drug Report Highlights Rise in New, Unregulated Drugs," *InSight Crime*, June 27, 2013.

BIBLIOGRAPHY

Alvito, Marcos. *As cores de Acari: Uma favela carioca*. Rio de Janeiro: Fundação Getulio Vargas, 2001.

Amorim, Carlos. *Comando Vermelho: A história secreta do crime organizado*. Rio de Janeiro: Editora Record, 1993.

Amorim, Carlos. *CV_PCC: A irmandade do crime*. Rio de Janeiro: Editora Record, 2003.

Andreas, Peter. "When Policies Collide: Market Reform, Market Prohibition, and the Narcotization of the Mexican Economy." In *The Illicit Global Economy and State Power*, ed. H. Richard Friman and Peter Andreas, 125–141. New York: Rowman and Littlefield, 1999.

Arias, Arturo, ed. *The Rigoberta Menchú Controversy*. Minneapolis: University of Minnesota Press, 2001.

Arias, Enrique Desmond. *Drugs and Democracy in Rio de Janeiro: Trafficking, Social Networks, and Public Security*. Chapel Hill: University of North Carolina Press, 2006.

Barcellos, Caco. *Abusado: O dono do Morro Dona Marta*. Rio de Janeiro: Editora Record, 2004.

Biehl, João. *Vita: Life in a Zone of Social Abandonment*. Berkeley: University of California Press, 2013.

Boiteux, Luciana. "Drugs and Prisons: The Repression of Drugs and the Increase of the Brazilian Penitentiary Population." In *Systems Overload: Drug Laws and Prisons in Latin America*, ed. Pien Metaal and Coletta Youngers, 30–38. Washington, DC: Transnational Institute / Washington Office on Latin America, 2011.

Bourgois, Phillipe. *In Search of Respect: Selling Crack in El Barrio*. Cambridge: Cambridge University Press, 2002.

Brune, Nancy. "The Brazil–Africa Narco Nexus." *Americas Quarterly* 5(4) (2011): 59–62.

Buarque de Hollanda, Cristina. *Polícia e direitos humanos: Política de segurança pública no Primeiro Governo Brizola.* Rio de Janeiro: Editora Revan, 2005.

Caldeira, Cesar. "A Última Jabuticaba: Presídio sem facções." *Insight/Inteligência* 32 (2006): 58–71.

Caldeira, Cesar. "Segurança pública e política penitenciária no Rio de Janeiro: Estudo do caso do Presídio Ary Franco." *Revista Rio de Janeiro* 12 (2004): 12–38.

Cano, Ignacio. *The Use of Lethal Force by Police in Rio de Janeiro.* Rio de Janeiro: ISER, 1997.

Carreira, Denise. *Relatoria Nacional para o Direito Humano à Educação: Educação nas Prisões Brasileiras.* São Paulo: Plataforma DhESCA Brasil, 2009.

Chazkel, Amy. *Laws of Chance: Brazil's Clandestine Lottery and the Making of Urban Public Life.* Durham, NC: Duke University Press, 2011.

Crandall, Russell, and Caroline McDermott. "City on the Hill: Letter from Medellín." *American Interest* (summer 2011): 117–122.

da Silva, Graziella Moraes, and Ignacio Cano. "The Case of Pavão-Pavãozinho-Cantagalo in Rio de Janeiro's Favelas." In *Legitimacy and Criminal Justice: International Perspectives,* ed. Tom Tyler, 186–214. New York: Russell Sage Foundation, 2007.

da Silva, Luiz Antônio Machado, ed. *Vida sob Cerco: Violência e rotinas nas favelas do Rio de Janeiro.* Rio de Janeiro: Nova Fronteira, 2008.

da Silva, William. *Quatrocentos contra um.* Rio de Janeiro: Vozes, 1991.

de Acosta, Joseph. *The Natural and Moral History of the Indies.* Edited by Clements Markham. Vol. 1, book 4, 245–246. London: The Lakluyt Society, 1880.

Dillehay, Tom, Jack Rossen, Donald Ugent, Anathasios Karathanasis, Víctor Vásquez, and Patricia J. Netherly. "Early Holocene Coca Chewing in Northern Peru." *Antiquity* 84(326) (2010): 939–953.

dos Santos, Myrian Sepúlveda. *Os porões da república: A barbárie nas prisões da Ilha Grande, 1894–1945.* Rio de Janeiro: Garamond, 2009.

Dowdney, Luke. *Crianças do tráfico: Um estudo de caso de crianças em violência armada organizada no Rio de Janeiro.* Rio de Janeiro: 7 Letras, 2003.

Everingham, Susan S., and C. Peter Rydell. *Modeling the Demand for Cocaine.* Santa Monica, CA: Rand Corporation, 1994.

Feitosa, Gustavo Raposo Pereira, and José Augusto de Oliveira Pinheiro. "Lei do Abate, guerra às drogas e defesa nacional." *Revista Brasileira de Política Internacional* 55(1) (2012): 66–92.

Fischer, Brodwyn. *A Poverty of Rights: Citizenship and Inequality in Twentieth-Century Rio de Janeiro.* Stanford: Stanford University Press, 2010.

Gay, Robert. *Lucia: Testimonies of a Brazilian Drug Dealer's Woman.* Philadelphia: Temple University Press, 2005.

Gay, Robert. *Popular Organization and Democracy: A Tale of Two Favelas.* Philadelphia: Temple University Press, 1994.

Godoy, Angelina Snodgrass. *Popular Injustice: Violence, Community, and the Law in Latin America.* Stanford, CA: Stanford University Press, 2006.

Goldstein, Donna. *Laughter Out of Place: Race, Class, Violence, and Sexuality in a Rio Shantytown.* Berkeley: University of California Press, 2003.

Gootenberg, Paul, ed. *Cocaine: Global Histories.* London: Routledge, 1999.

Holston, James. *Insurgent Citizenship: Disjunctions of Democracy and Modernity in Brazil.* Princeton, NJ: Princeton University Press, 2008.

Kuhlmann, Paulo Roberto Loyolla. "O serviço militar, democracia e defesa nacional: Razões da permanência do modelo de recrutamento no Brasil." Master's thesis, Universidade de São Paulo, 2001.

Leeds, Elizabeth. "Cocaine and Parallel Polities in the Brazilian Urban Periphery." *Latin American Research Review* 31(3) (1996): 47–83.

Love, Joseph. *The Revolt of the Whip.* Stanford: Stanford University Press, 2012.

McCann, Bryan. *Hard Times in the Marvelous City: From Dictatorship to Democracy in the Favelas of Rio de Janeiro.* Durham, NC: Duke University Press, 2014.

Metaal, Pien, and Coletta Youngers, eds. *Systems Overload: Drug Laws and Prisons in Latin America.* Washington, DC: Transnational Institute / Washington Office on Latin America, 2011.

Misse, Michel. "Malandros, marginais e vagabundos & a acumulação social da violência no Rio de Janeiro." PhD diss., IUPERJ, 1999.

Monteiro, Lício Caetano do Rego. "O curto vôo da Lei do Abate." *Revista Eletrônica Boletim do* TEMPO 3(27) (2008).

Penglase, Ben. "The Bastard Child of the Dictatorship: The Comando Vermelho and the Birth of 'Narco-Culture' in Rio de Janeiro." *Luso-Brazilian Review* 45(1) (2008): 118–145.

Perlman, Janice. *Favela: Four Decades of Living on the Edge in Rio de Janeiro.* New York: Oxford University Press, 2010.

Ramos, Graciliano. *Memórias do cárcere.* São Paulo: Livraria Martins, 1953.

Soares, Luiz Eduardo. *Meu casaco de general: 500 dias no front da segurança pública do estado do Rio de Janeiro.* Rio de Janeiro: Cia. das Letras, 2000.

Soares e Souza, Taiguara Libano. "Constituição, segurança pública e estado de exeção permanente: A biopolítica dos autos de resistência." Master's thesis, PUC, Rio de Janeiro, 2011.

Spillane, Joseph F. *Cocaine: From Medical Marvel to Modern Menace in the United States, 1884–1920.* Baltimore, MD: Johns Hopkins University Press, 2000.

Wacquant, Loïc. "The Militarization of Urban Marginality: Lessons from the Brazilian Metropolis." *International Political Sociology* 2 (2008): 56–74.

Willis, Graham Denyer. "Antagonistic Authorities and the Civil Police in São Paulo." *Latin American Research Review* 49(1) (2014): 3–22.

Wright, Joanna. "Cocaine Traffickers Develop New Routes from Brazil." *Jane's Intelligence Review* 18(1) (2006): 6–12.

Zaluar, Alba. *Condomínio do diablo*. Rio de Janeiro: UFRJ, 1995.

Zaluar, Alba. *Integração perversa: Pobreza e tráfico de drogas*. Rio de Janeiro: Fundação Getulio Vargas, 2004.

Zdun, Steffen. "Difficulties Measuring and Controlling Homicide in Rio de Janeiro." *International Journal of Conflict and Violence* 5(1) (2011): 188–199.

INDEX